# Intimate Vermont

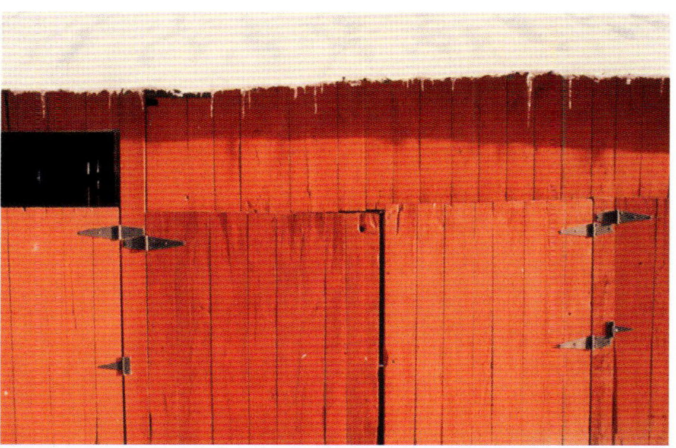

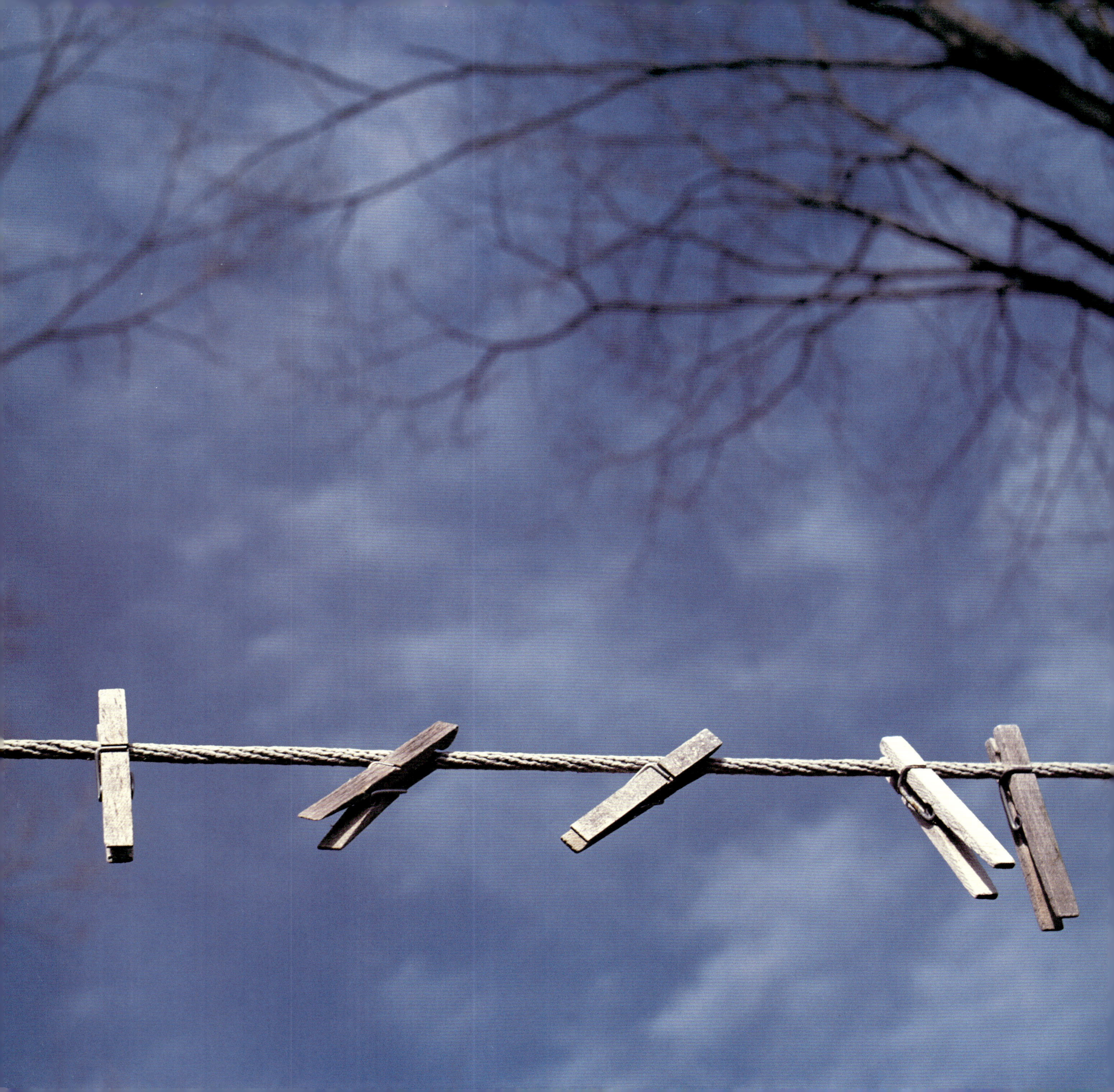

# Intimate Vermont

*Photographs by*

**Jon Gilbert Fox**

University Press of New England

Hanover and London

Published by University Press of New England,

One Court Street, Lebanon, NH 03766

www.upne.com

© 2005 by University Press of New England

Printed in Korea

5 4 3 2 1



*Library of Congress Cataloging-in-Publication Data*

Fox, Jon Gilbert.
Intimate Vermont / photographs by Jon Gilbert Fox.
   p.  cm.
ISBN 1-58465-408-2 (cloth : alk. paper)
1. Vermont—Pictorial works.  I. Title.
F50.F69 2005
974.3'0022'2—dc22           2004022783

To My Mother

Who First Put a Camera in My Hands


*and*



To Darrell Hotchkiss

Who Has Kept My Focus Steady

*Intimate Vermont* was my publisher's idea of a title. I had less poetic titles in mind. I was thinking of calling the book *Road Kill* to commemorate all the times I "braked for" show-stopping images on the highways and back roads of Vermont. Or maybe *Vermont Safari*—but that would have implied more deliberation and an awareness of specific prey, and maybe even a guide. But I was after nothing specific, and there was no guide. Instead, these are images that simply appeared uninvited and stopped me in my tracks, images that captured me before I captured them. I was not even on assignment when I snapped most of these photographs.

This method began when I received my first camera from my mother when I was eight years old. That summer we were on a family sojourn, accompanying my father on a business trip from our house in upstate New York through all of the New England states. Somewhere on the Maine coast, my mother gave me her old Kodak (a foldable version with a lens attached to a leather bellows you had to pull out before photographing), which she had been given upon her graduation from high school. The first two black-and-white photographs I produced (on film you can no longer buy) were of a burro and a weathered barn. Both burro and barn stood beside a country road. On that fateful road trip, I was introduced to photography and some of my favorite subjects, including Vermont, at the same time. I swore then that someday I would live in the state.

I moved to Vermont in 1978. Many years, and many, many miles later, I've made tens of thousands of photographs of

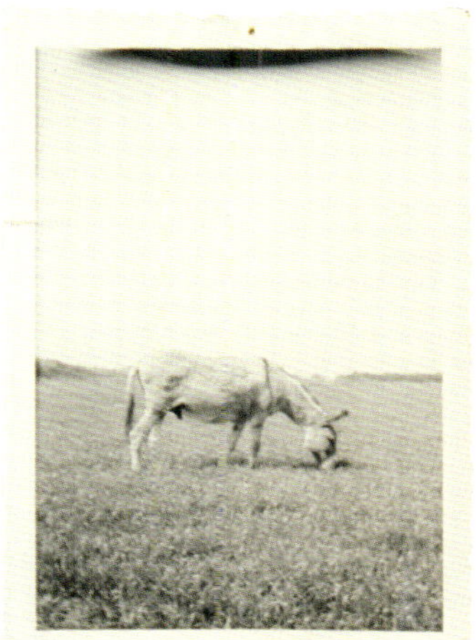

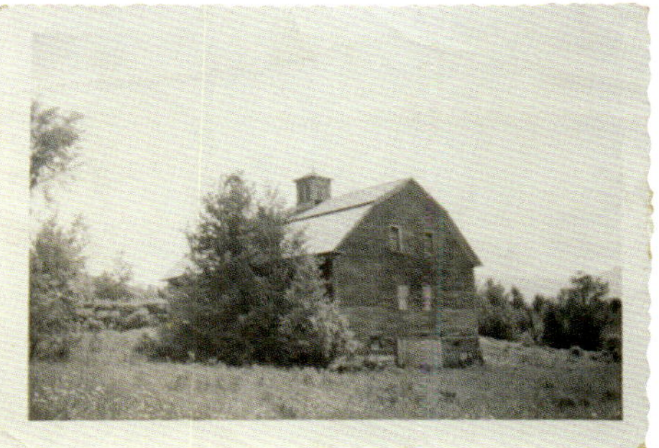

the state and its people. Living in Vermont has opened my eyes and heart to the wonderful scenery and warm reception by friends and neighbors, which have made me feel at home. Looking back on it, I can see that what I braked for were unrehearsed scenes—scenes in which the quality of light, the angle of the shadows, or the tints of color illuminated moments of human introspection or shared experience and in which animals and inanimate objects were painted with rich emotional hues. Maybe this collection of images is more of a "family album" of the extended family formed around me by this unique state. I guess *Intimate Vermont* is just right for the title.

I hope you will enjoy this road I've traveled through the state and will linger with me while looking at some of my favorite places and people.

# Intimate Vermont

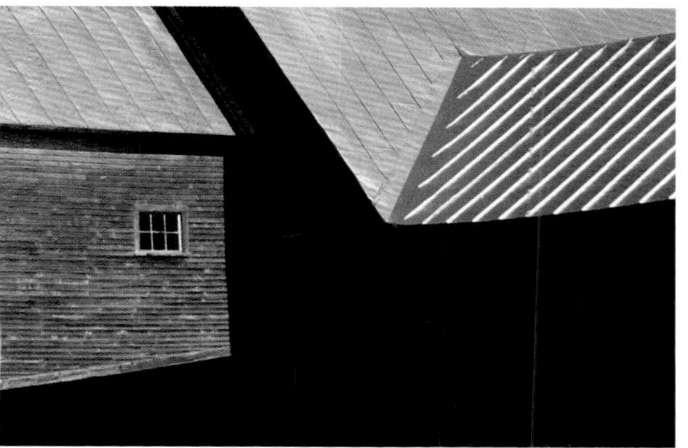

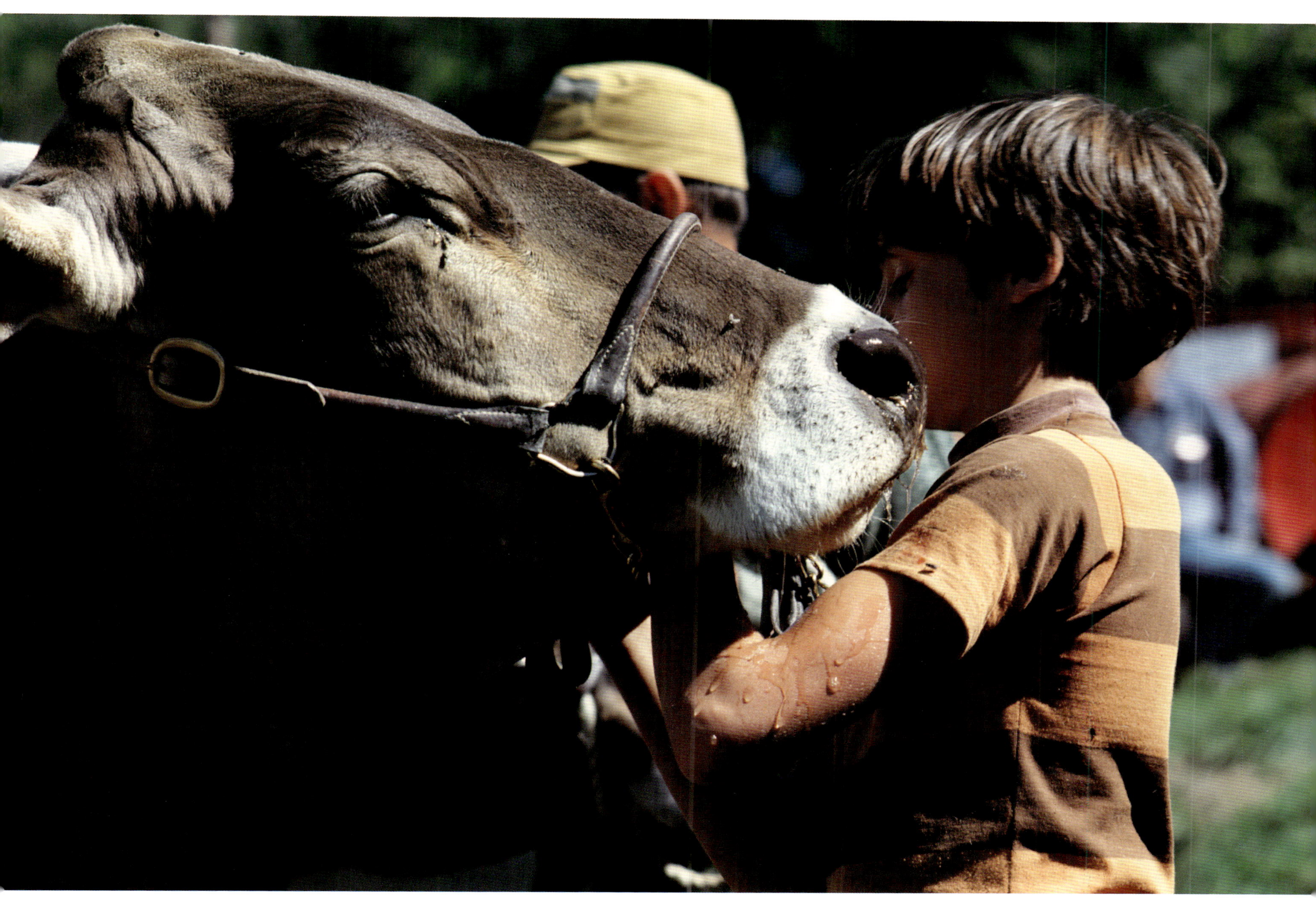

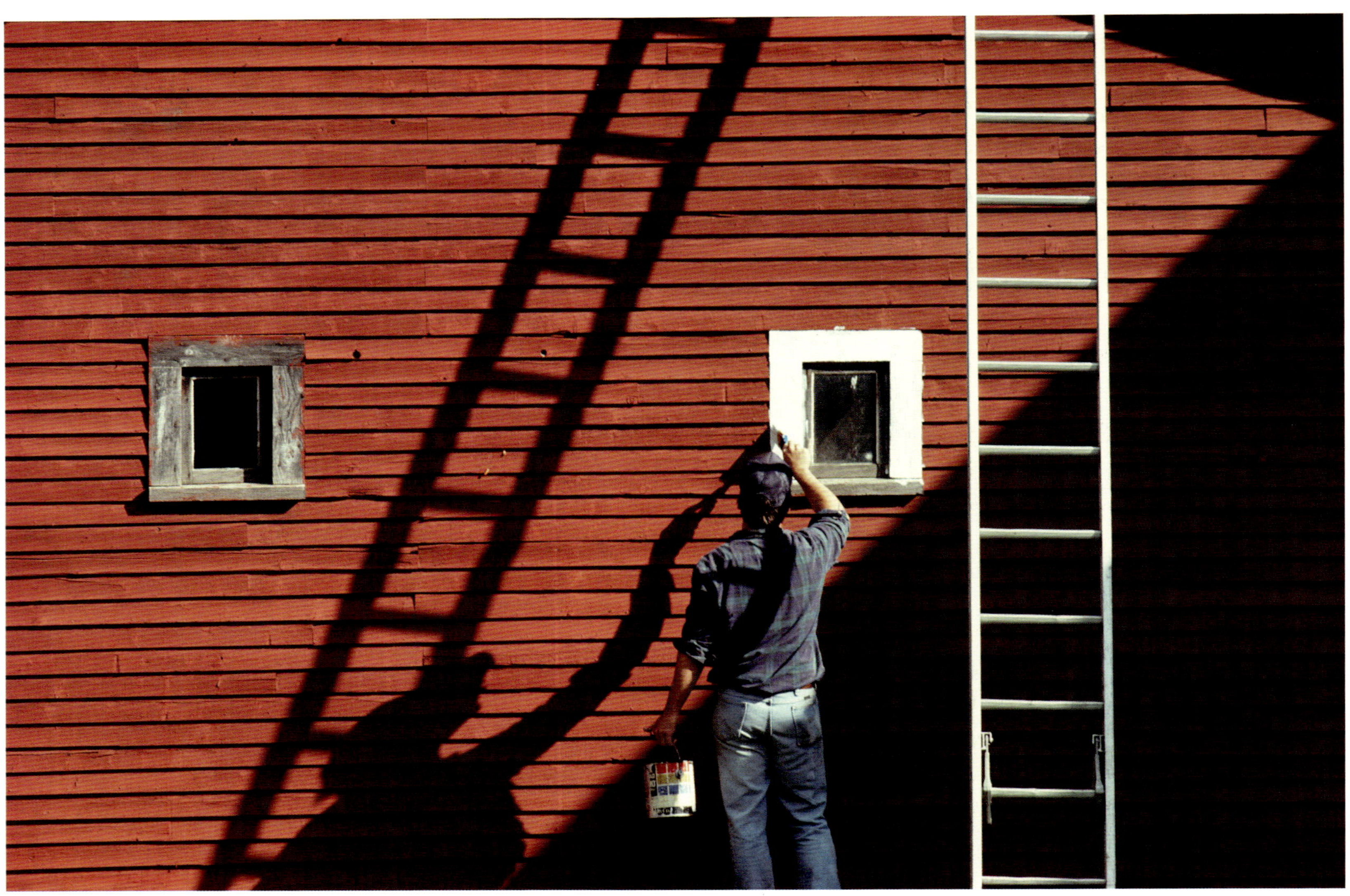

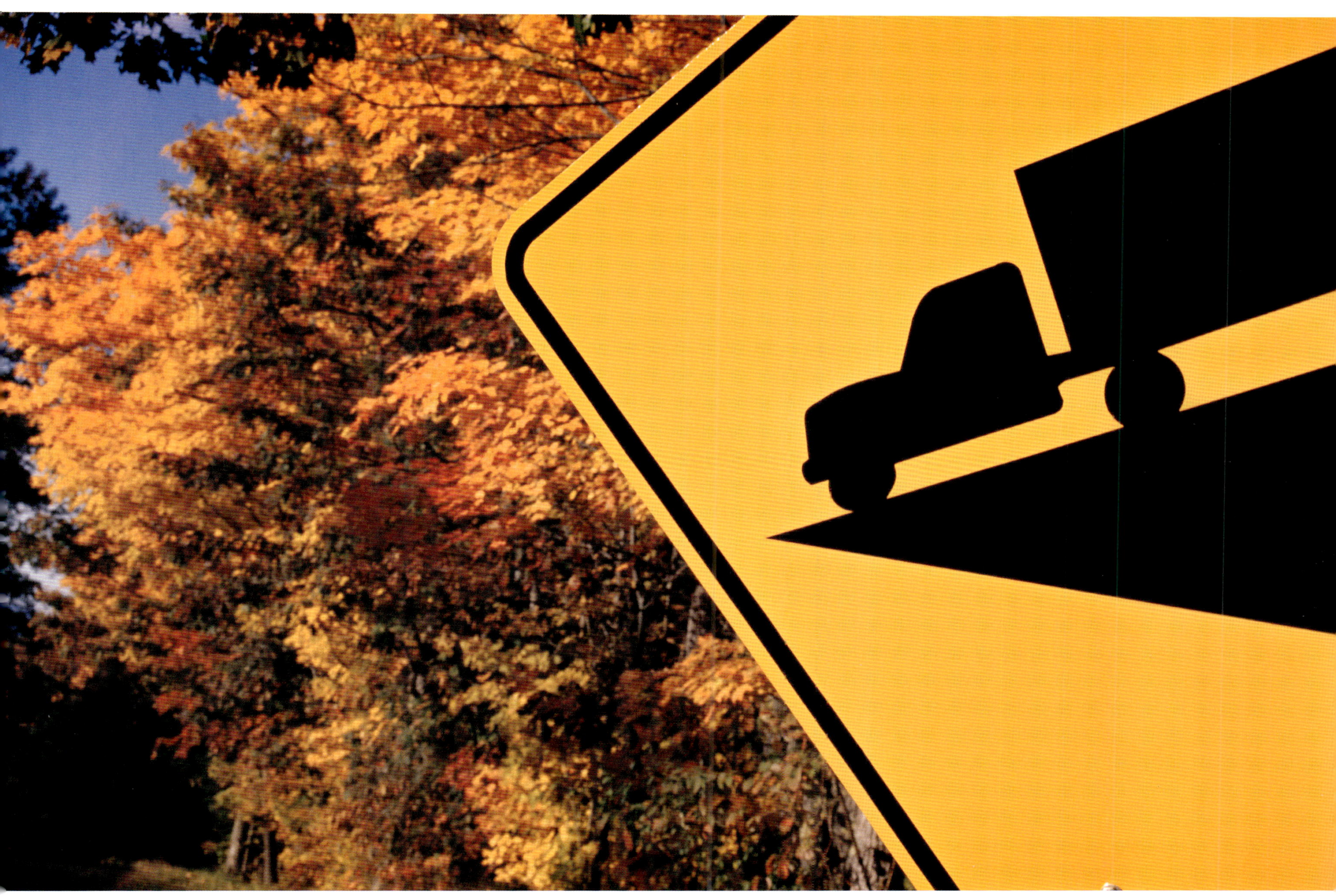

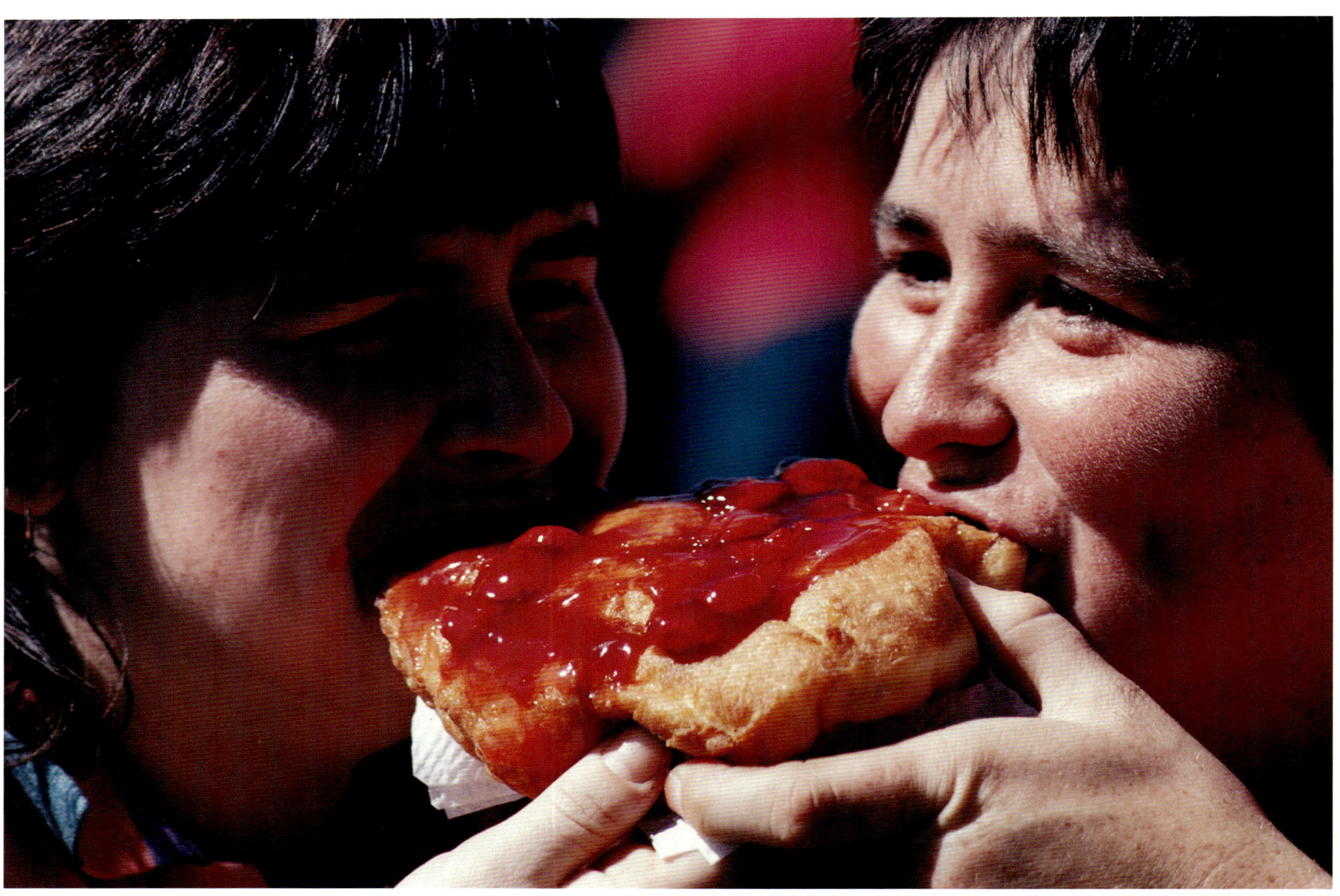

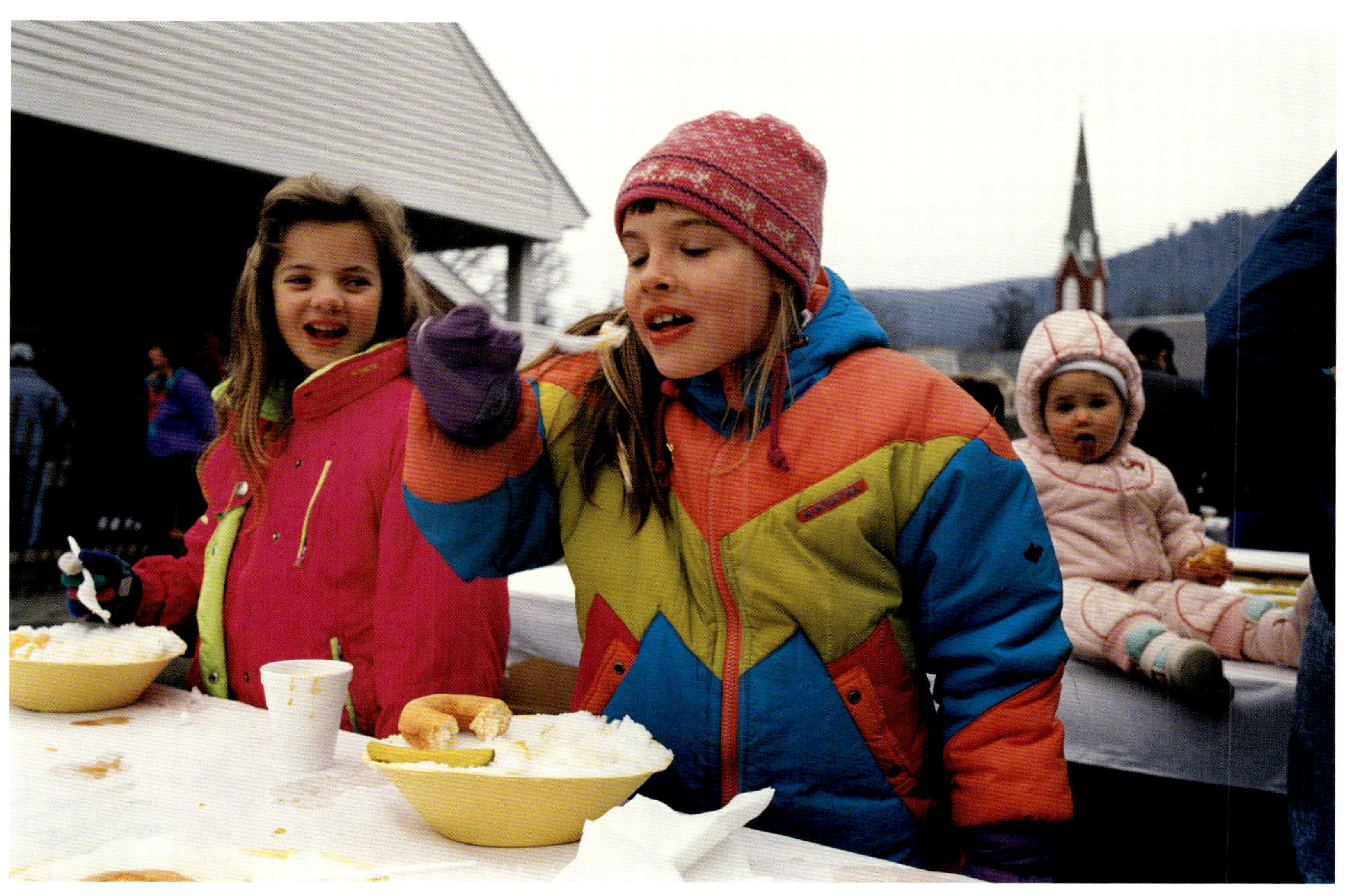

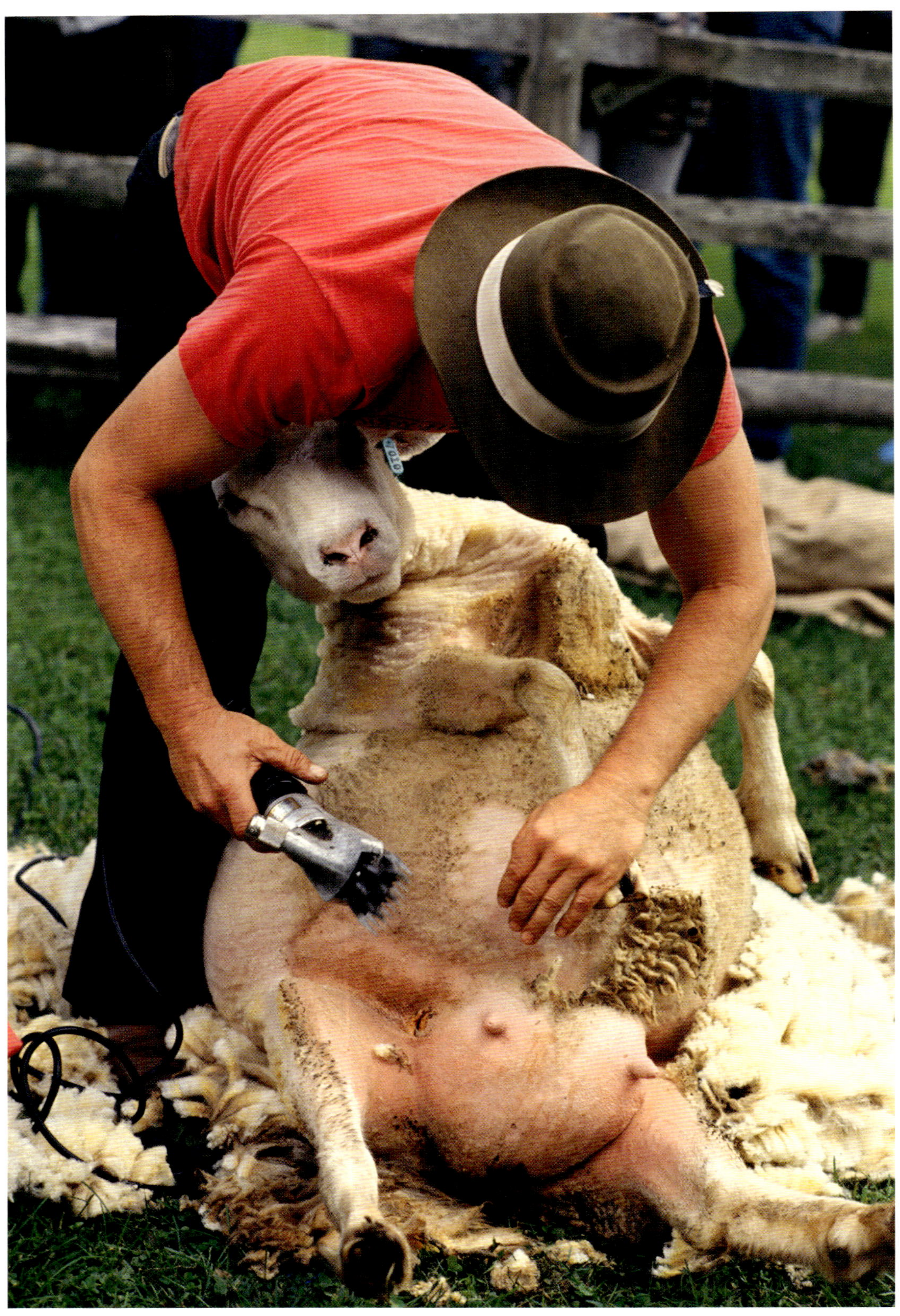

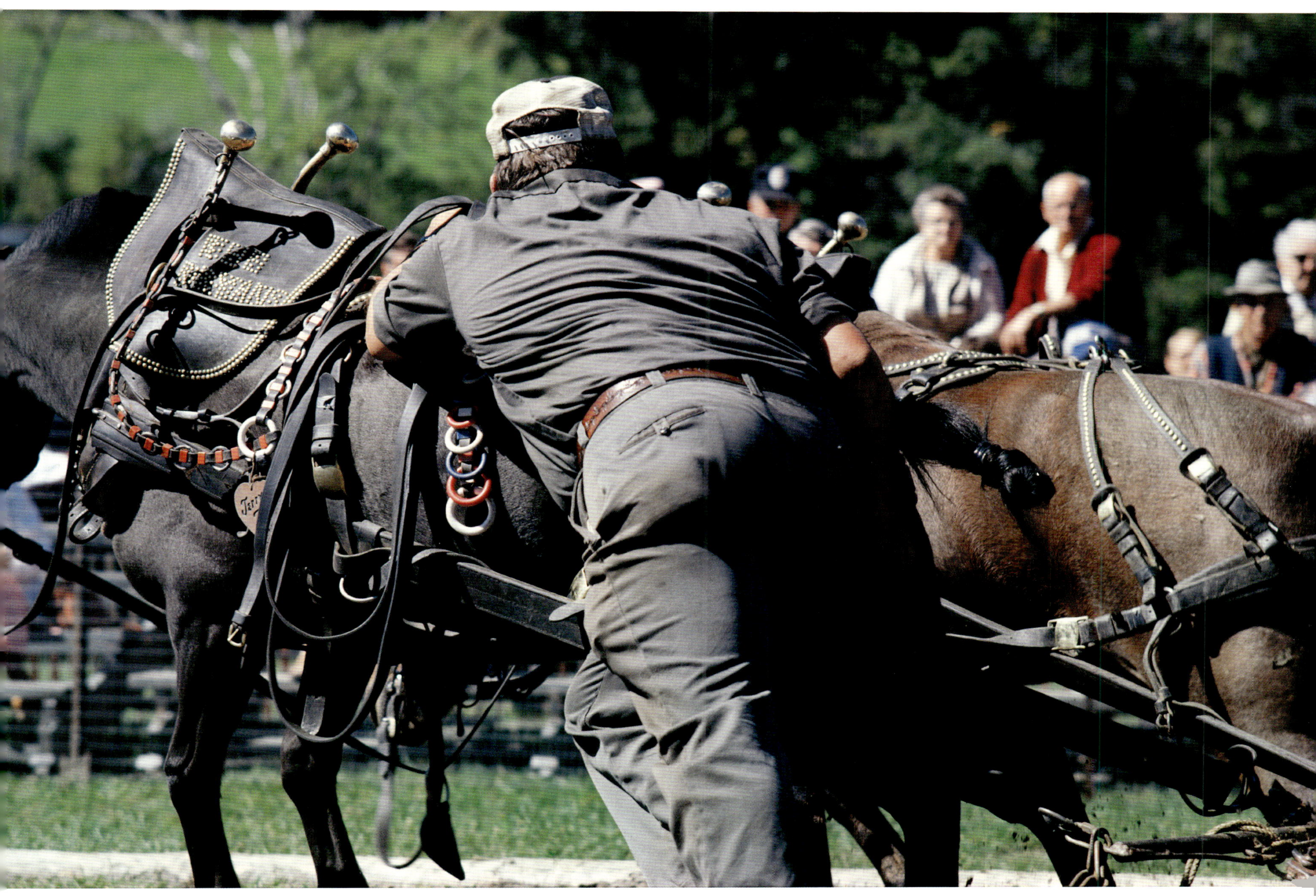

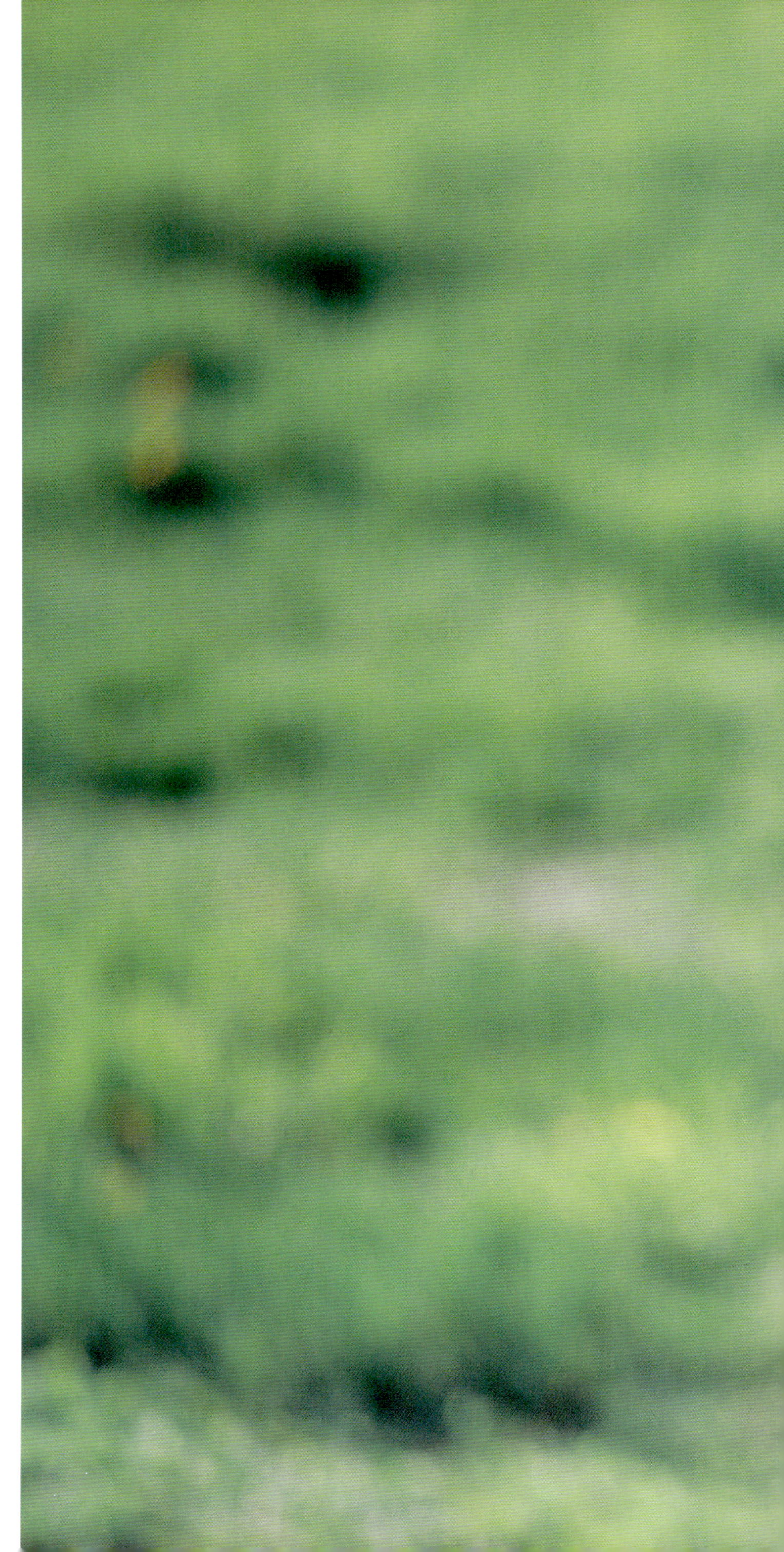

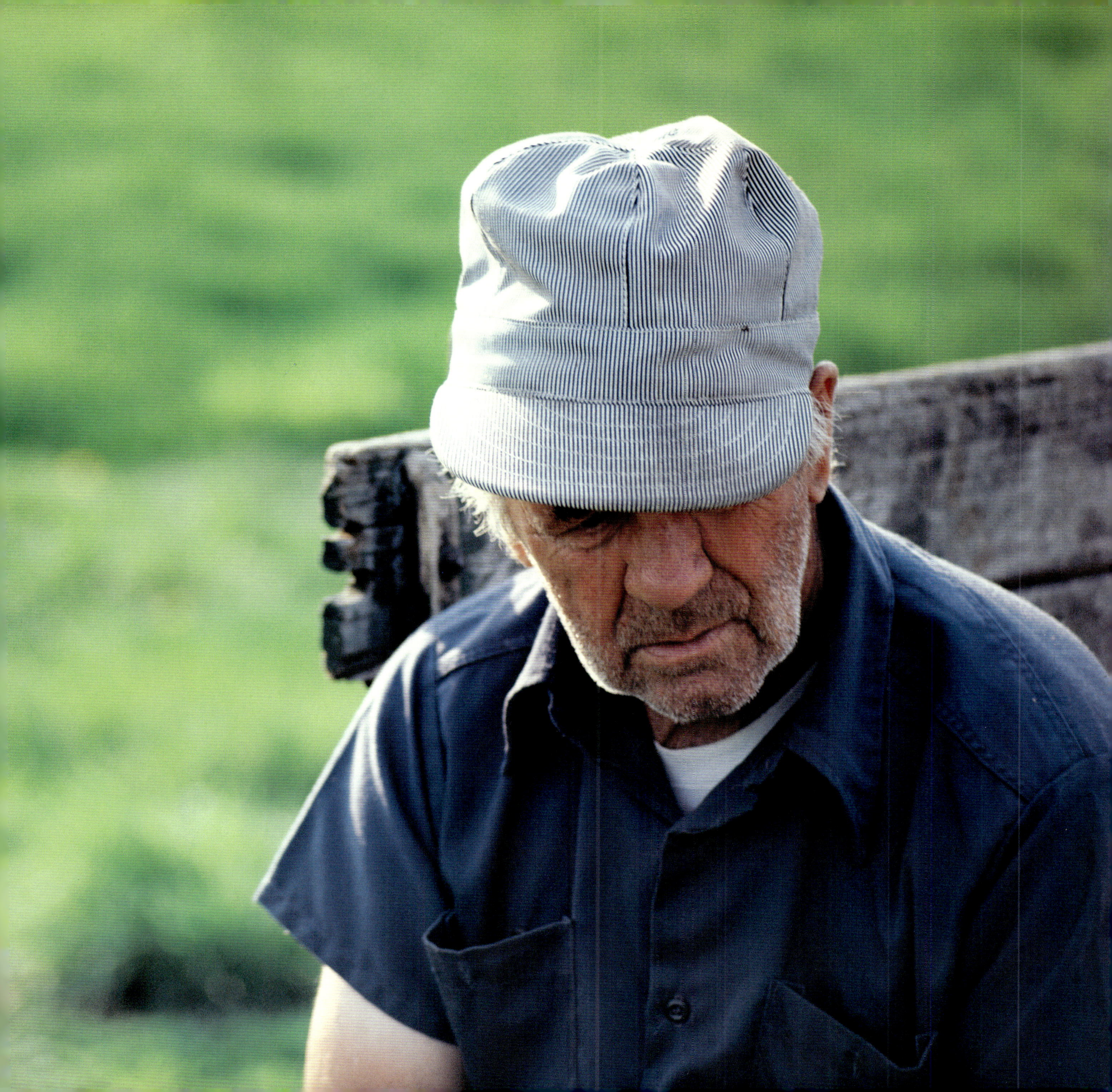

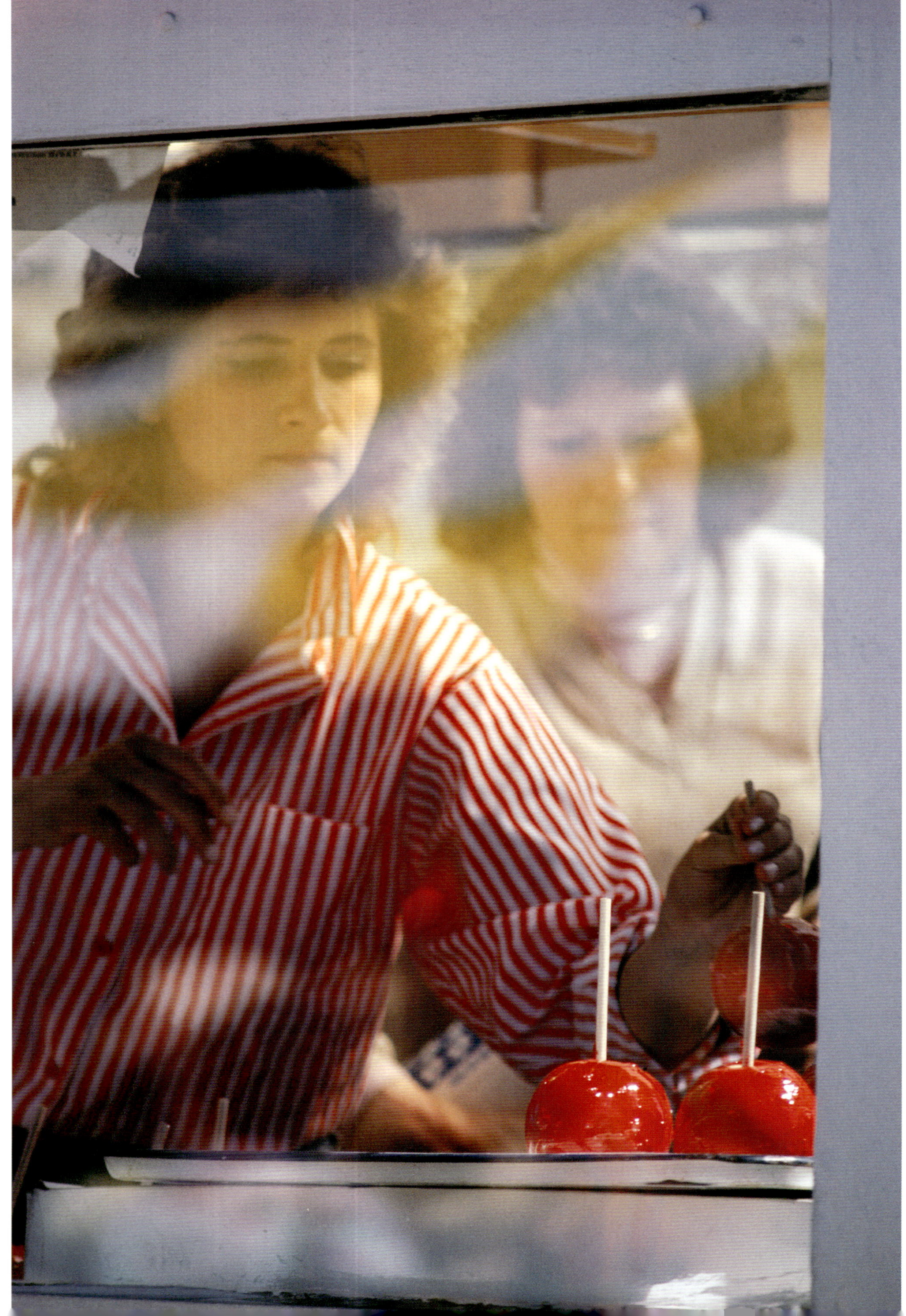

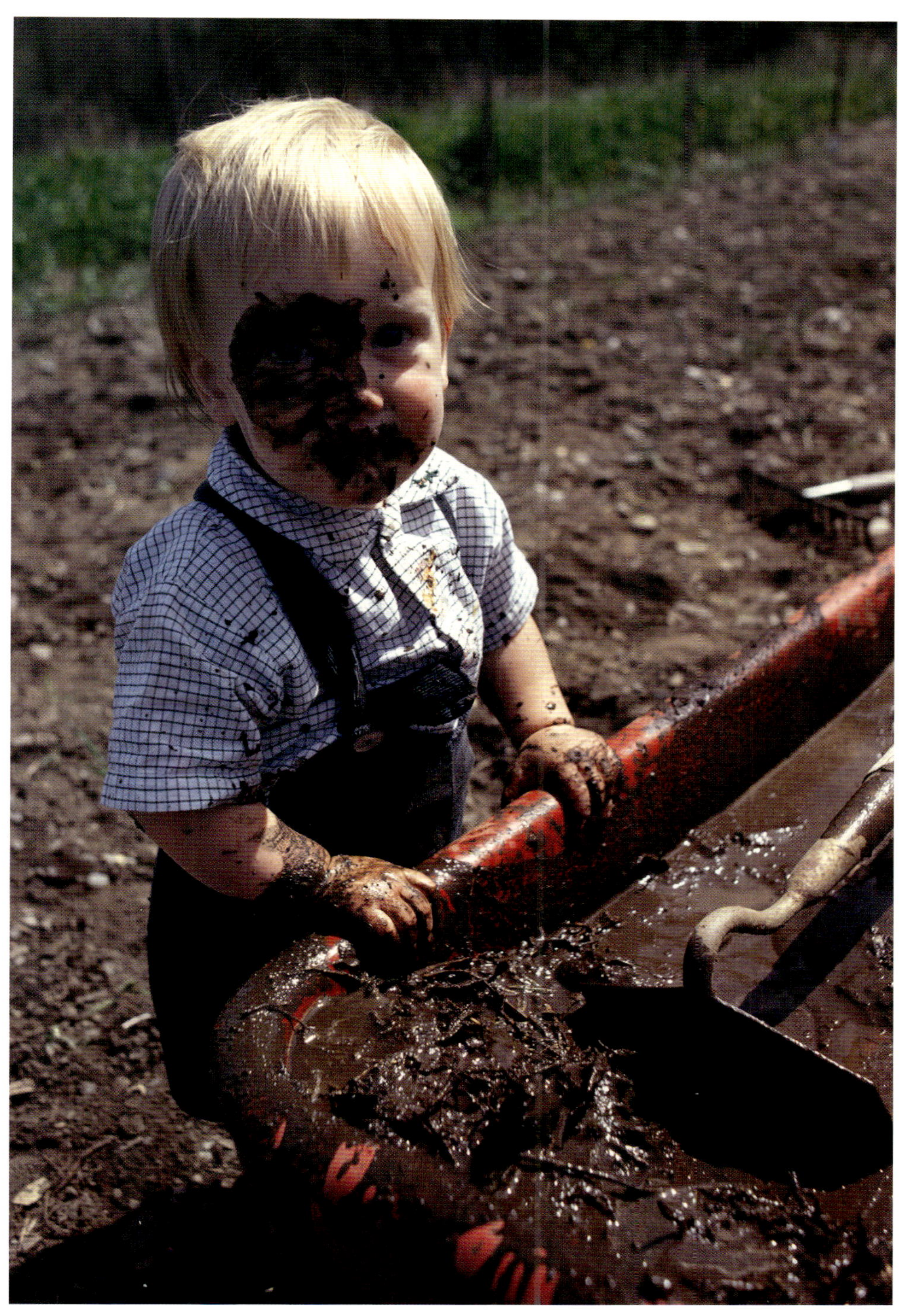

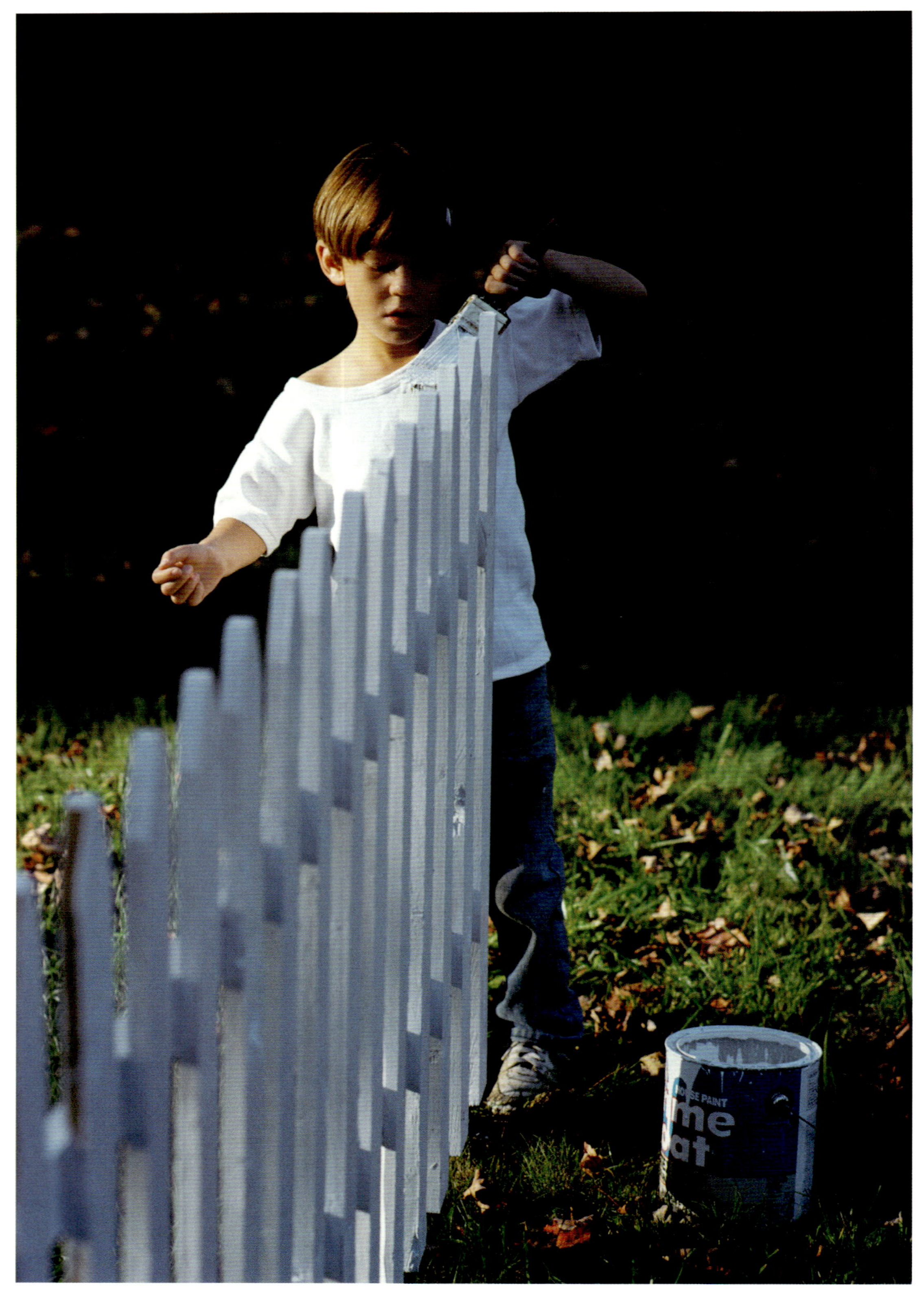
HOUSE PAINT
me
at

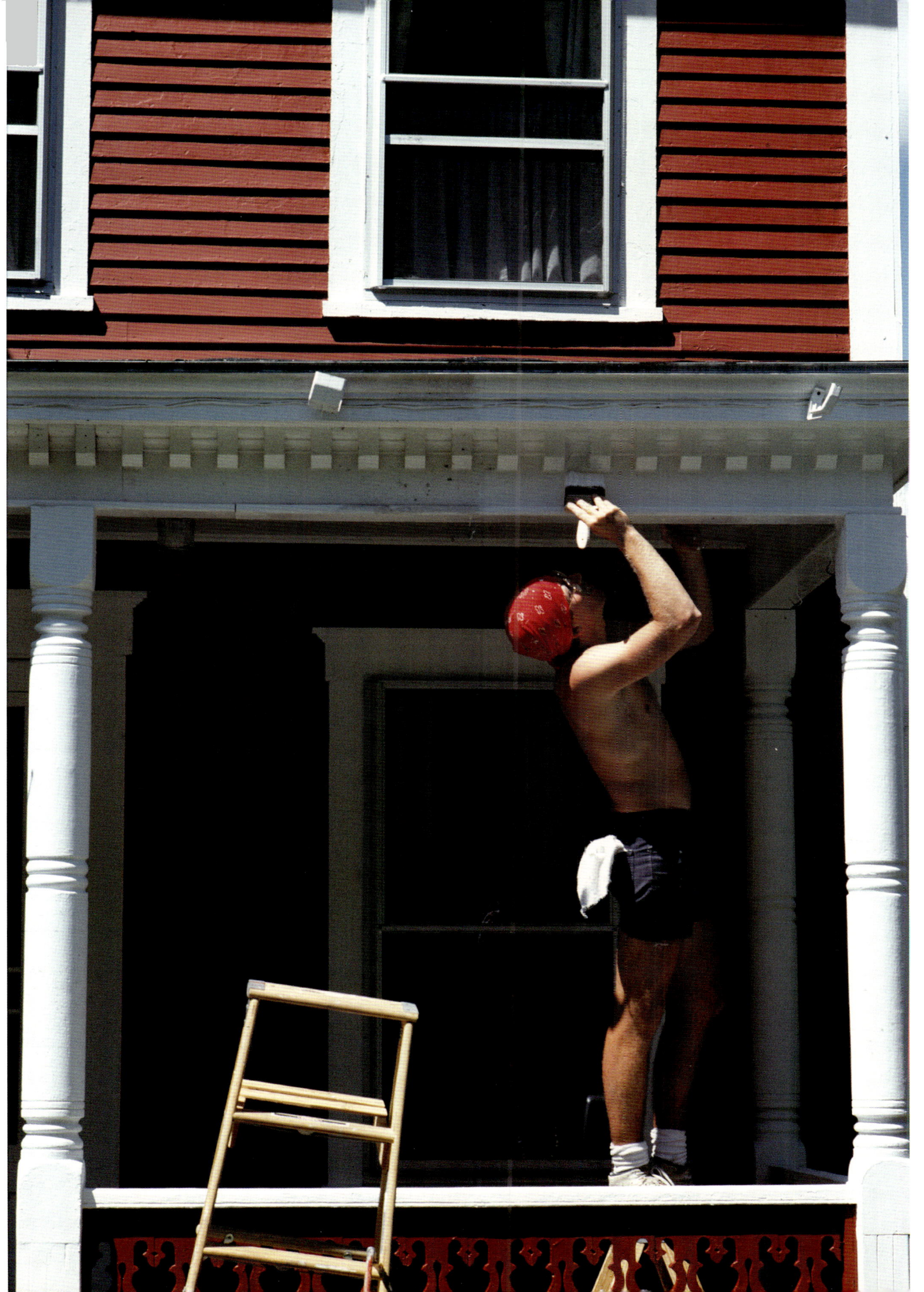

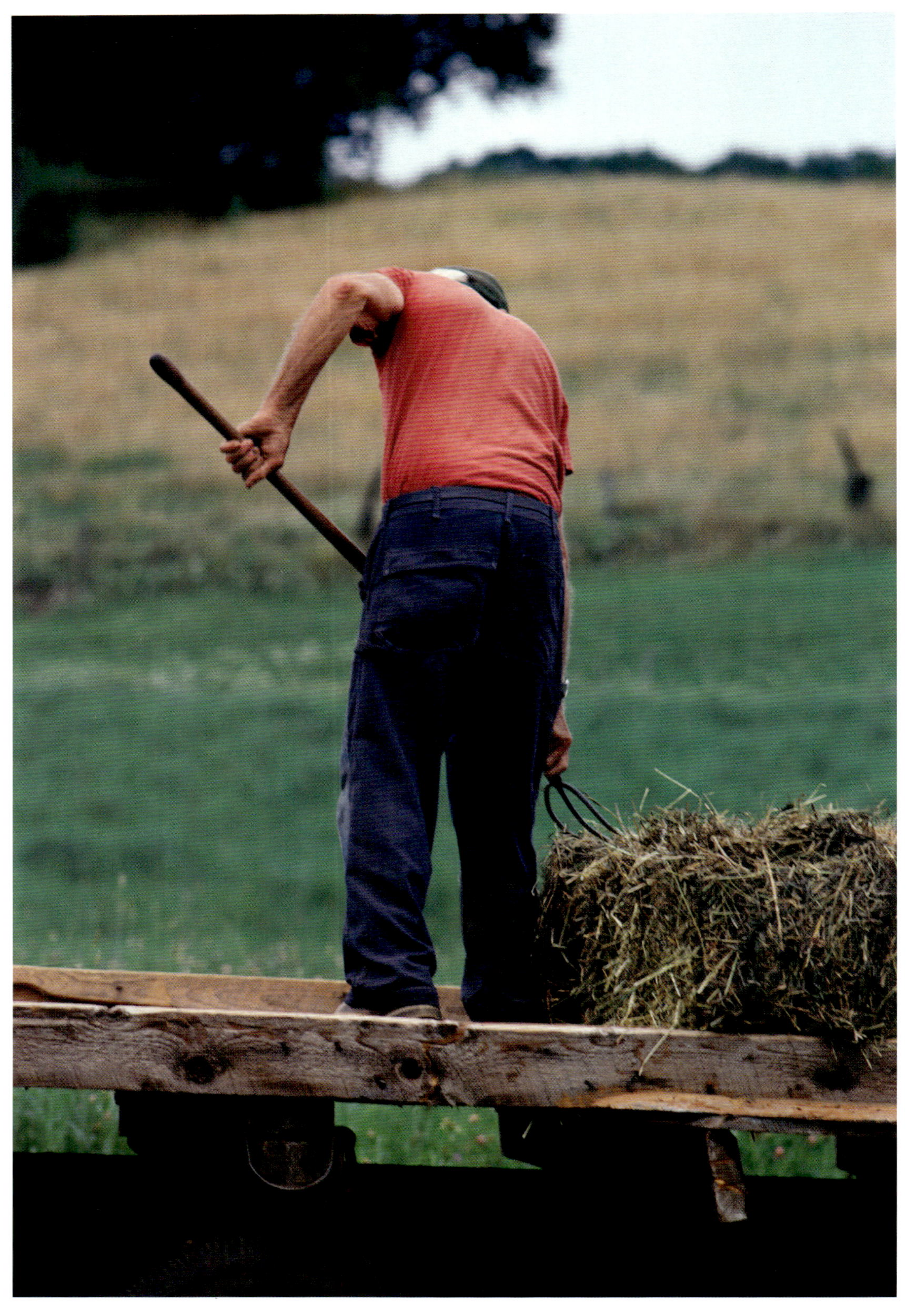

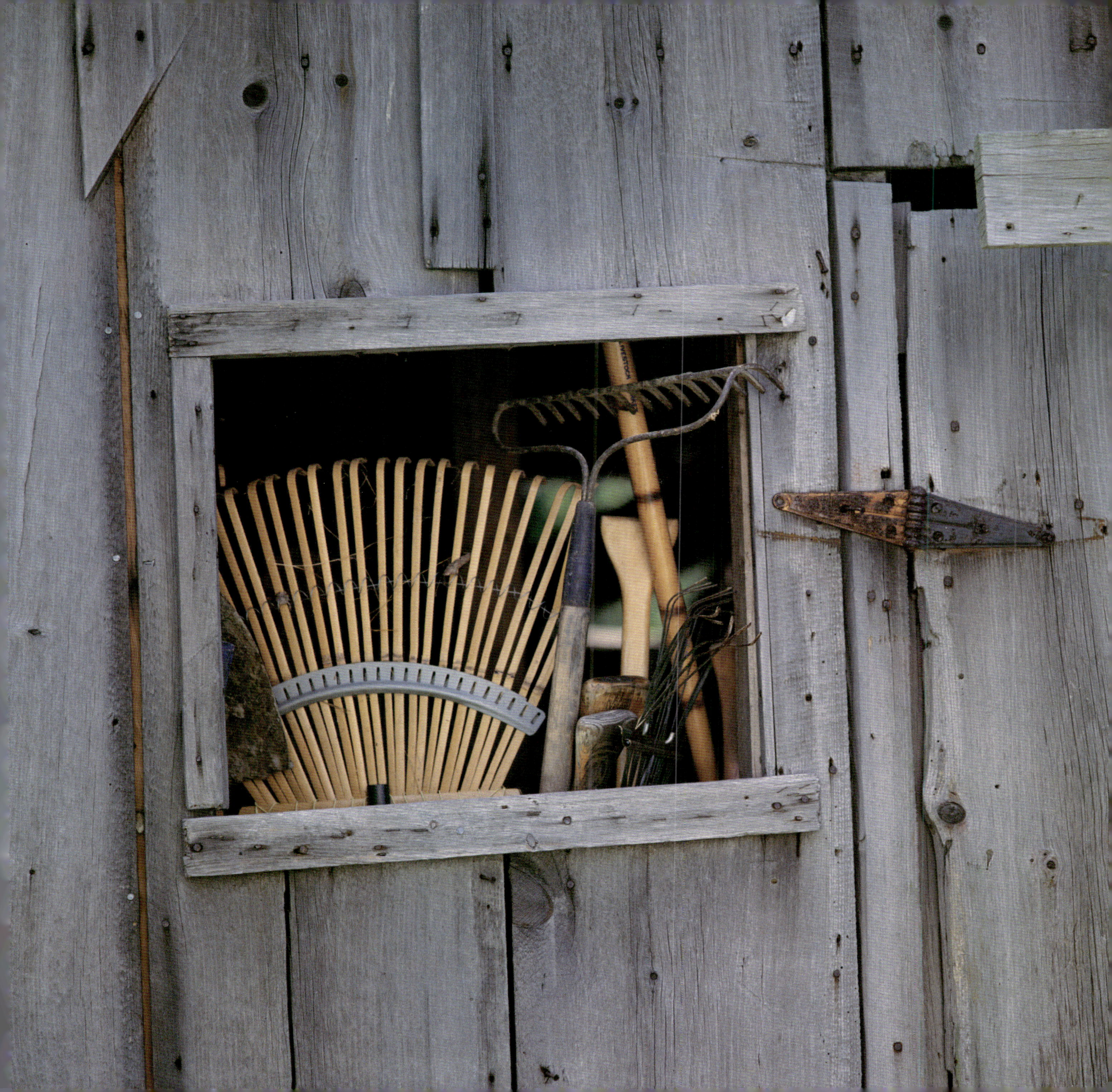

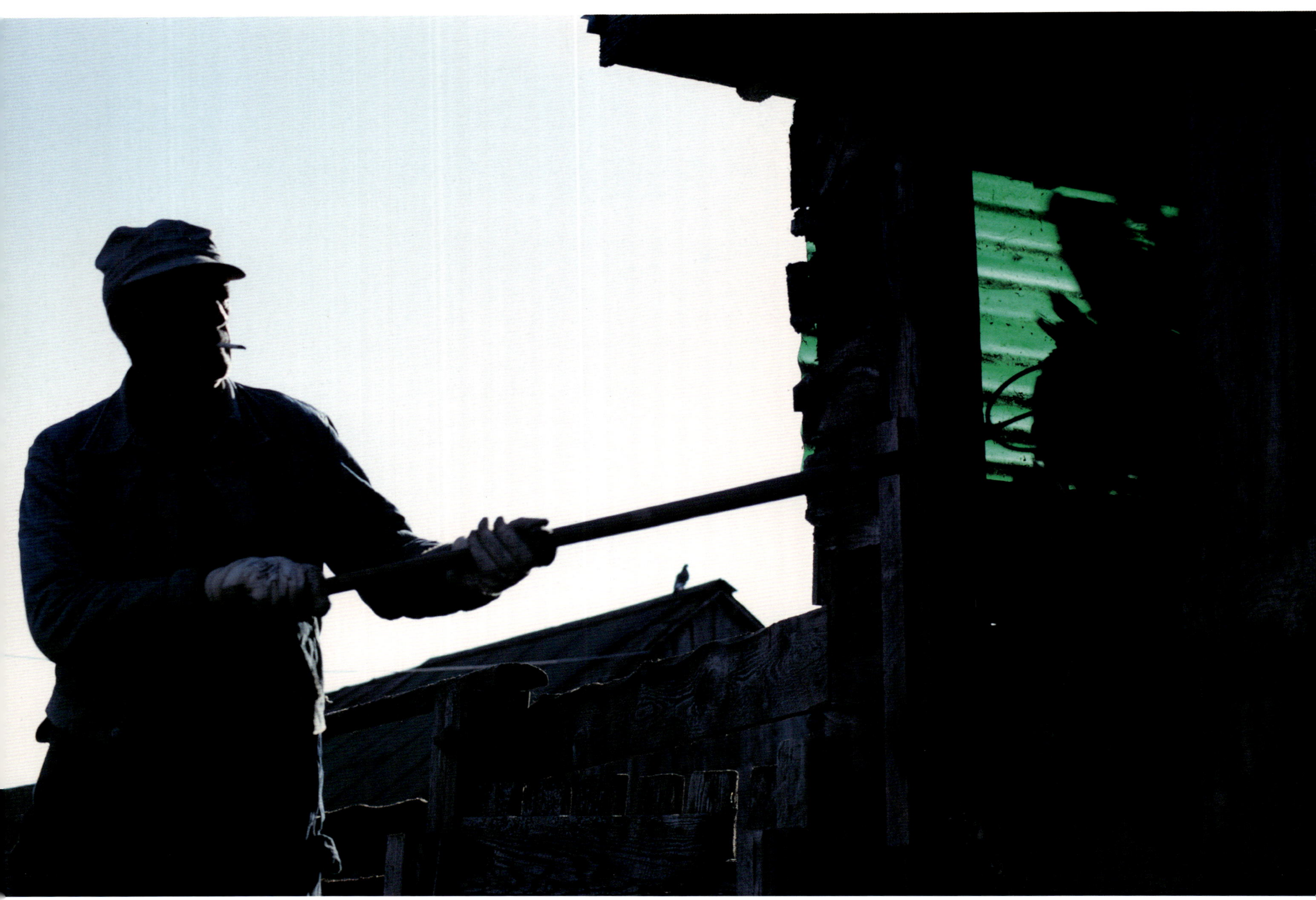

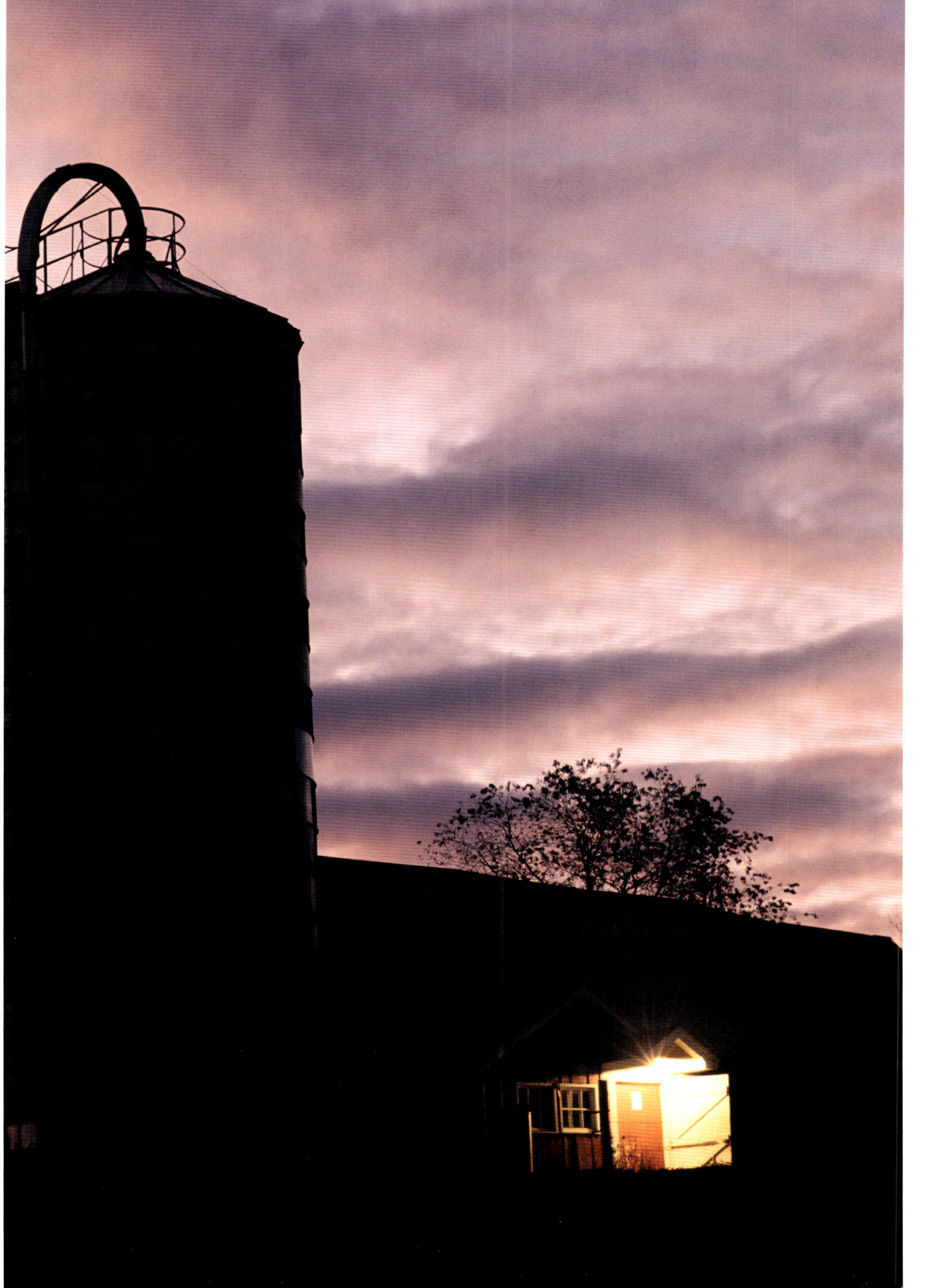

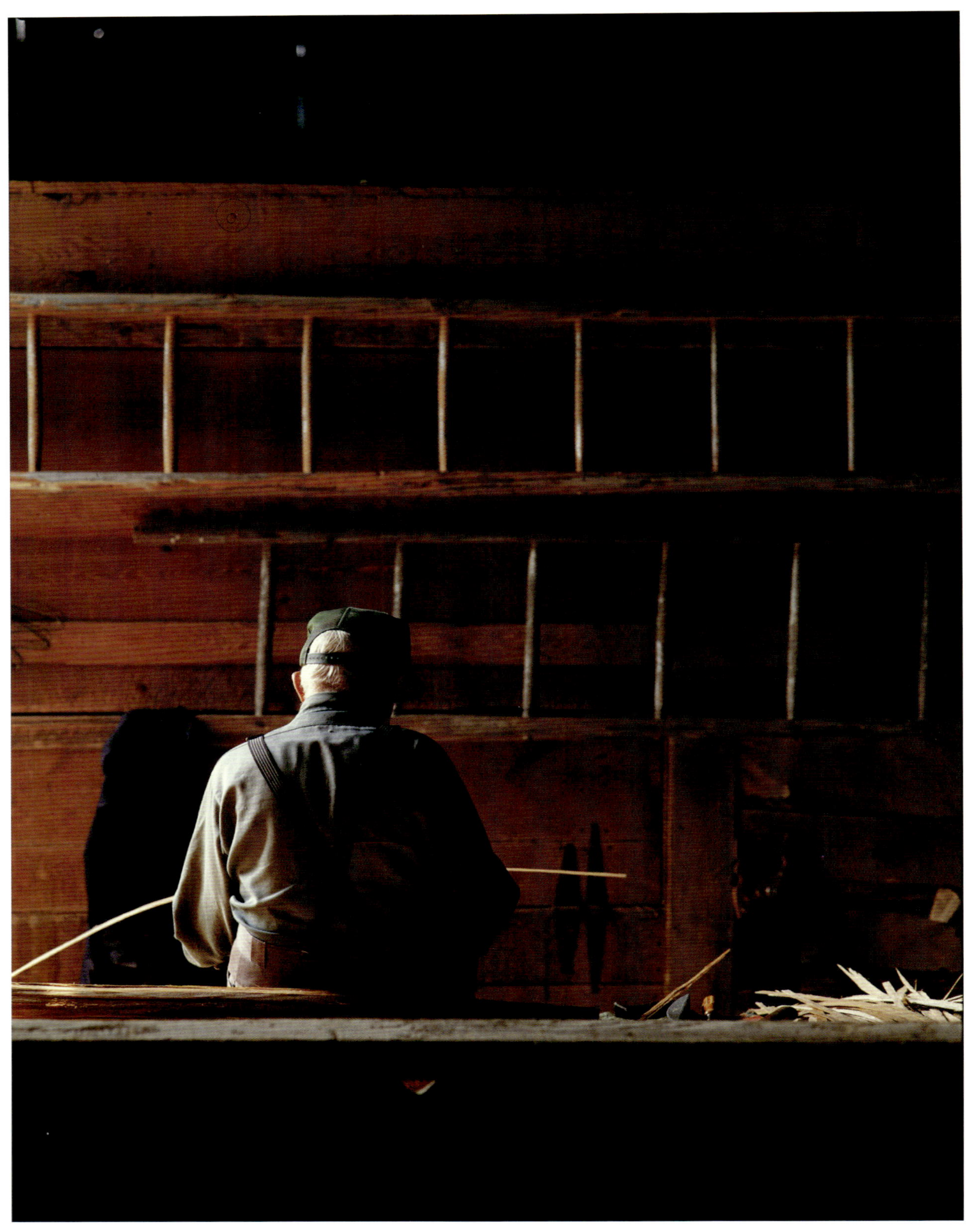

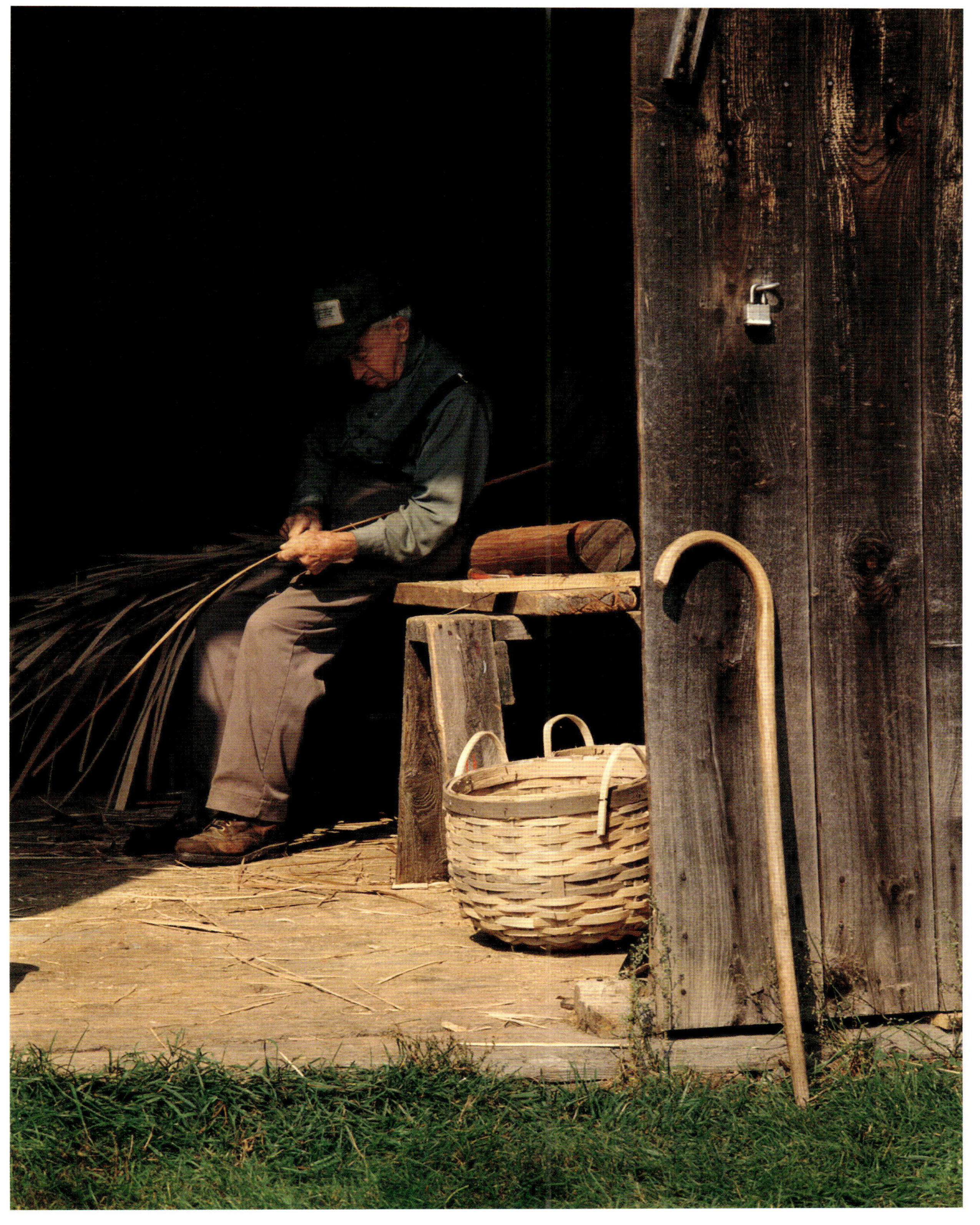

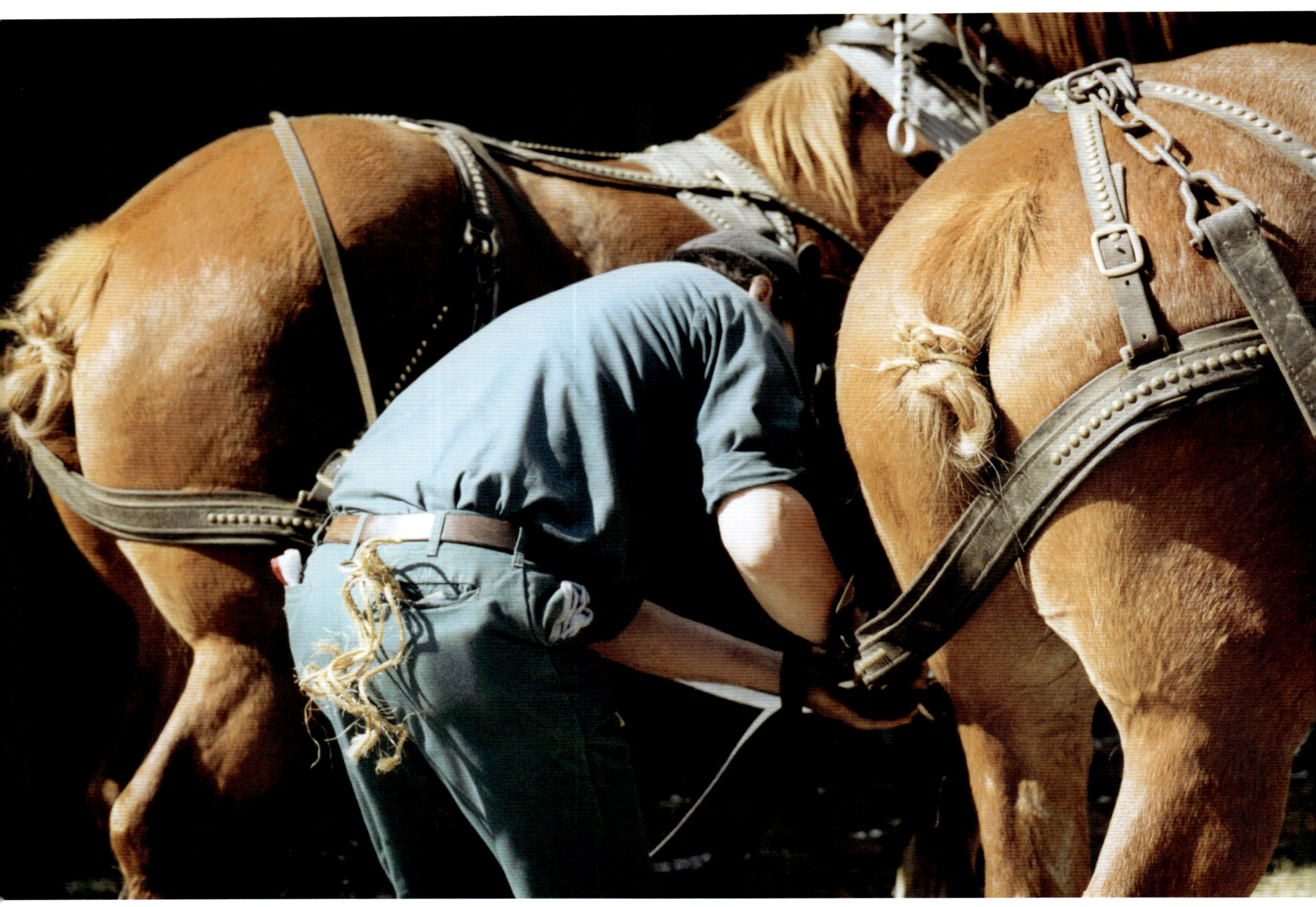

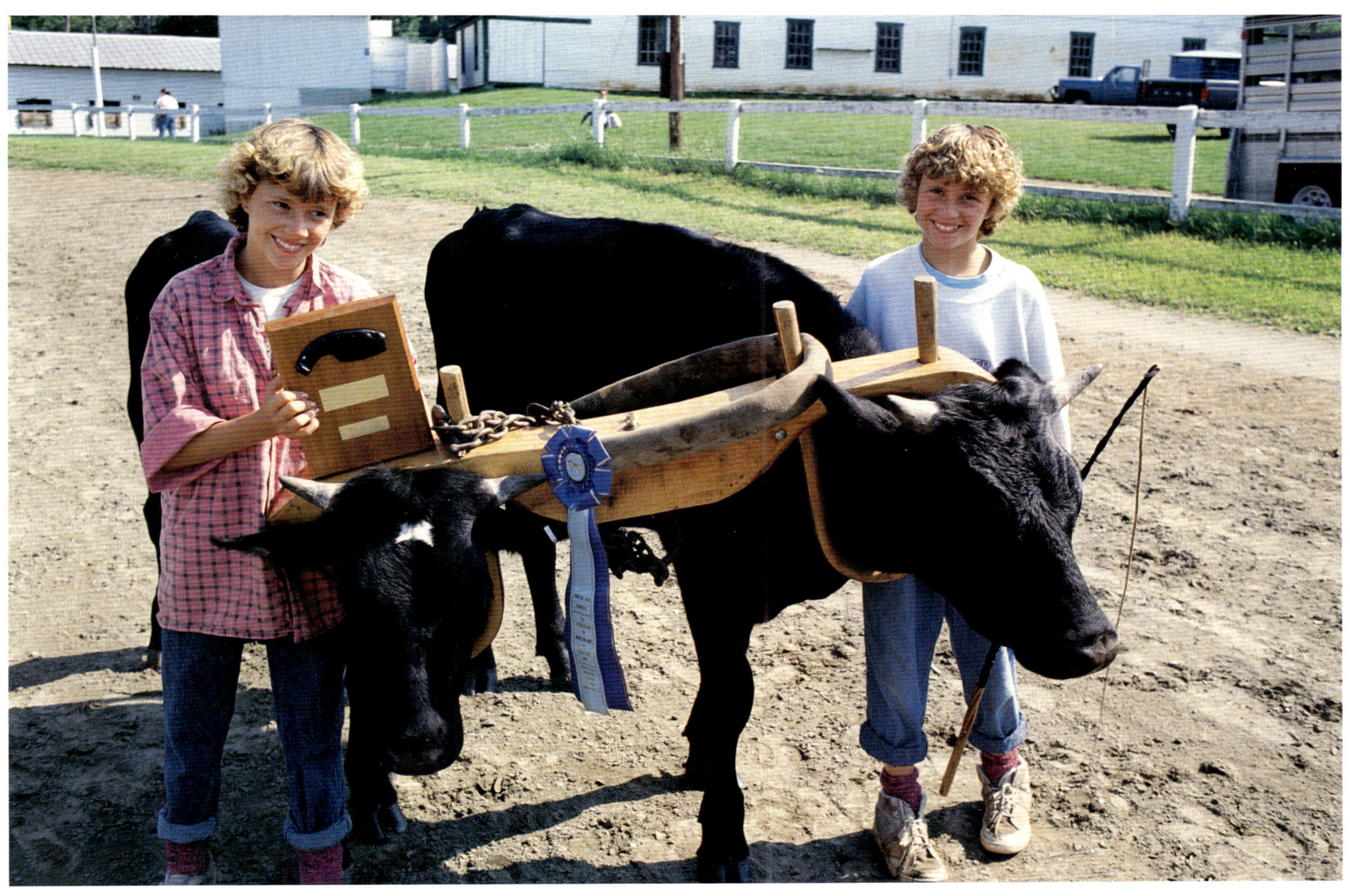

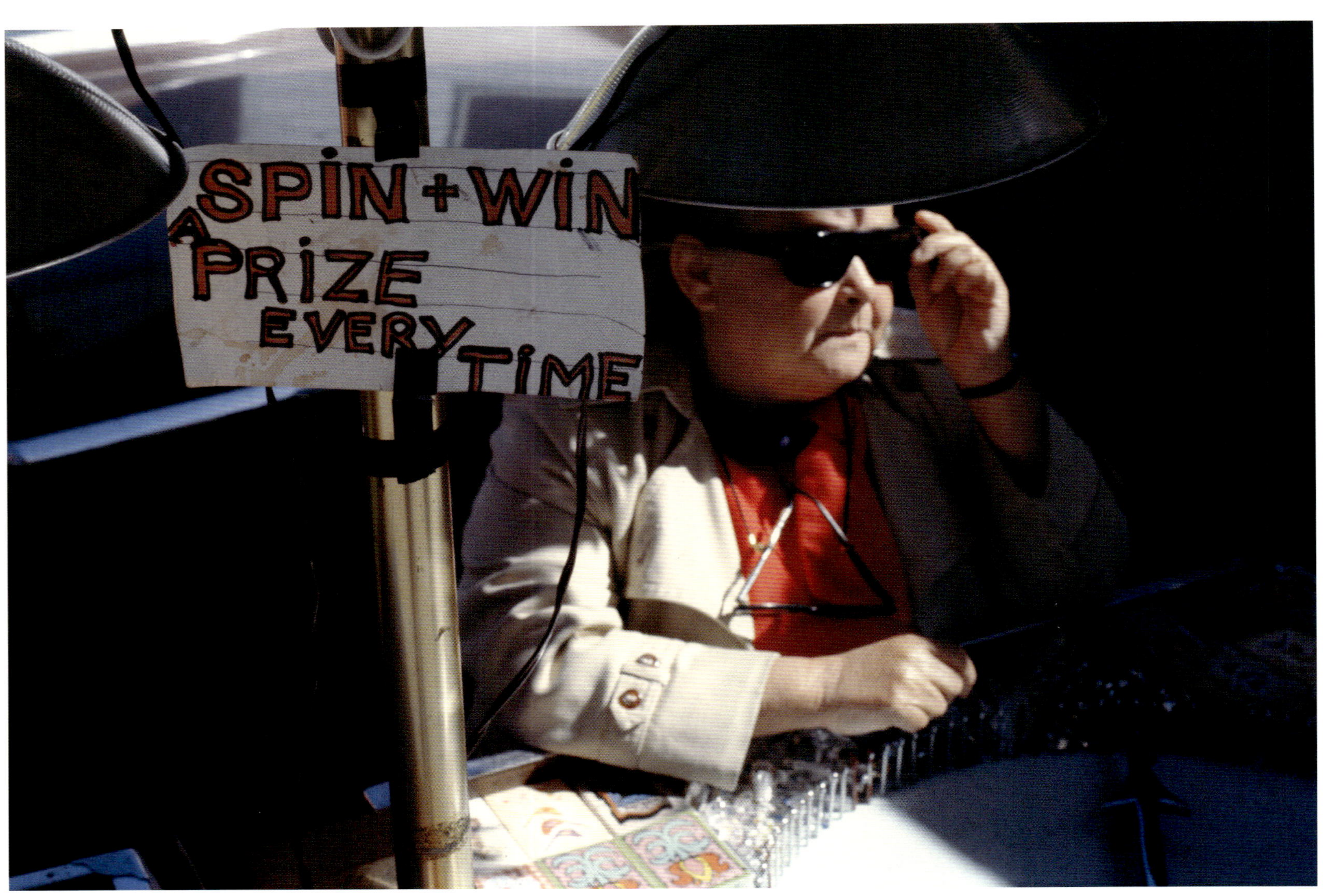

SPIN + WIN
A PRIZE
EVERY TIME

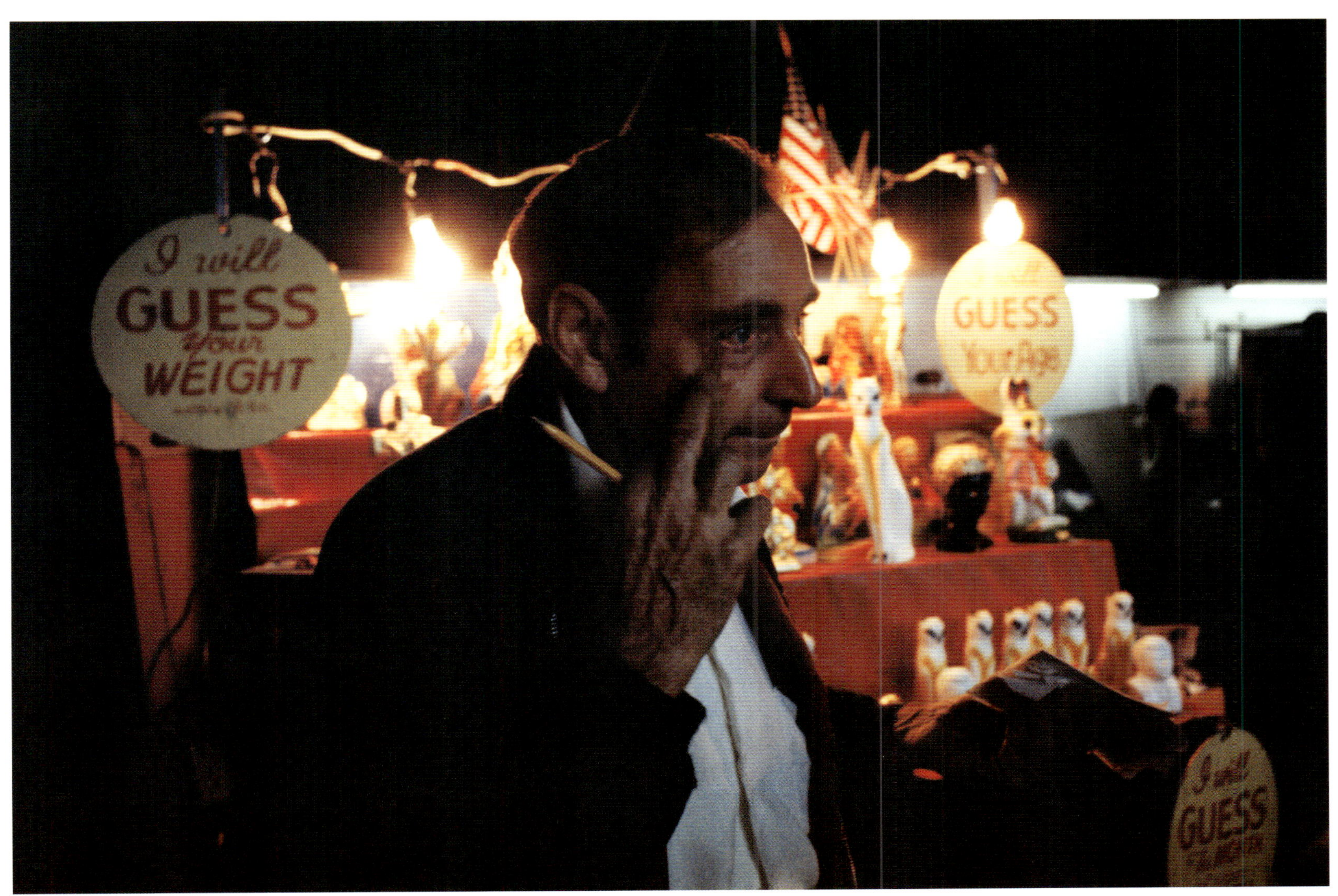

I will
GUESS
your
WEIGHT


GUESS
Your Age


I will
GUESS

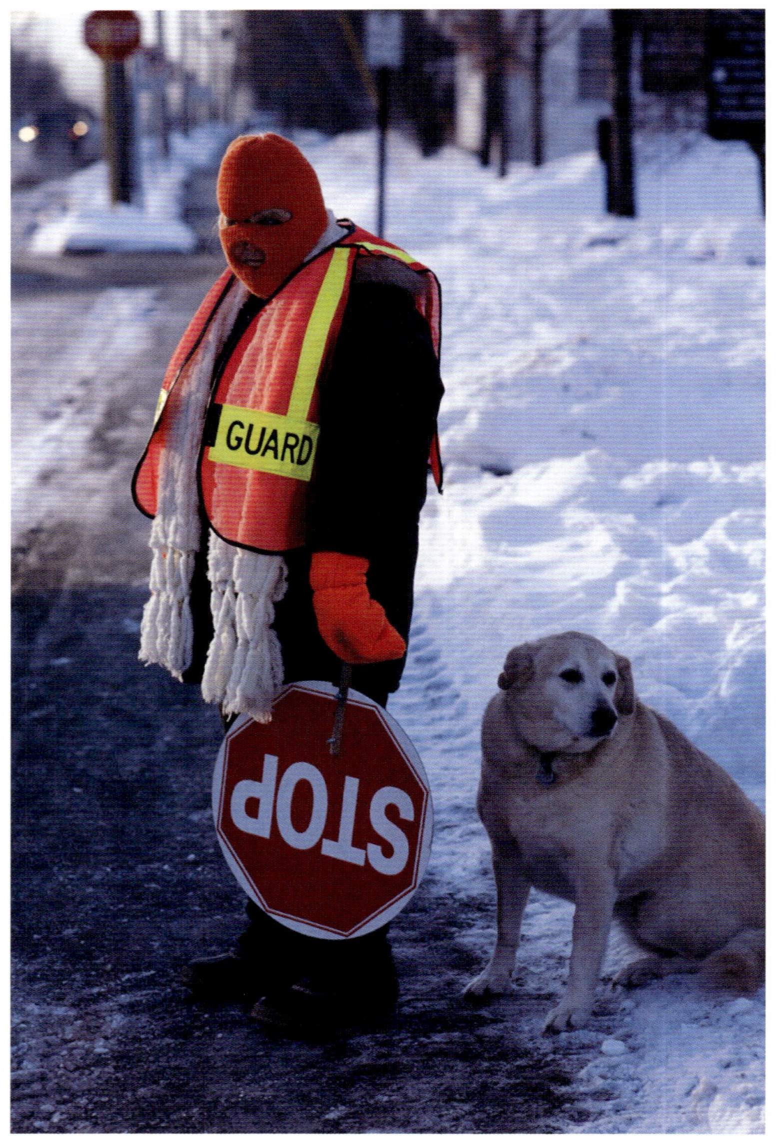

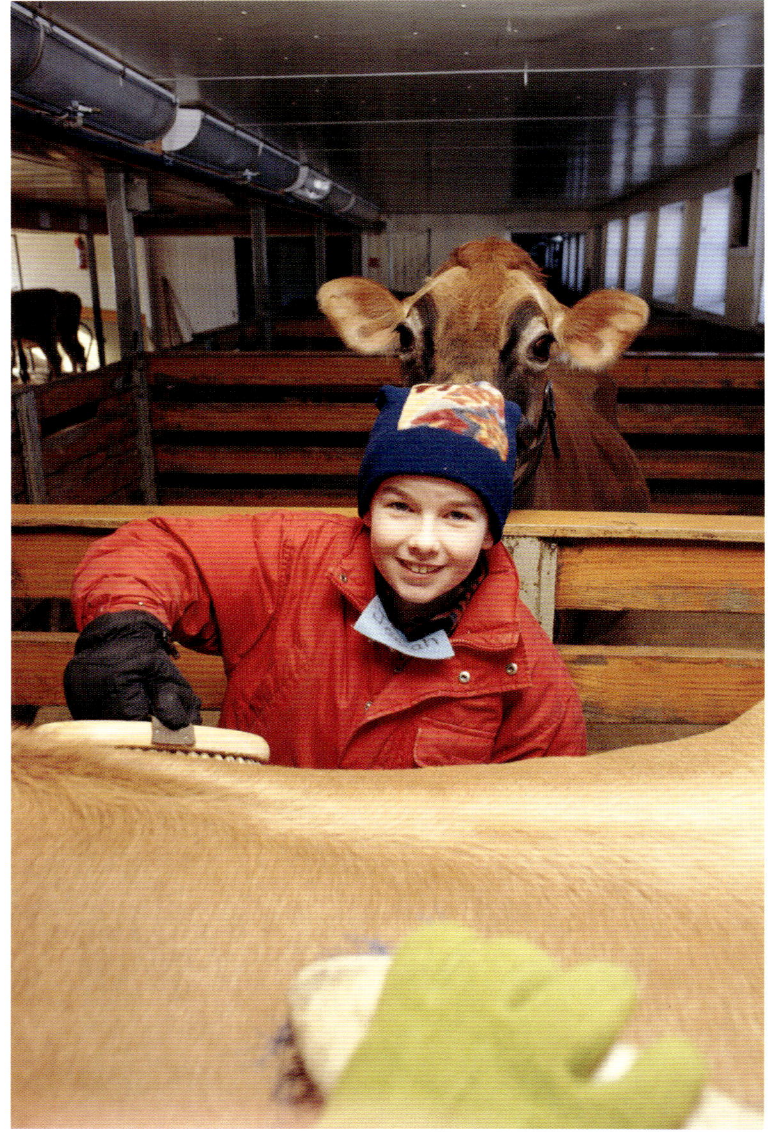

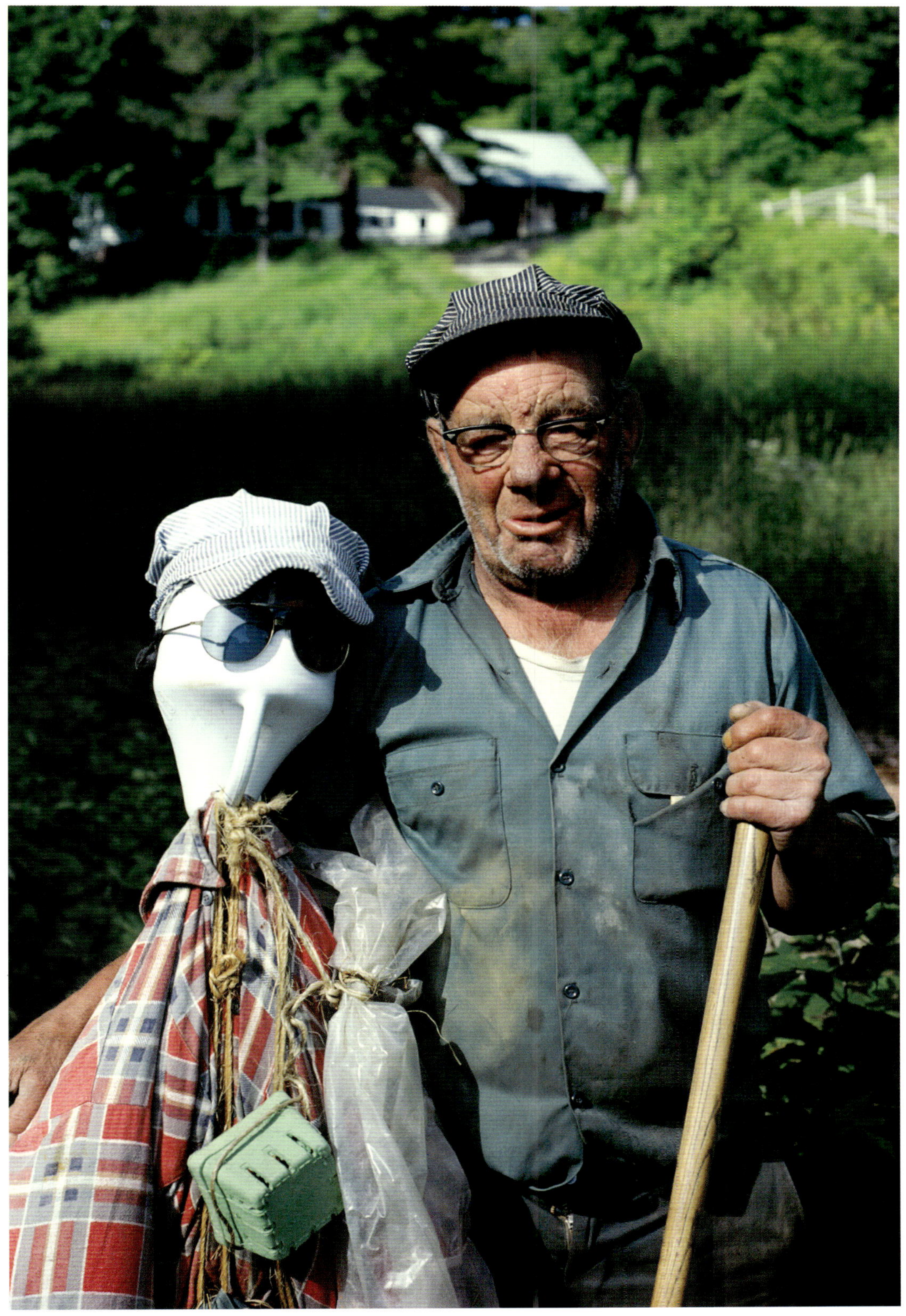

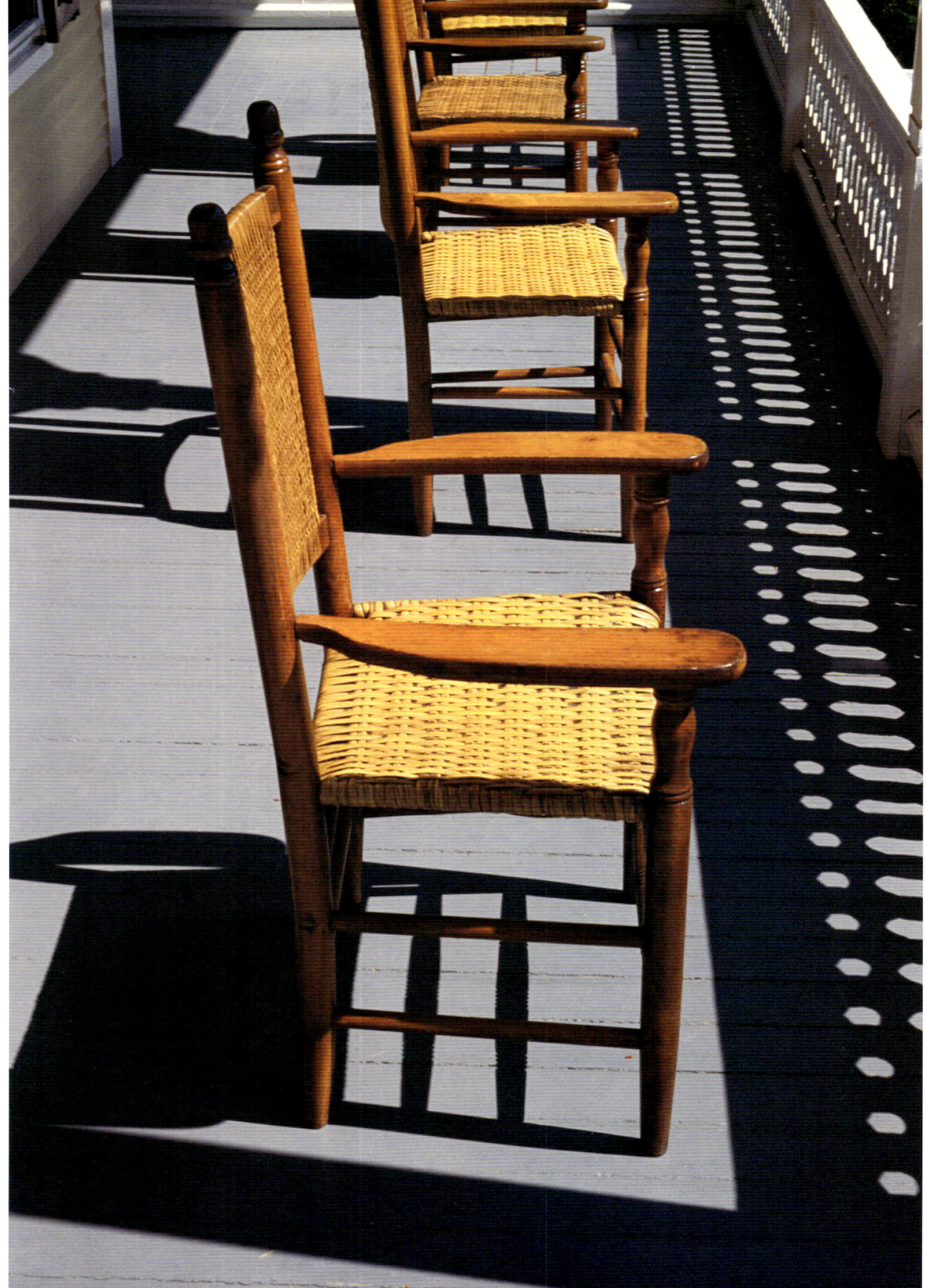

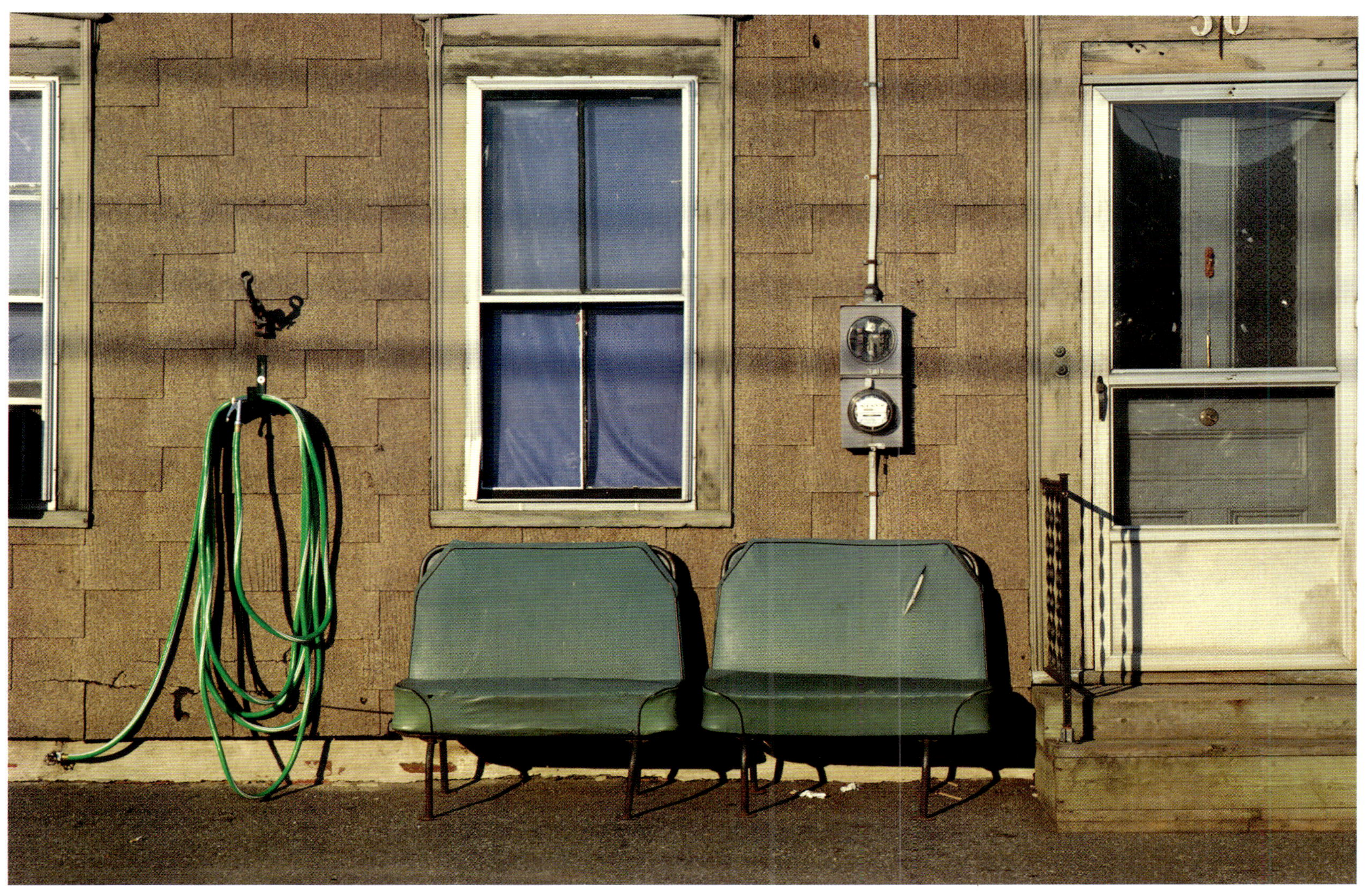

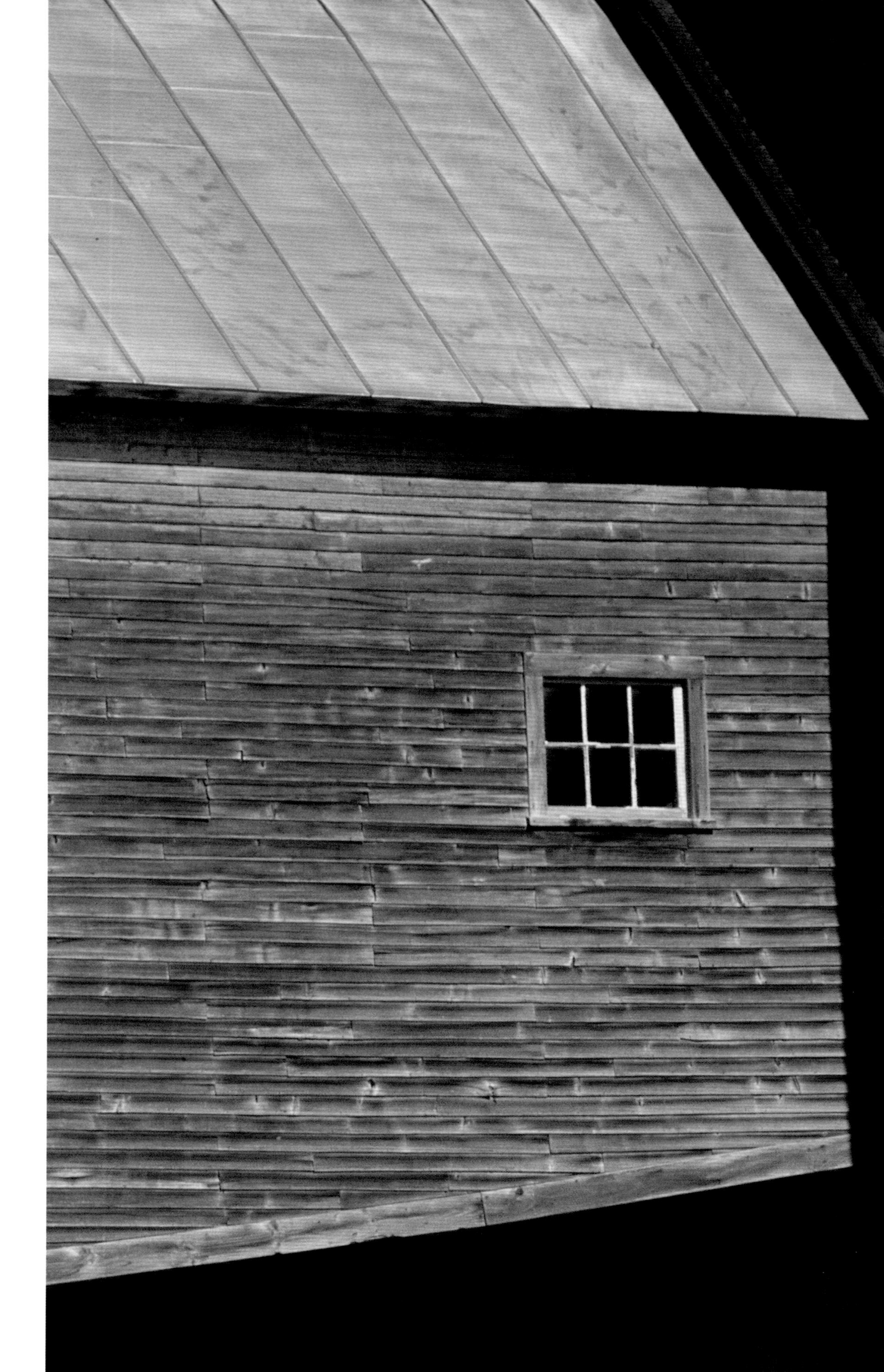

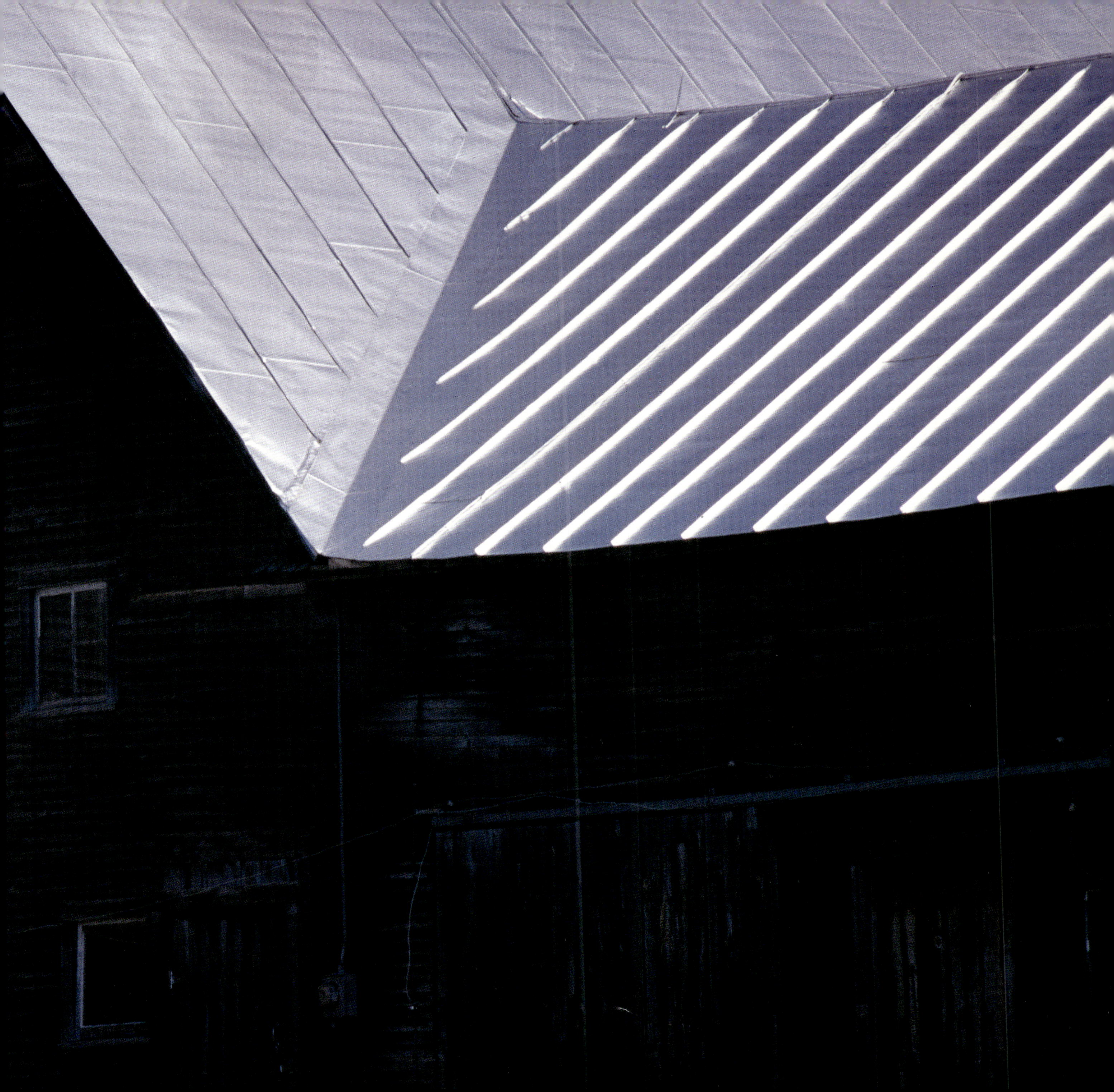

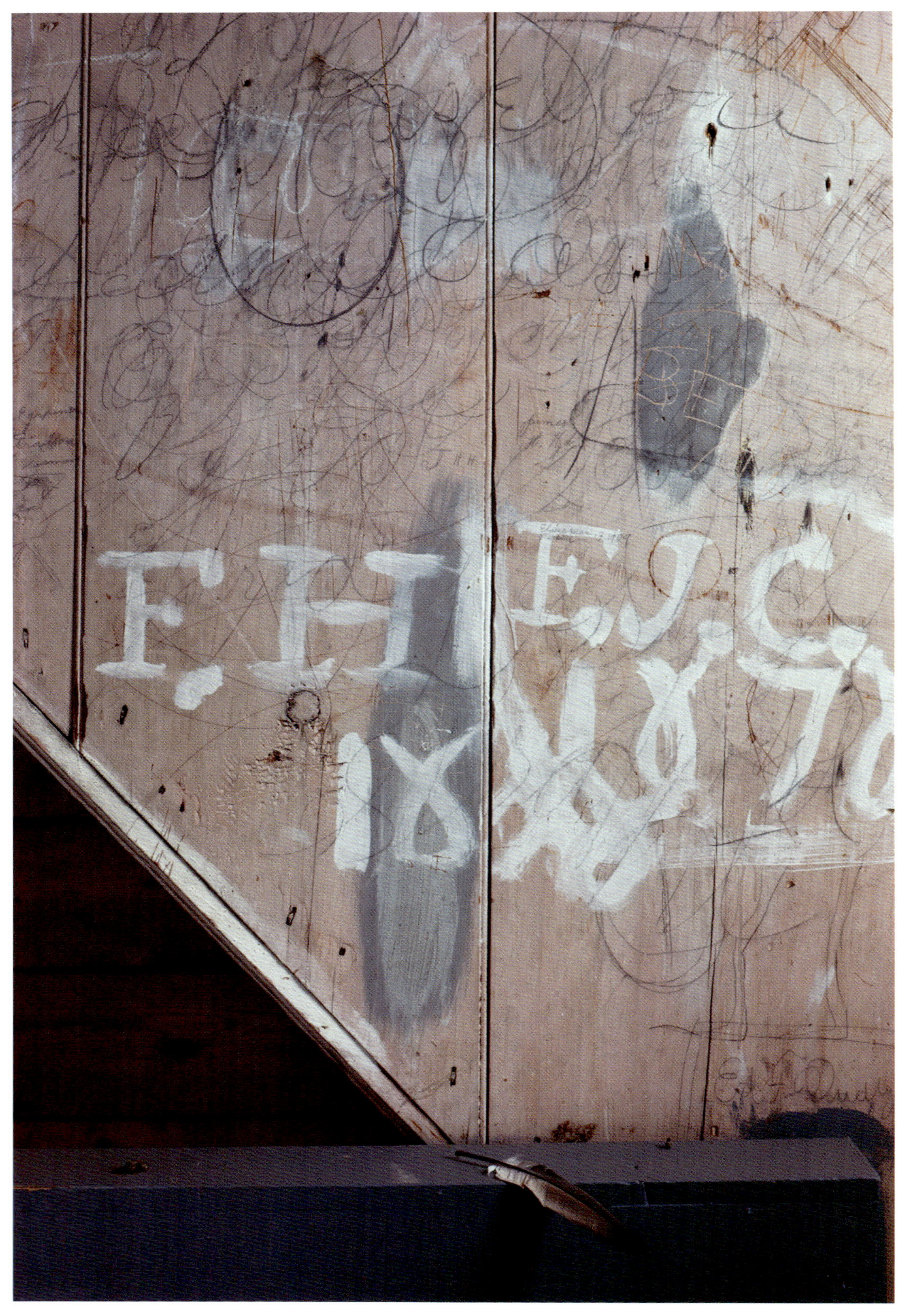

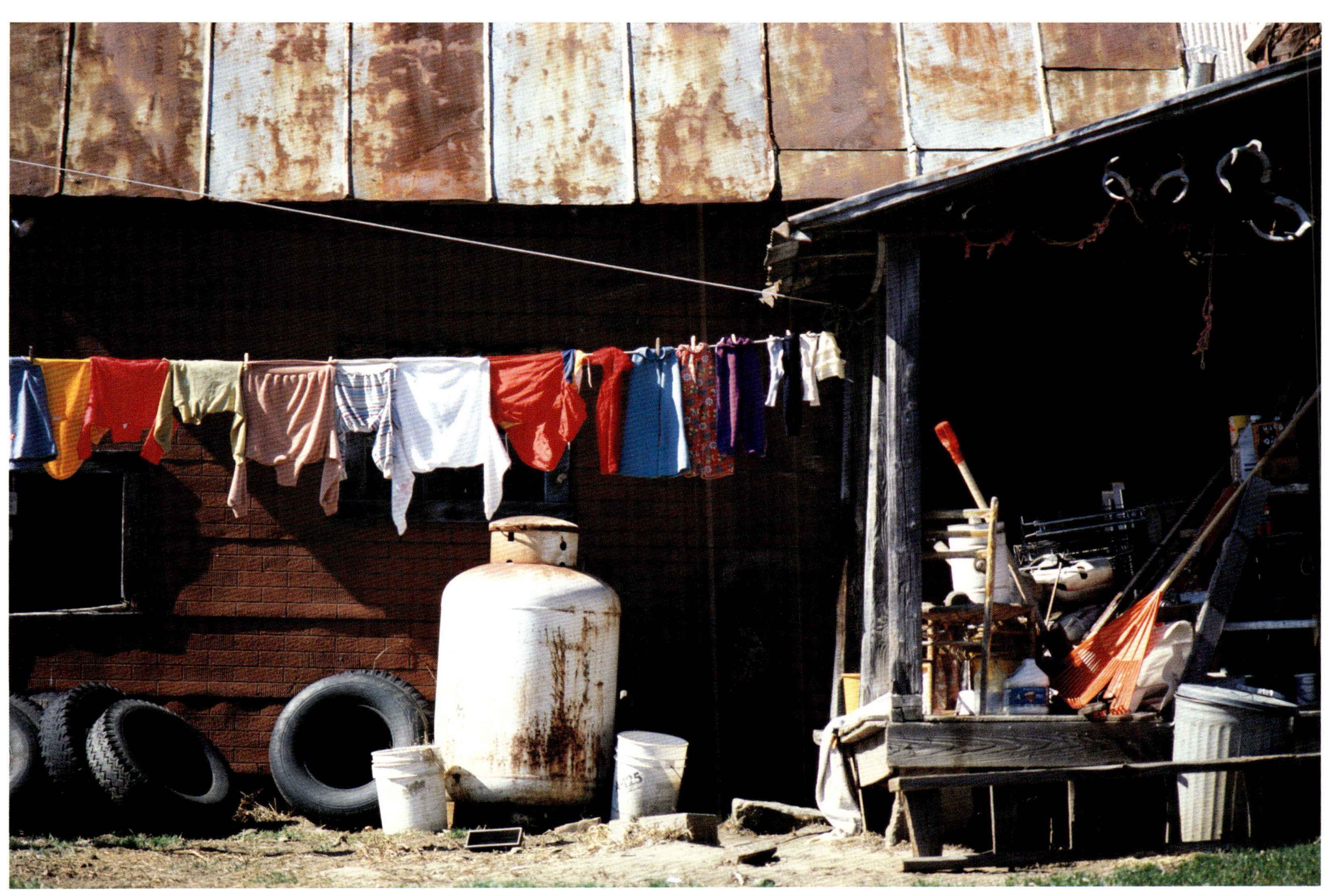

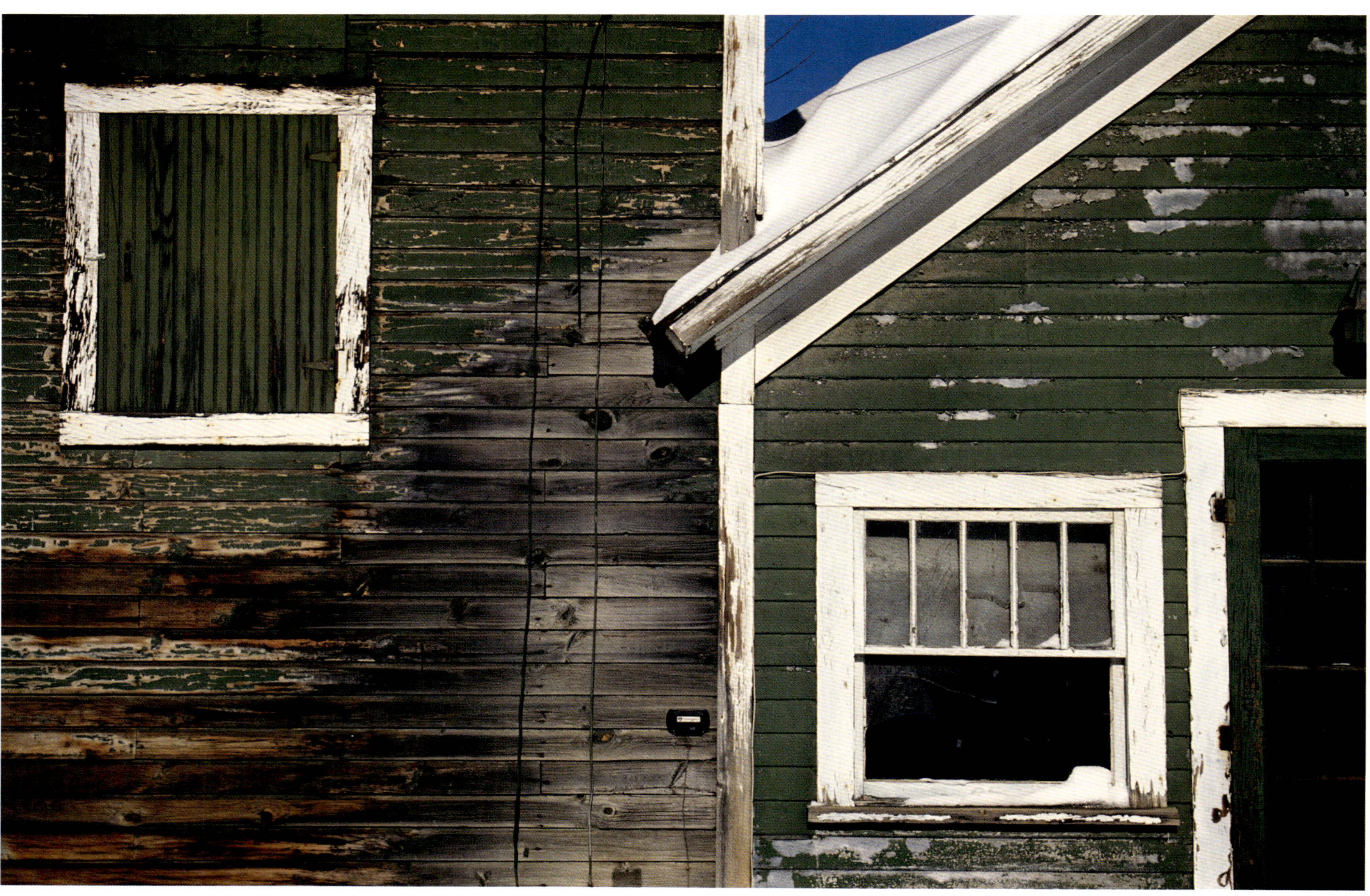

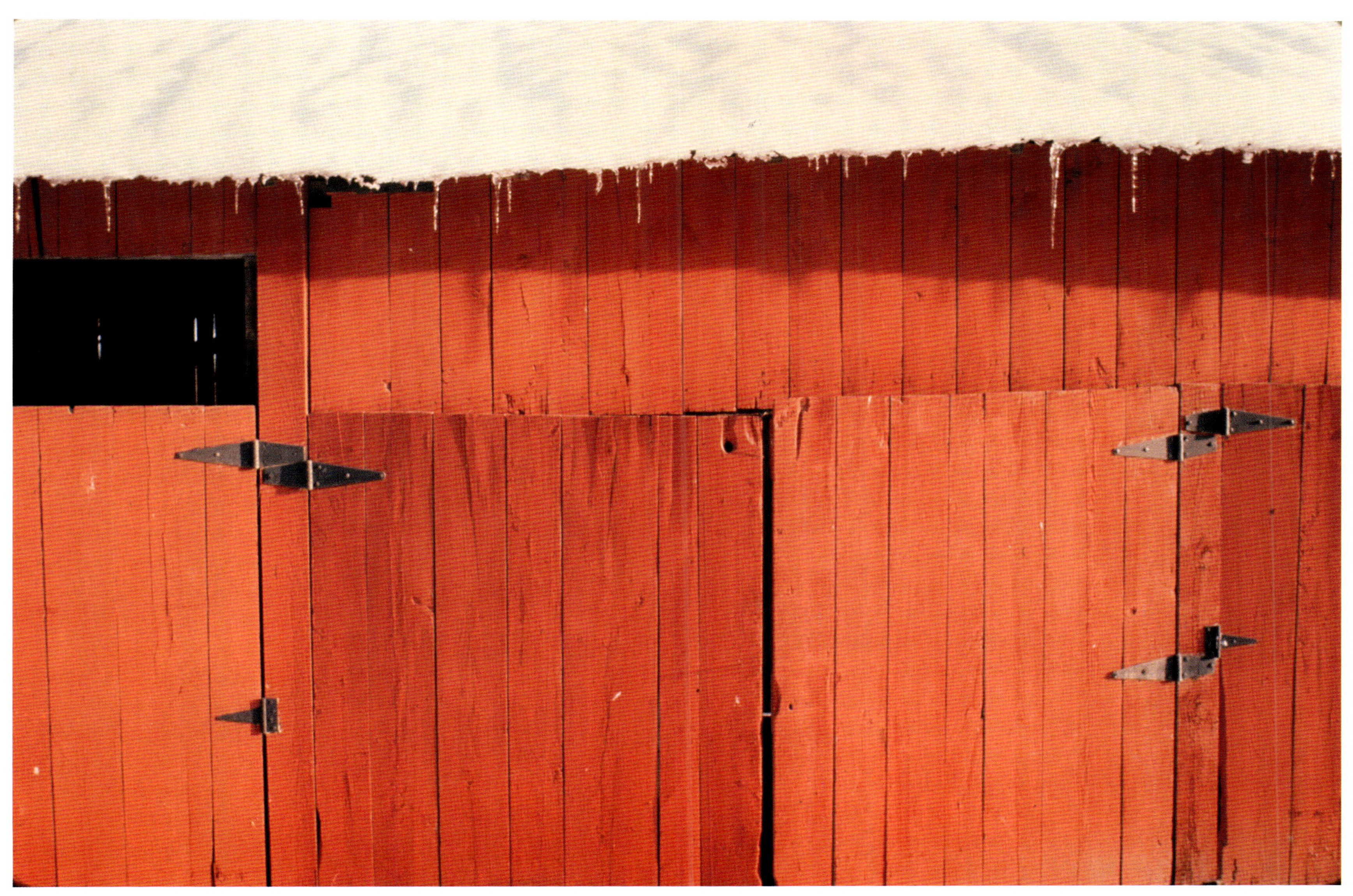

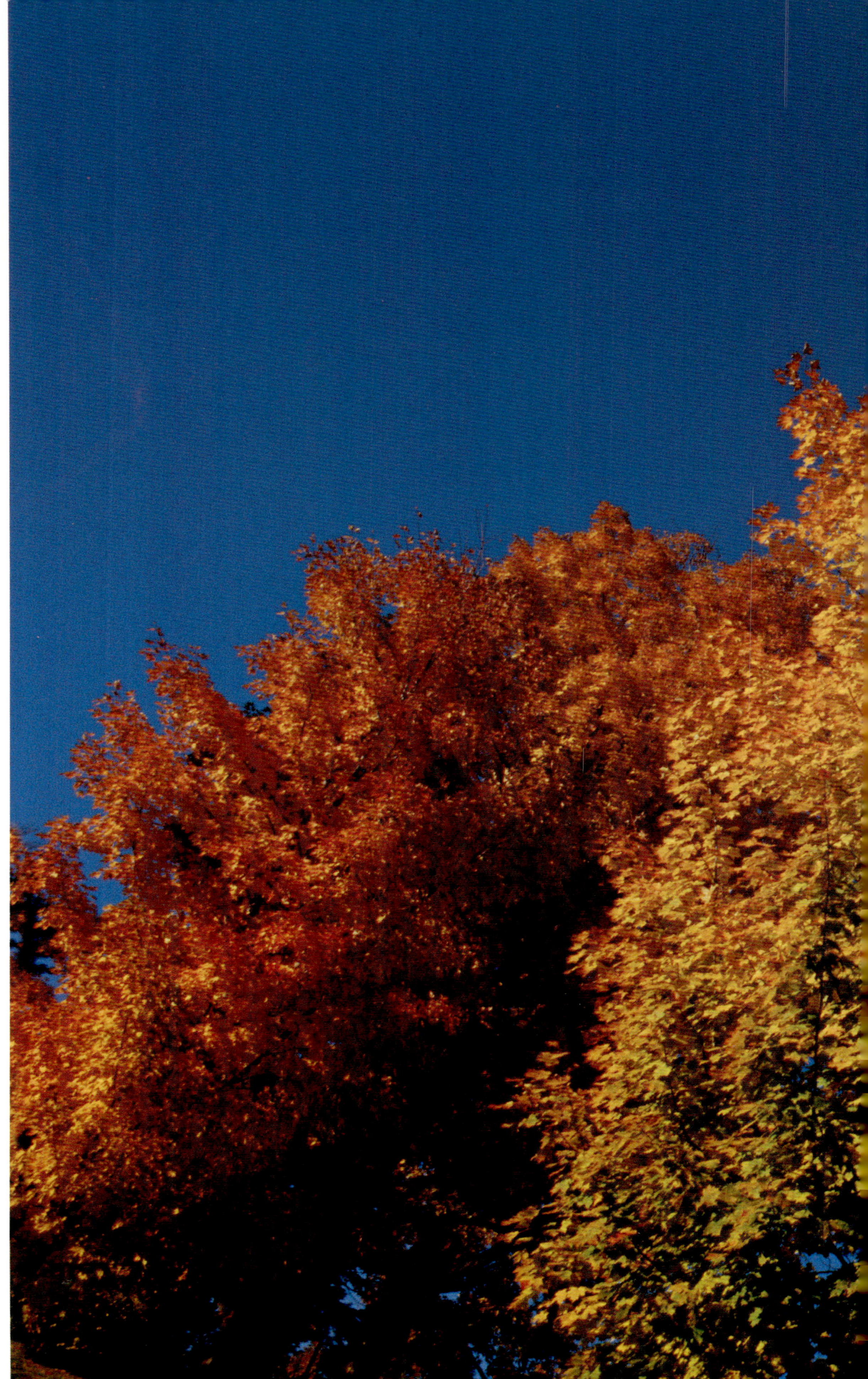

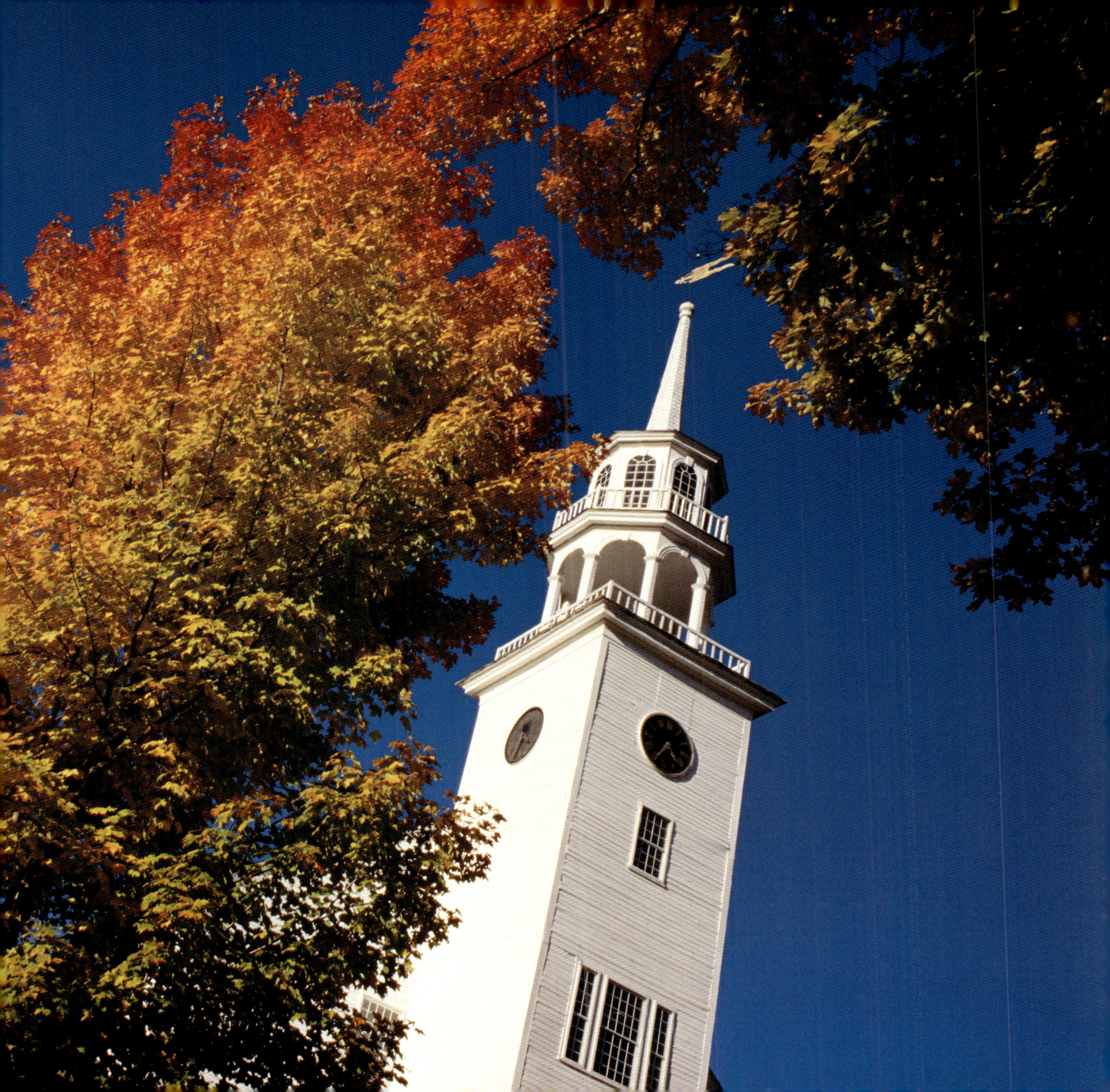

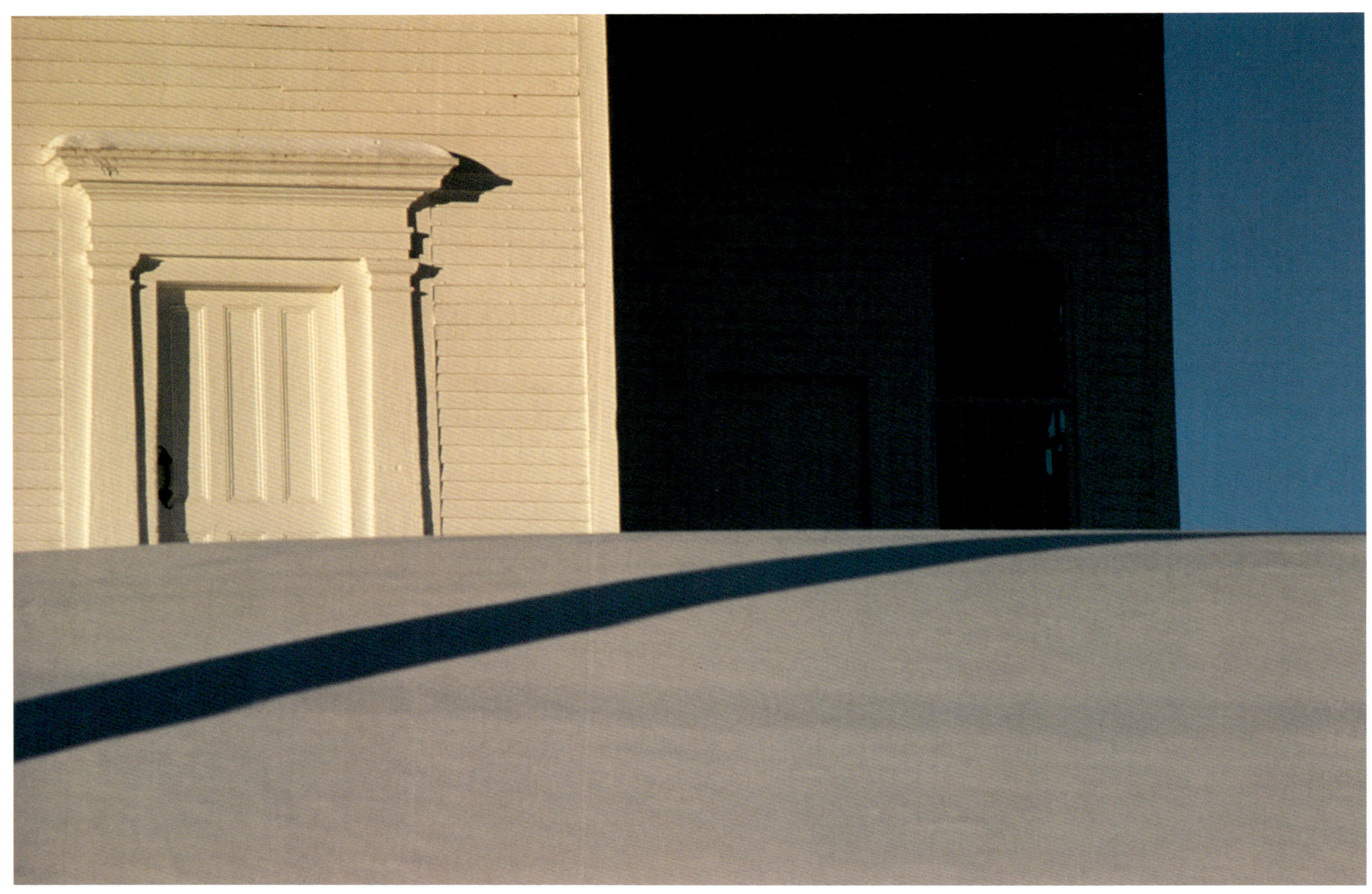

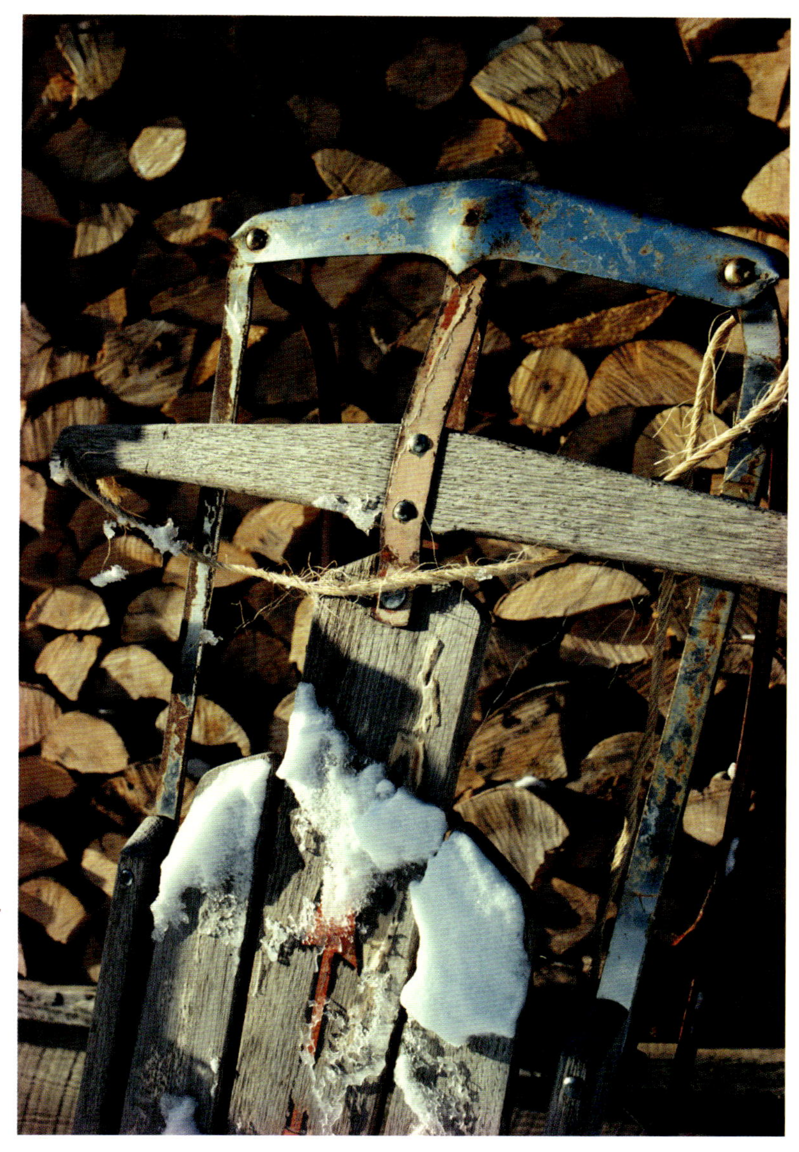
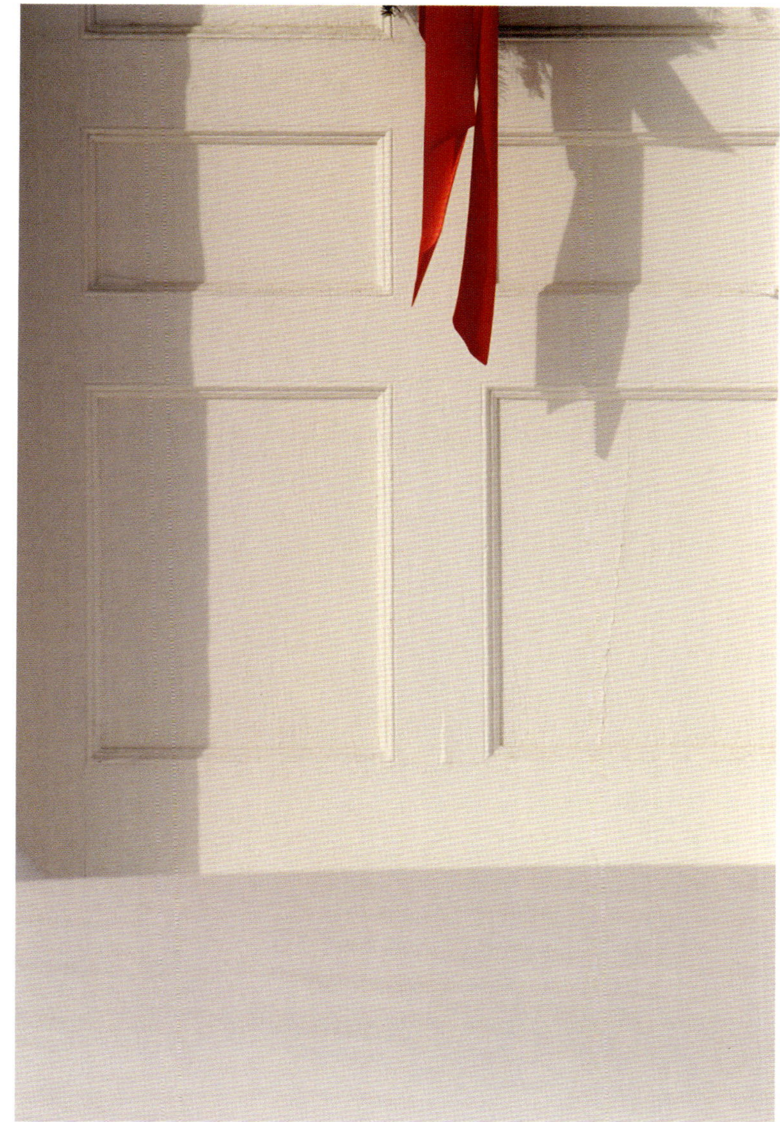

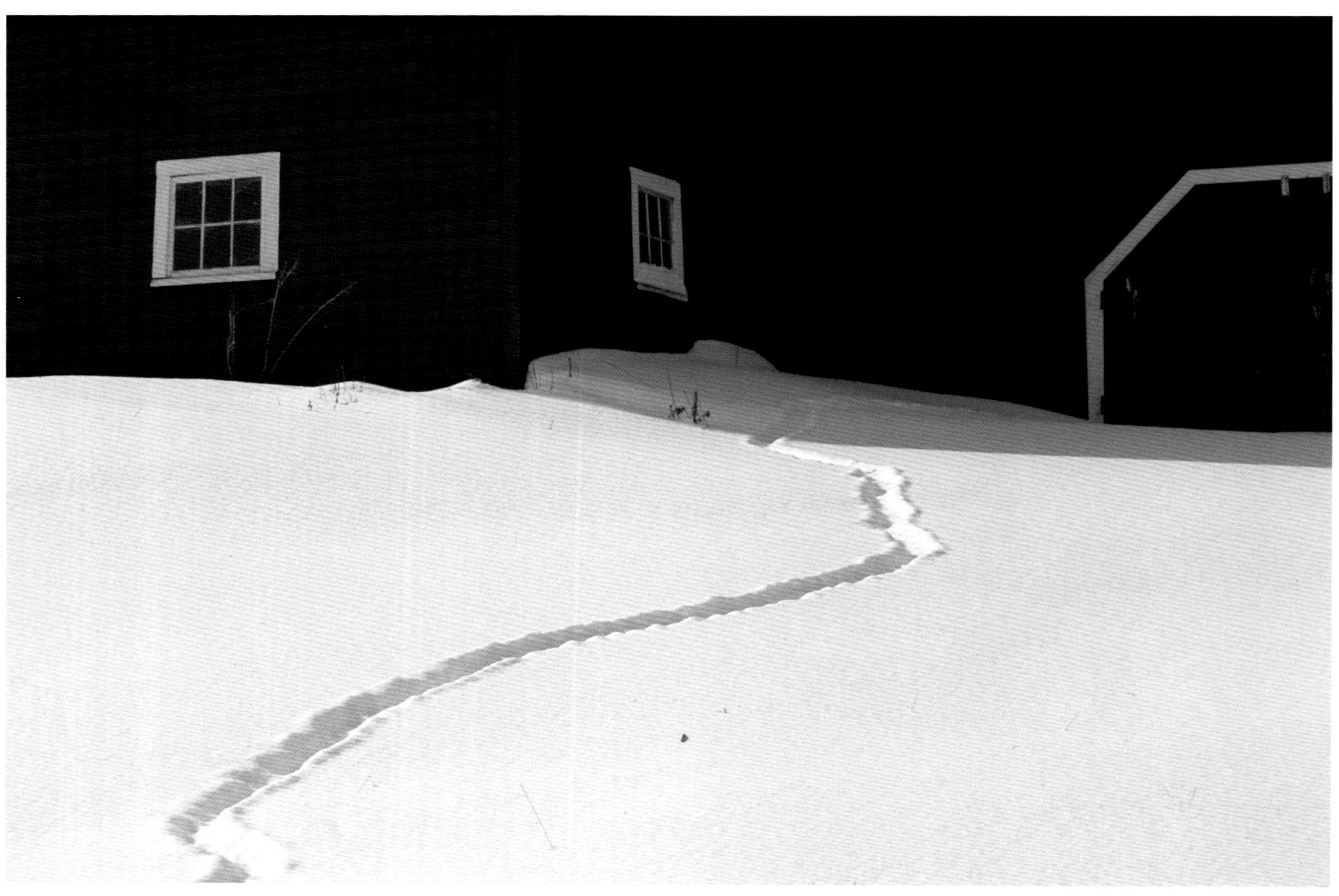

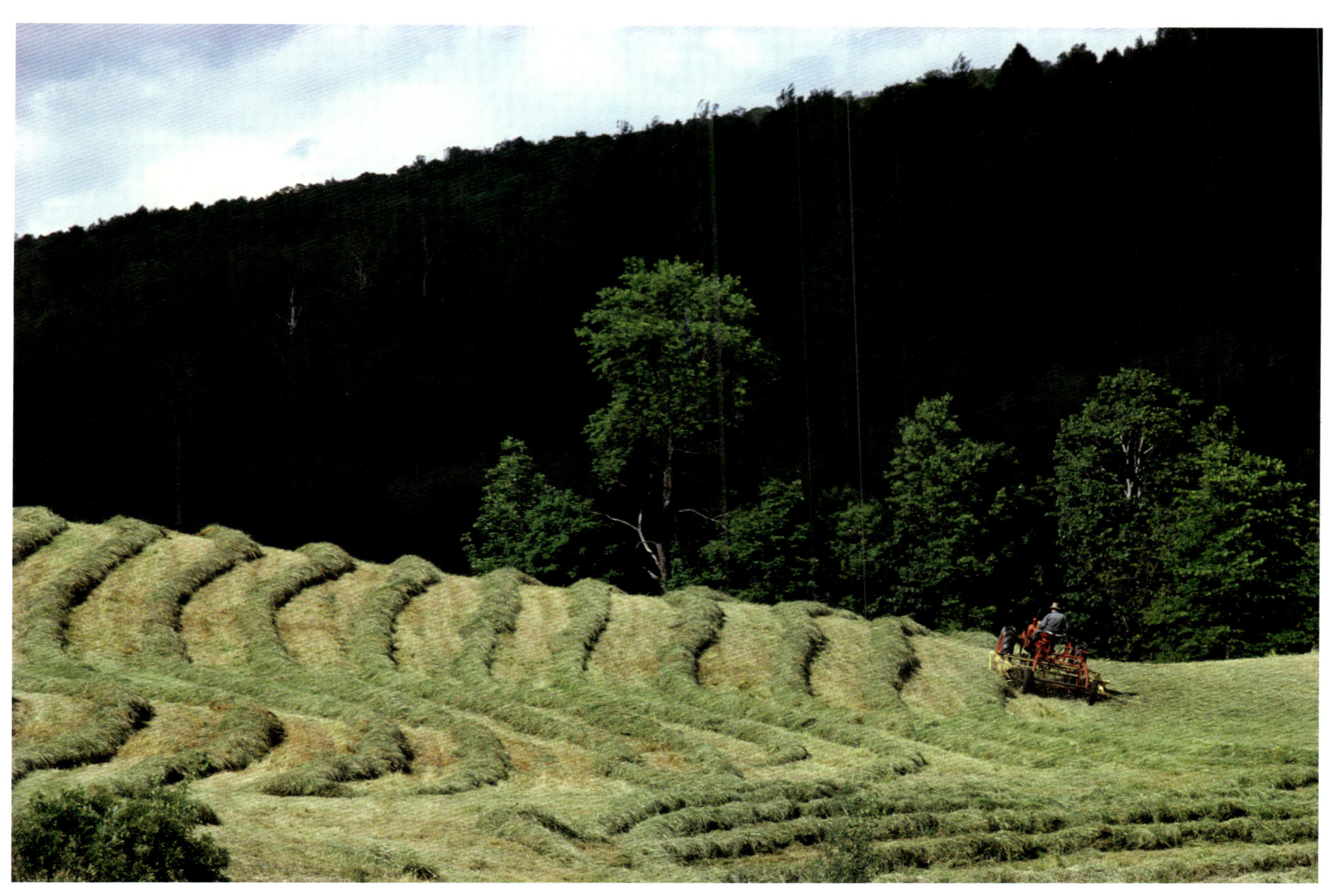

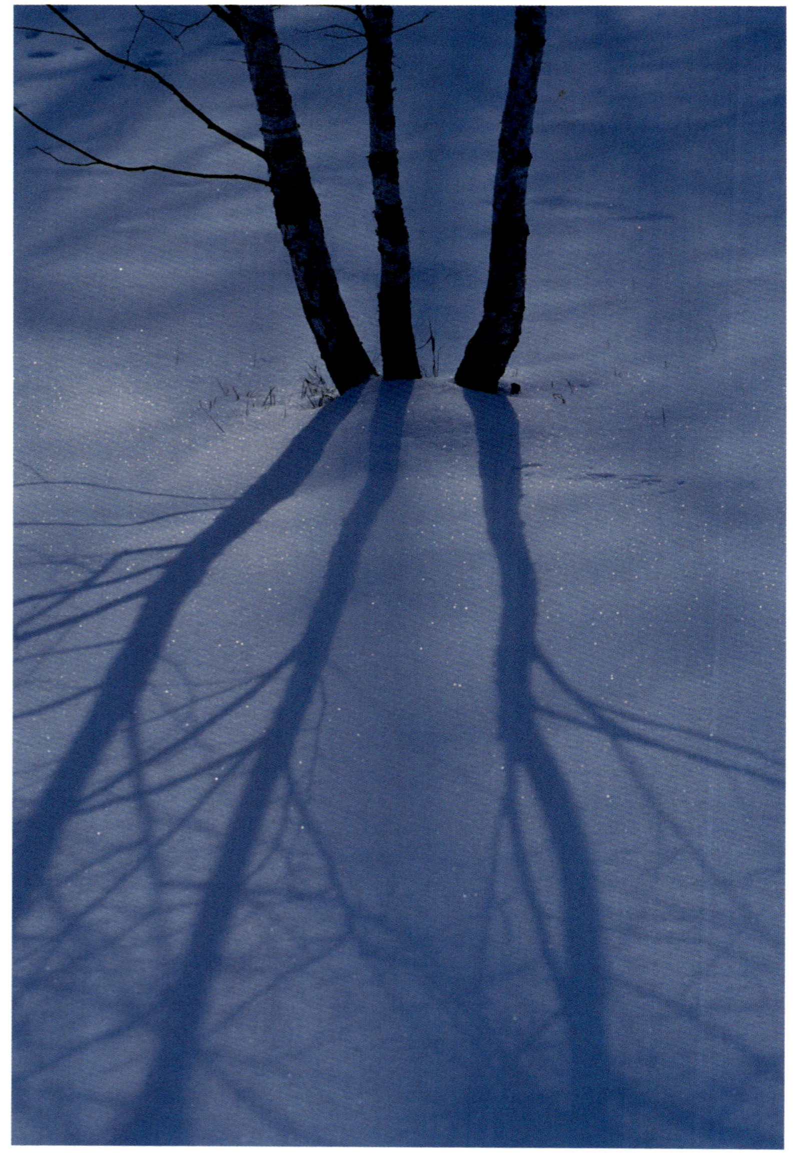
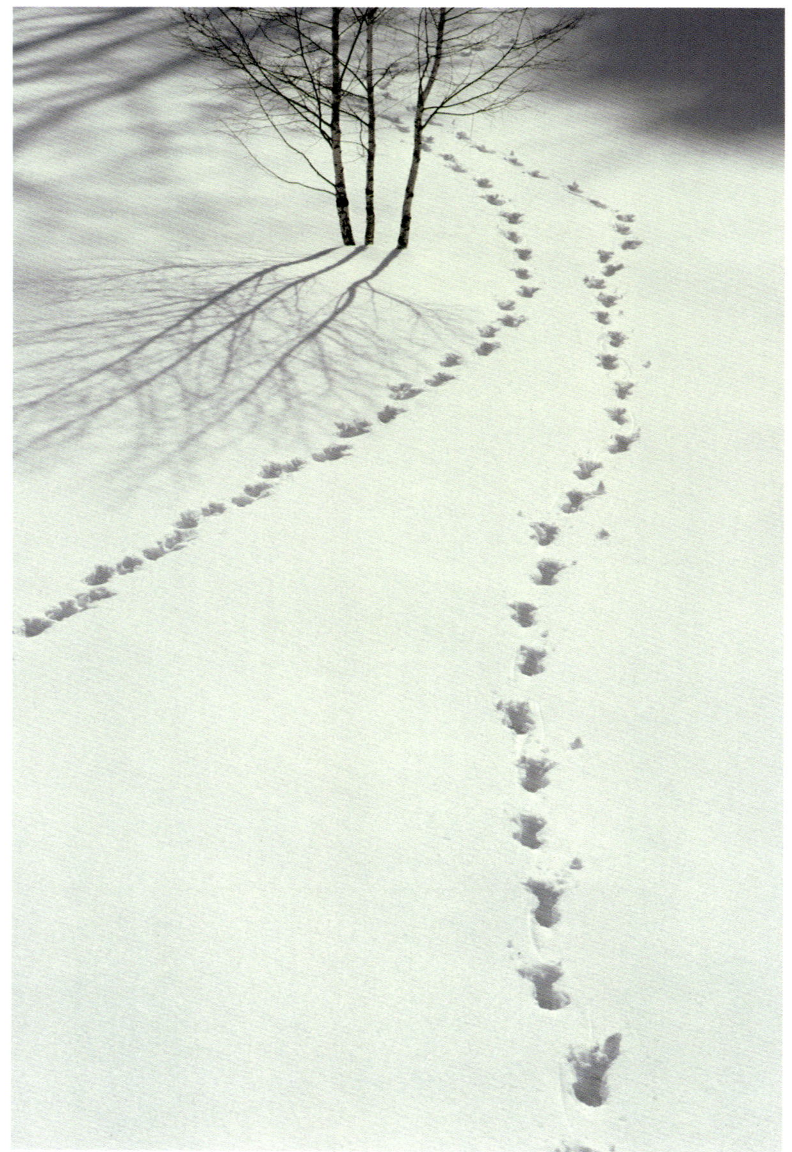

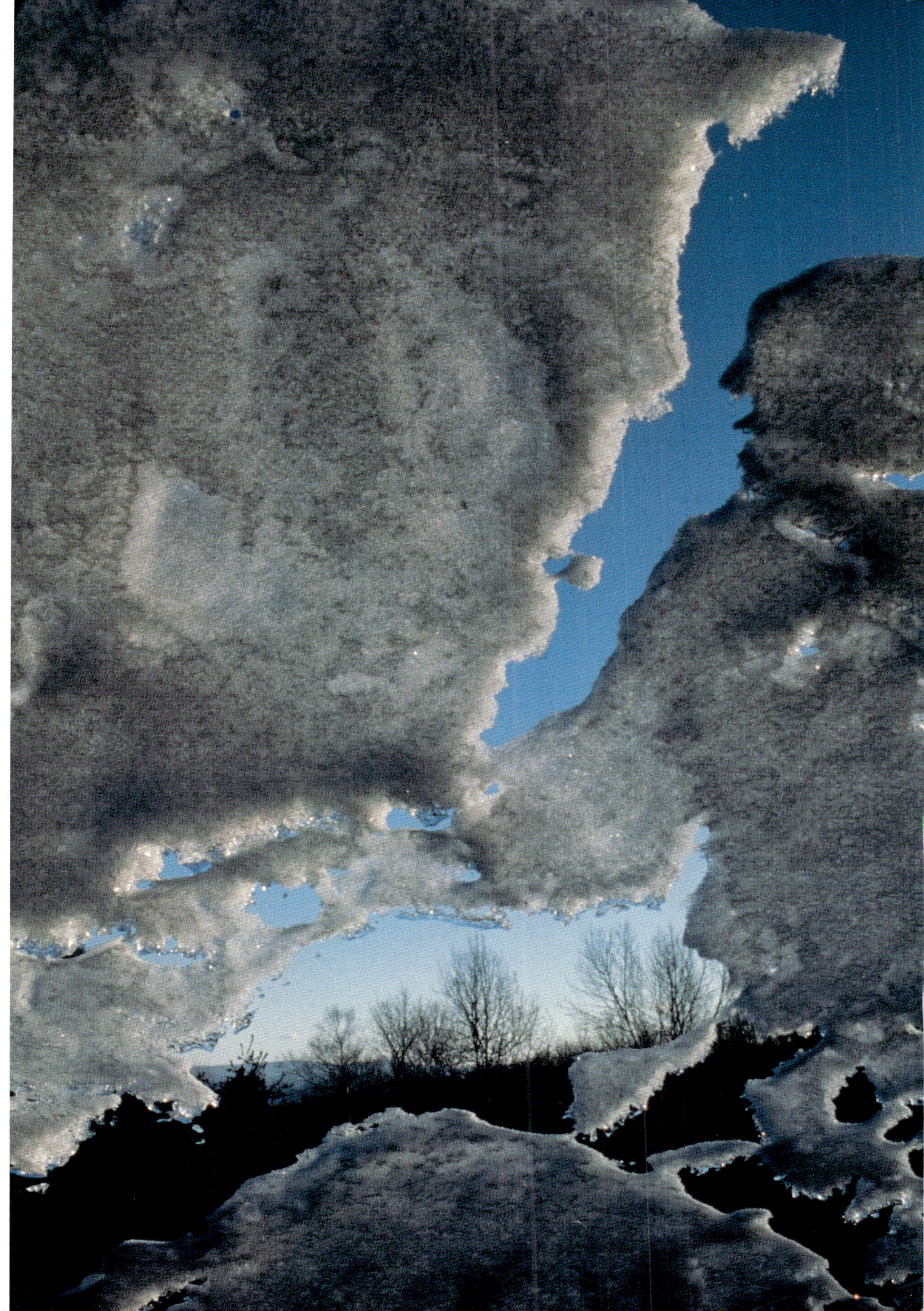

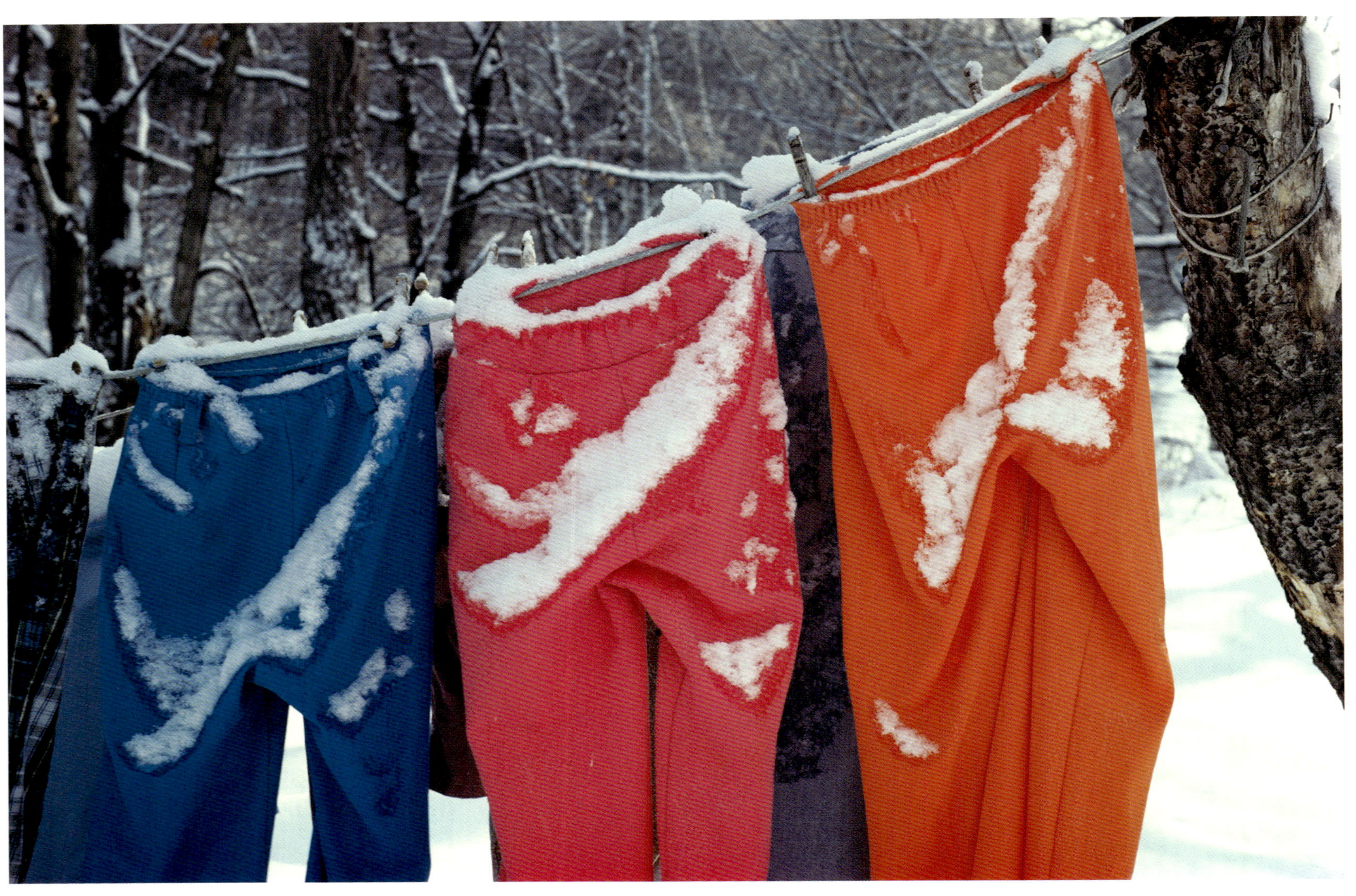

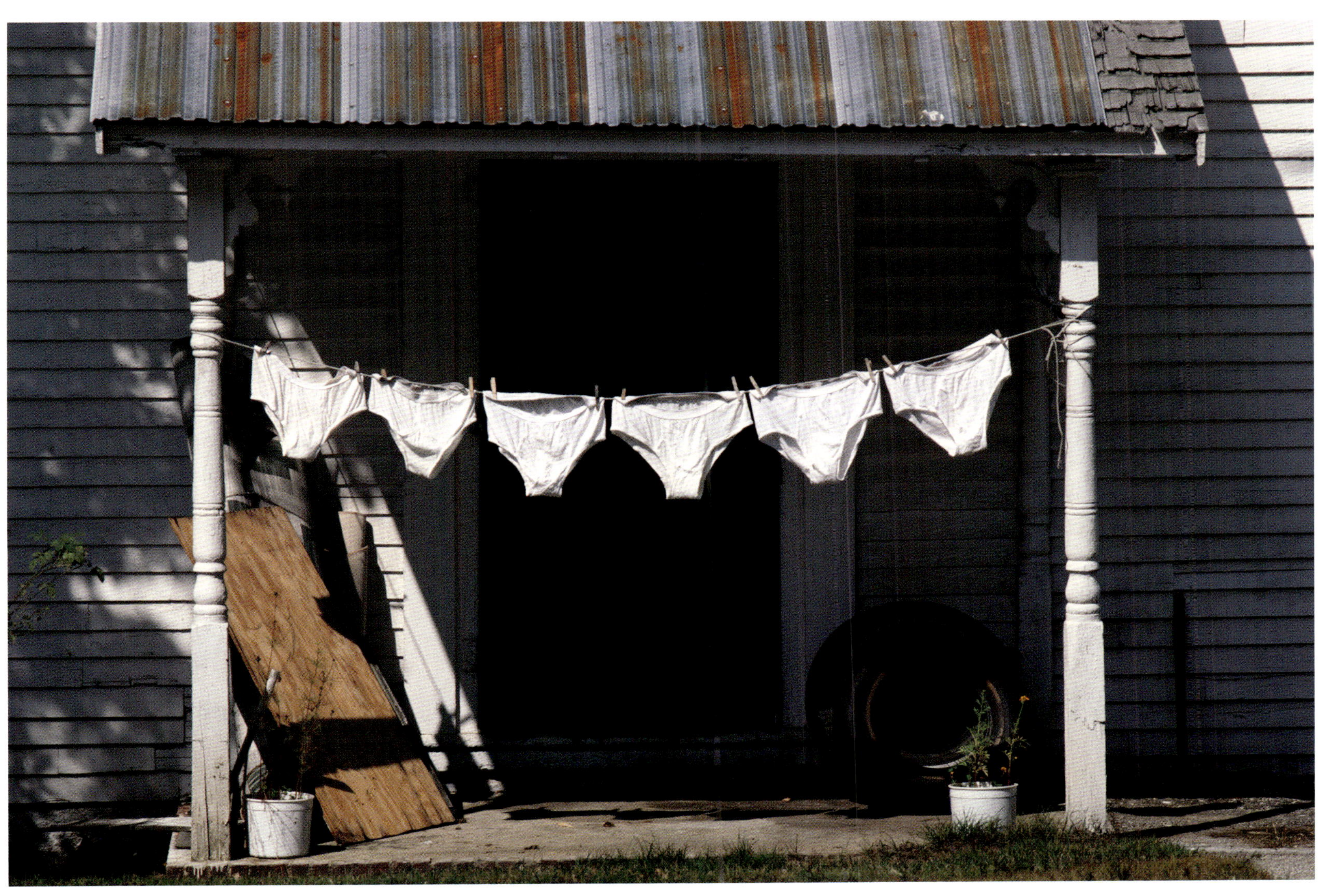

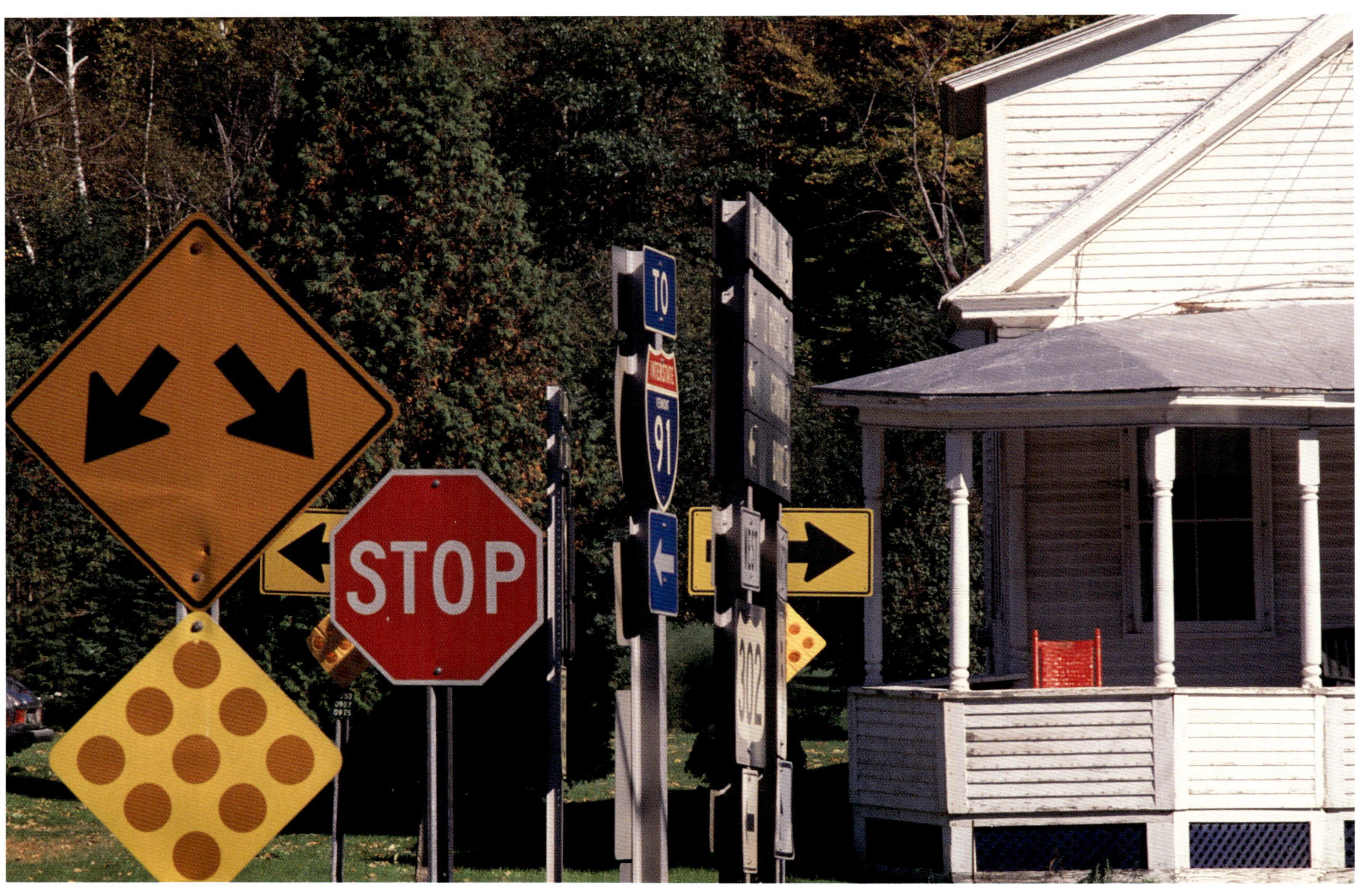


44

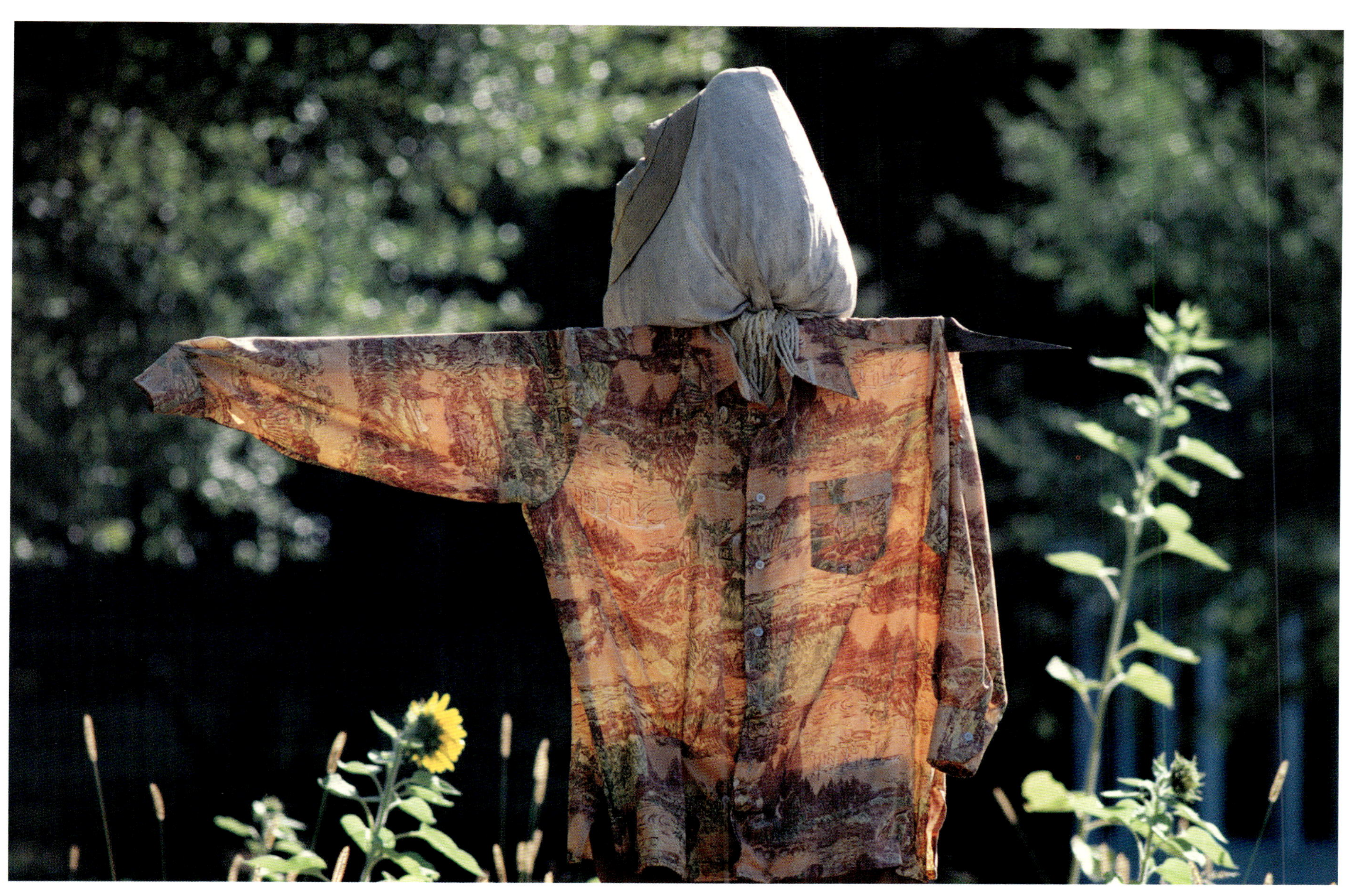

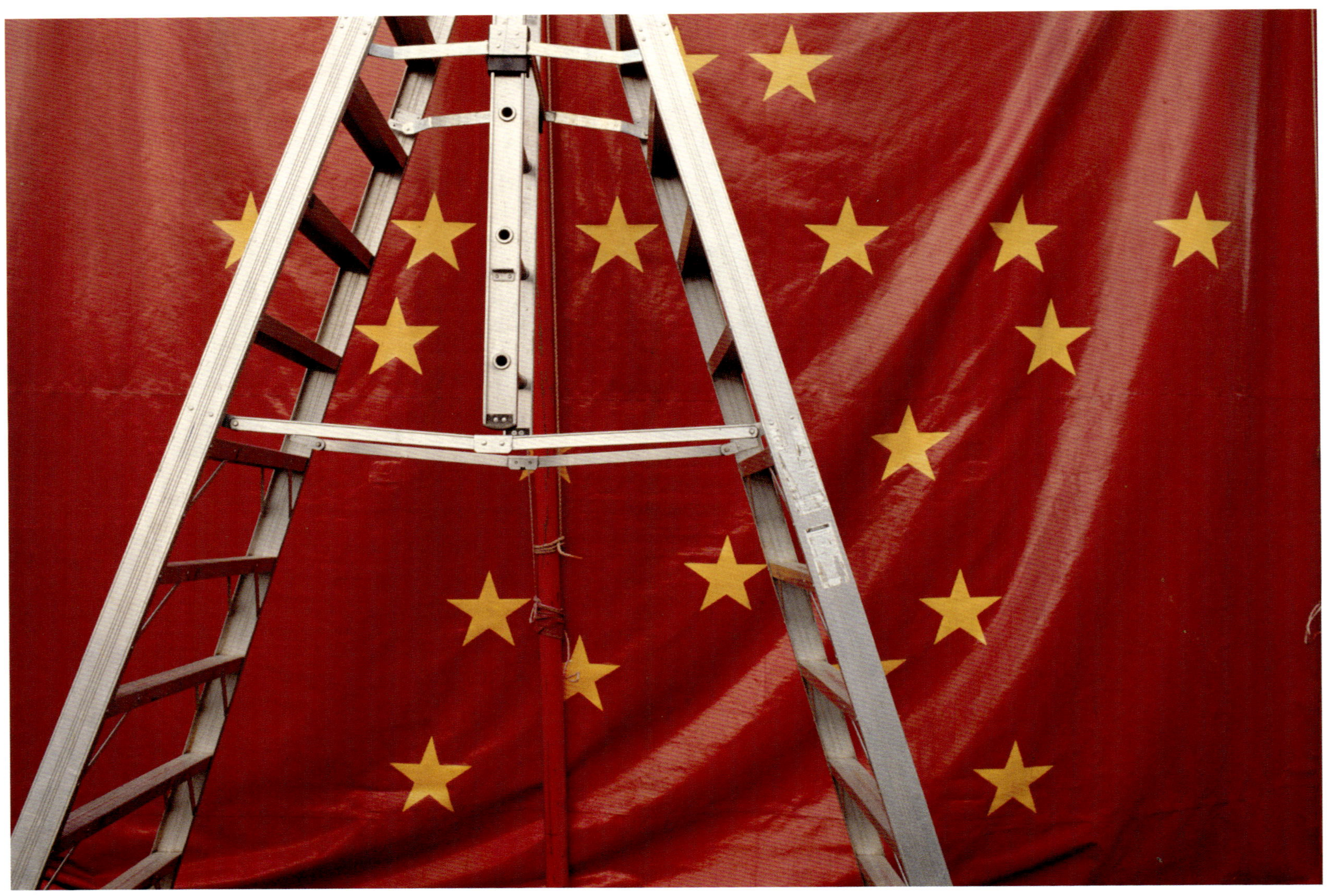

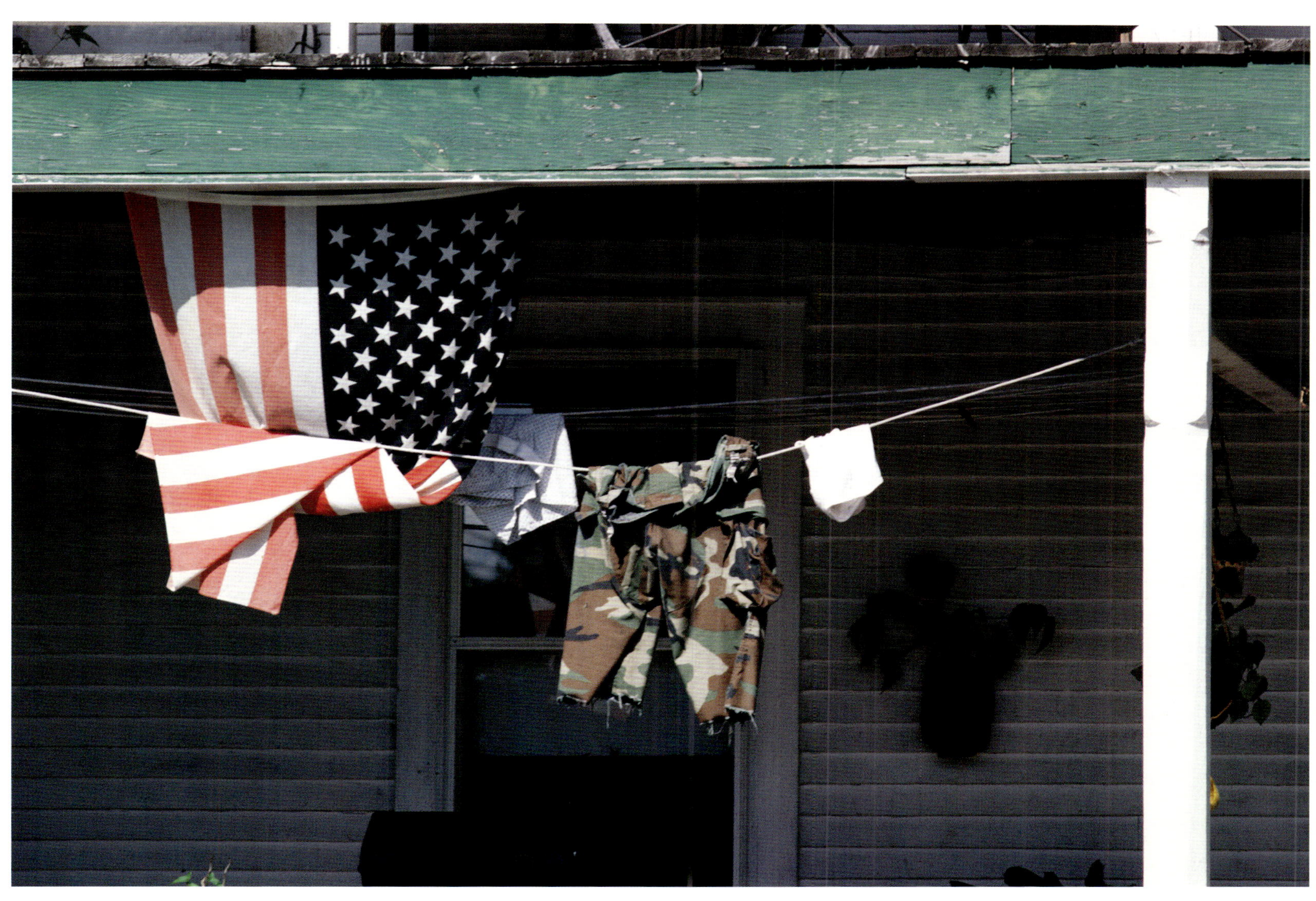

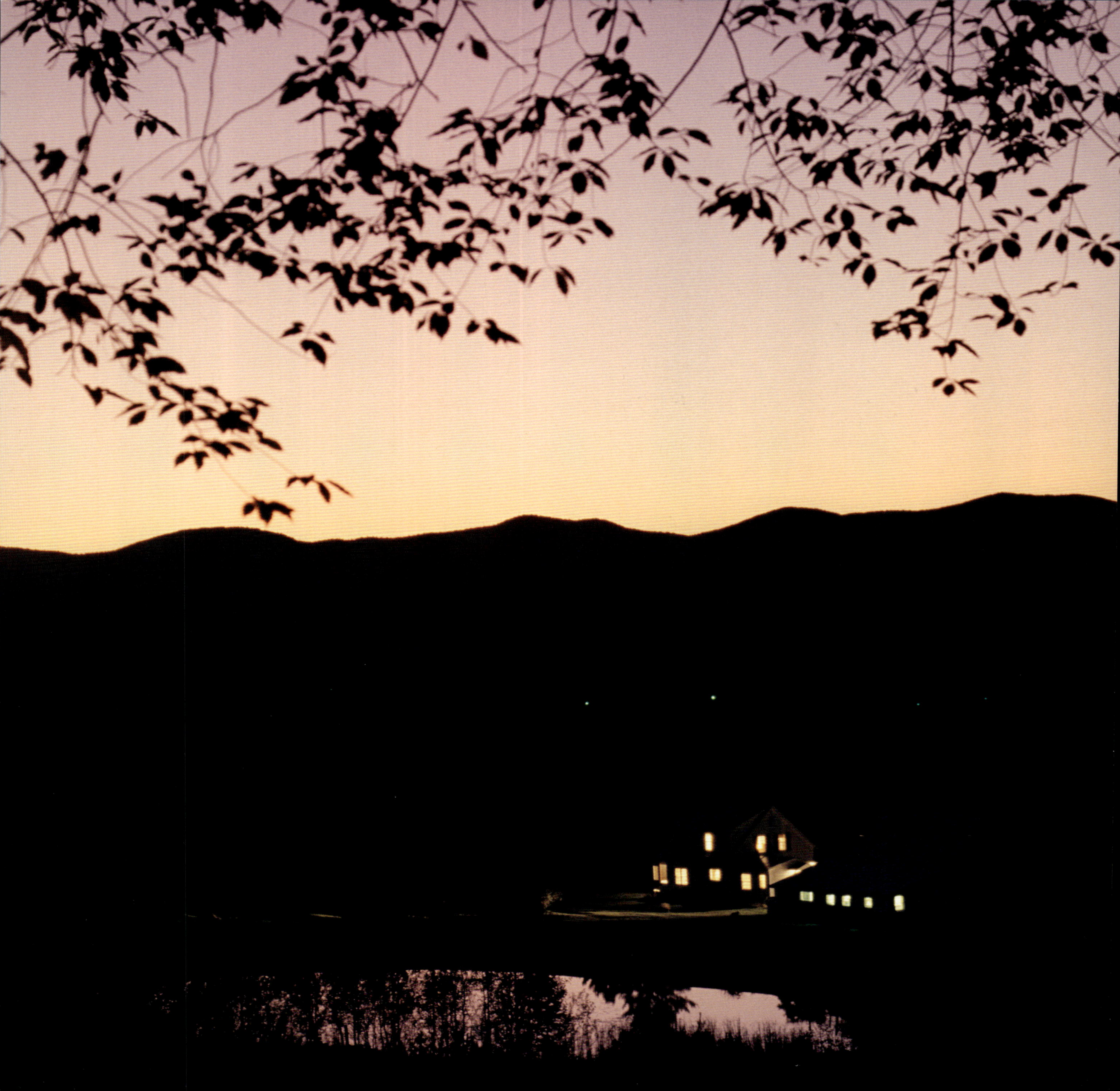

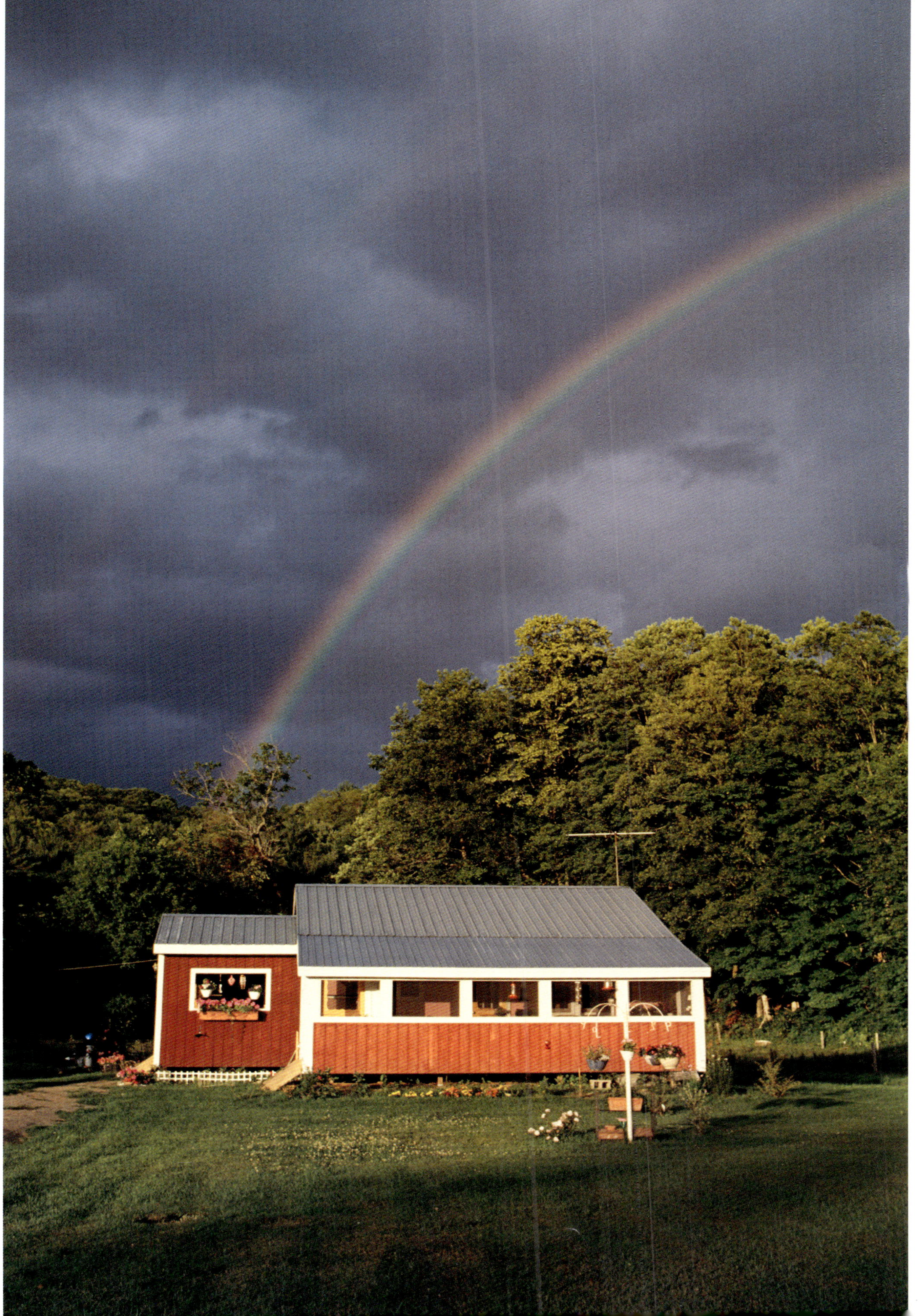

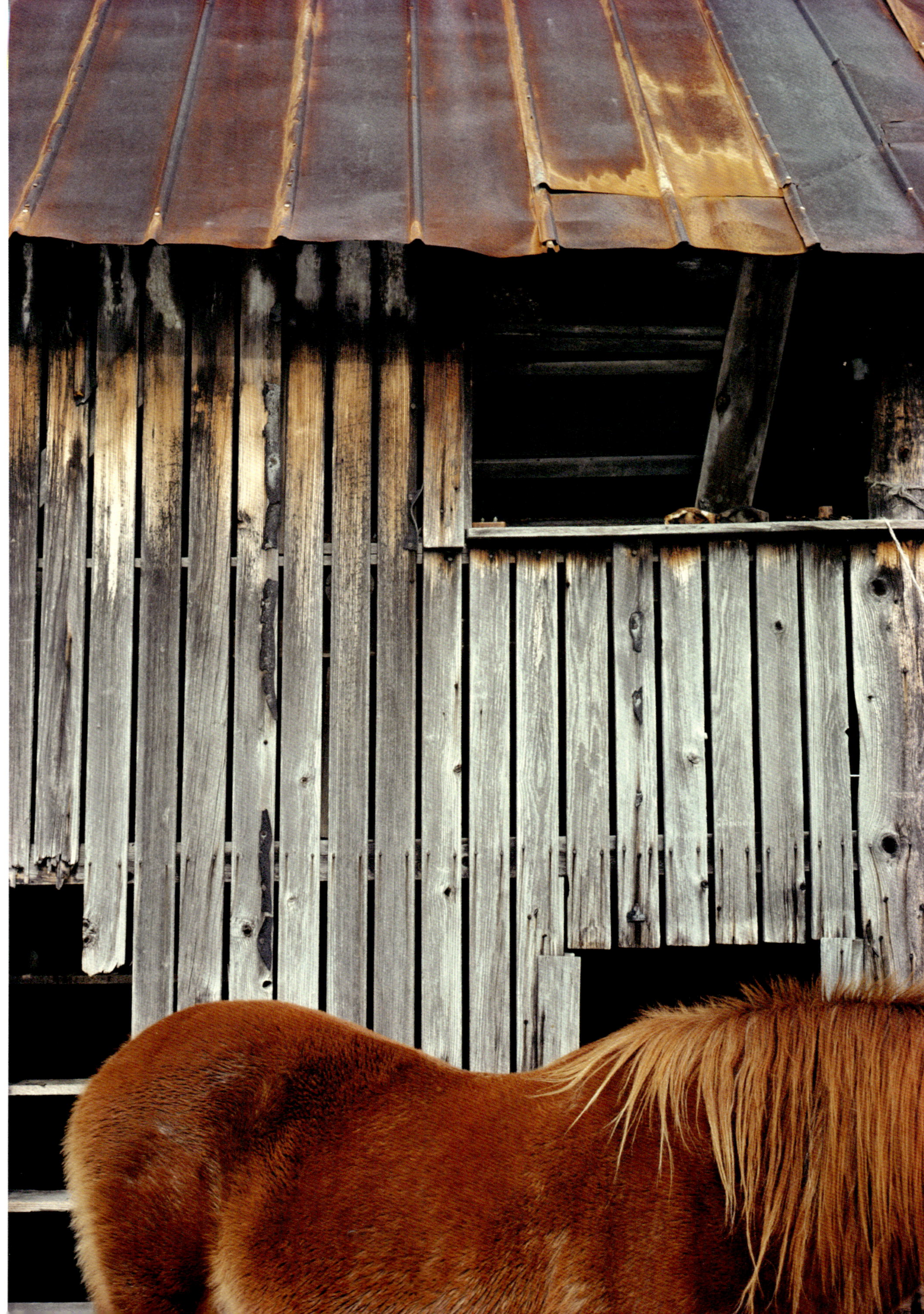

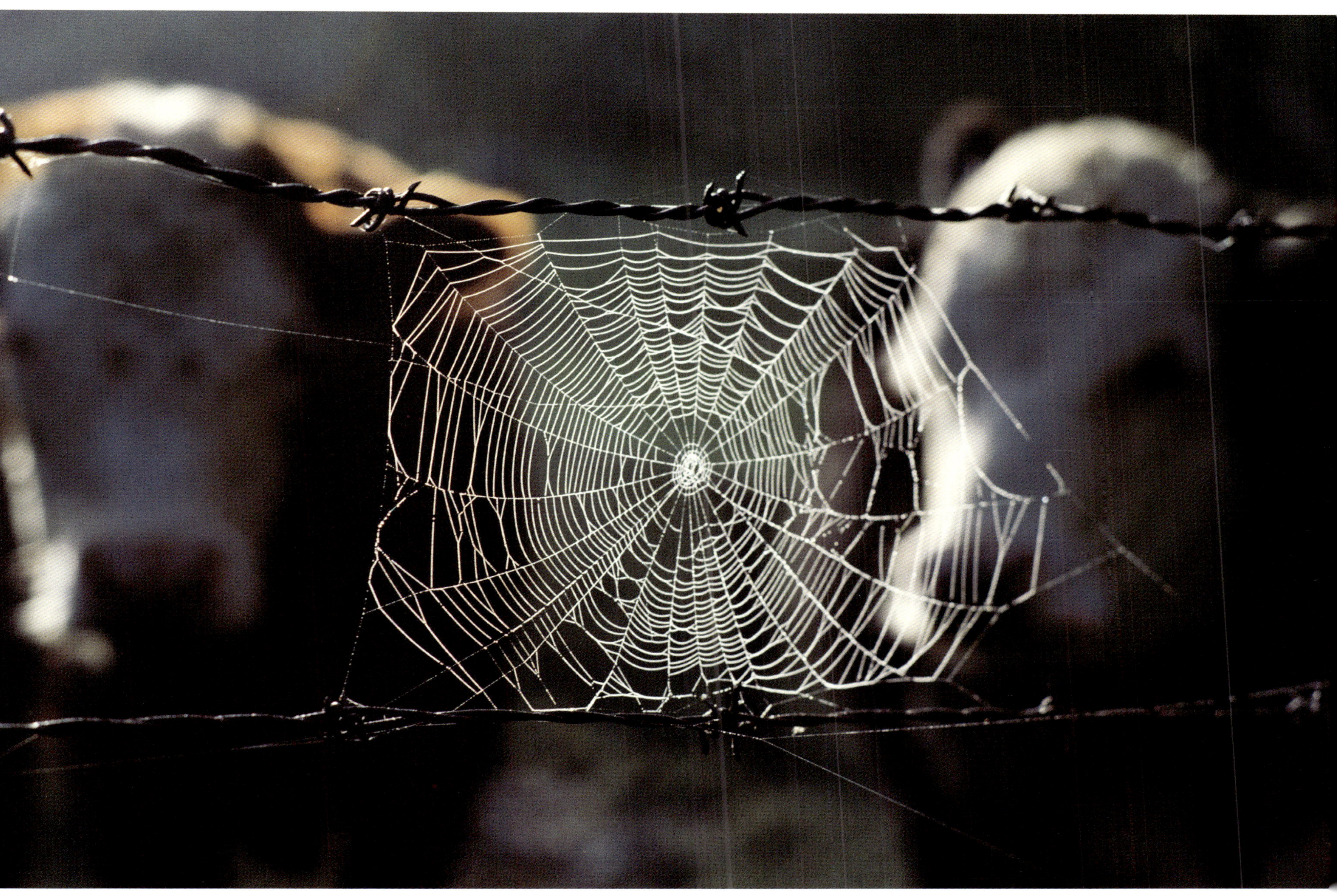

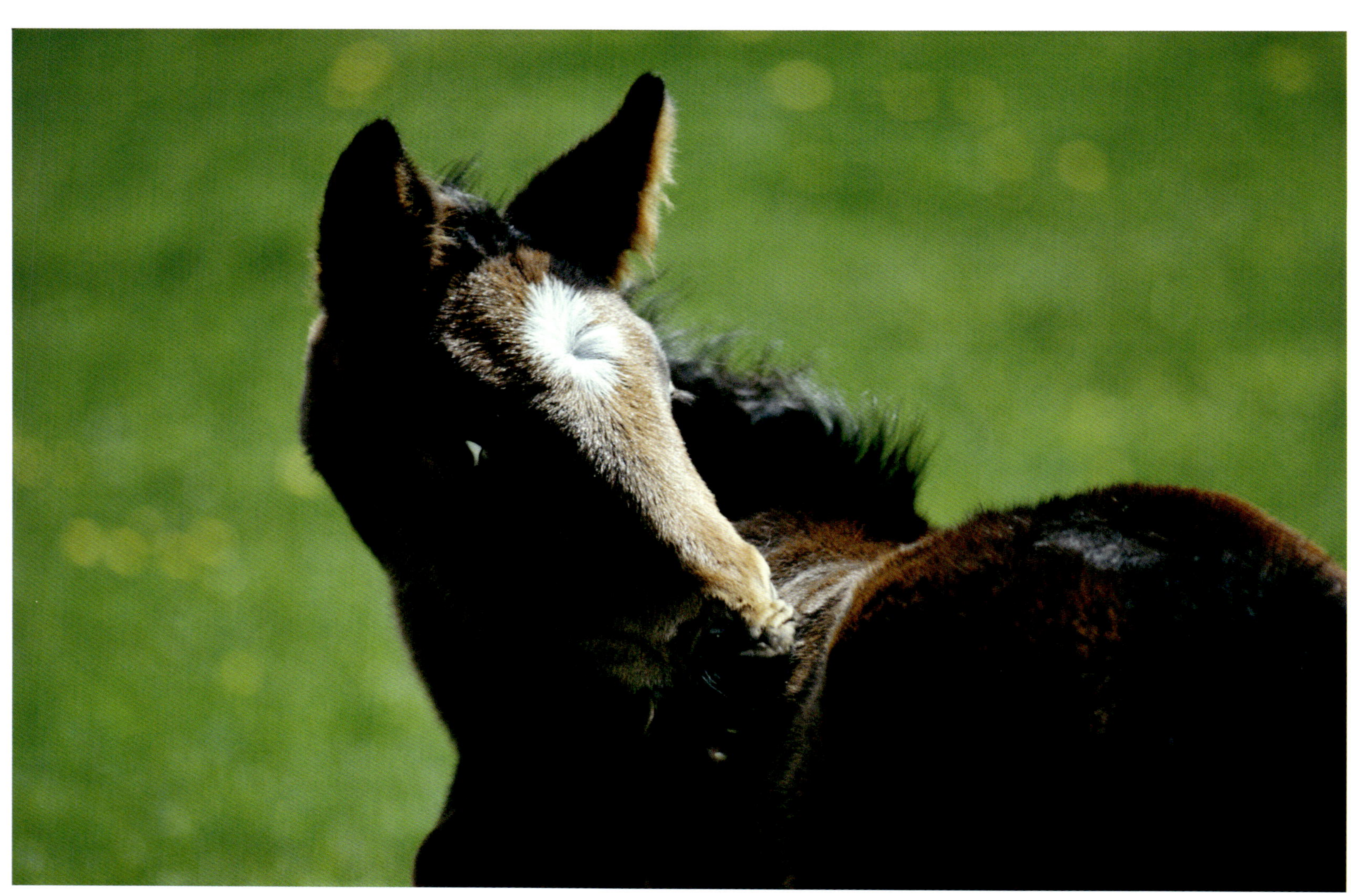

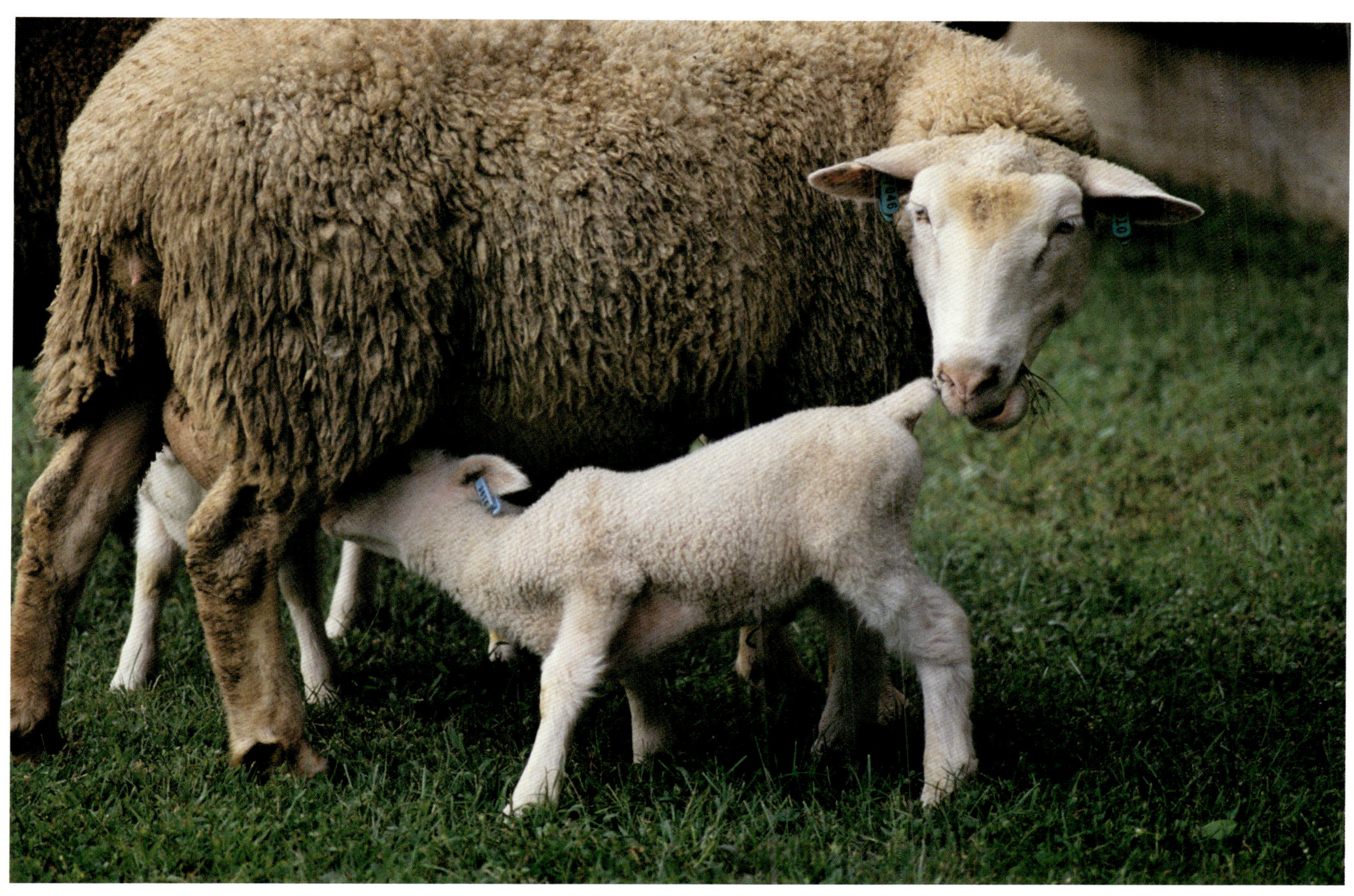

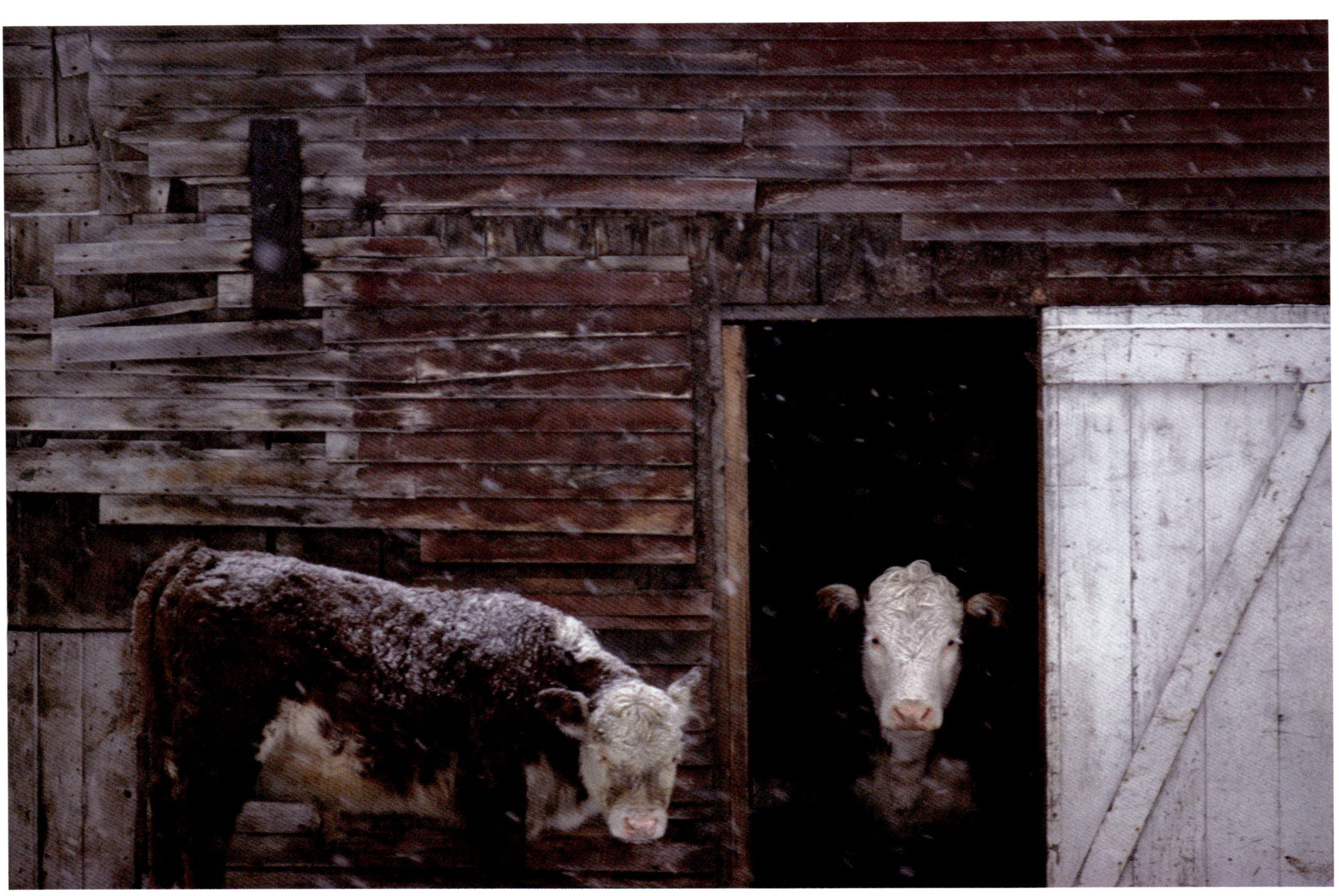

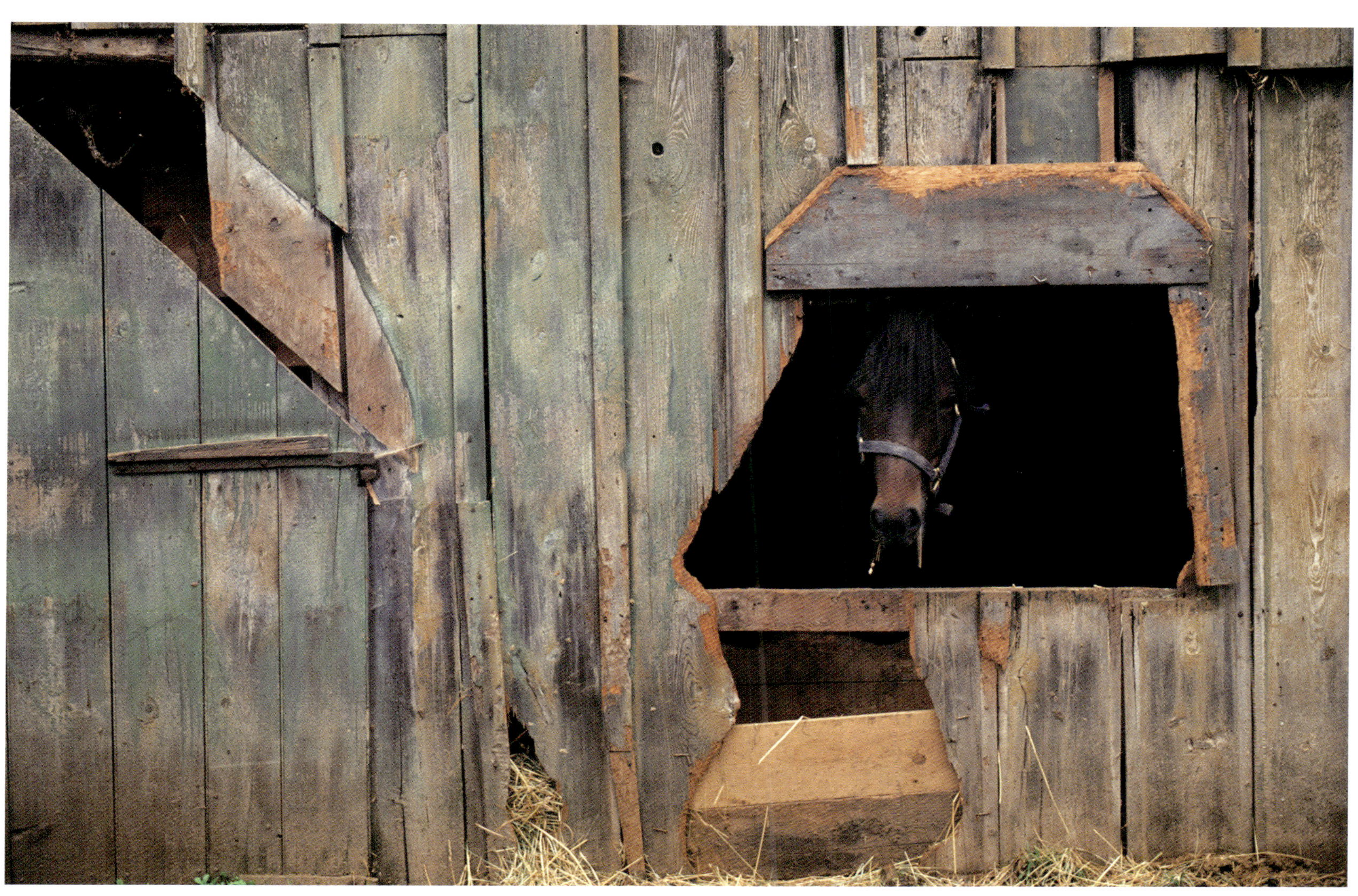

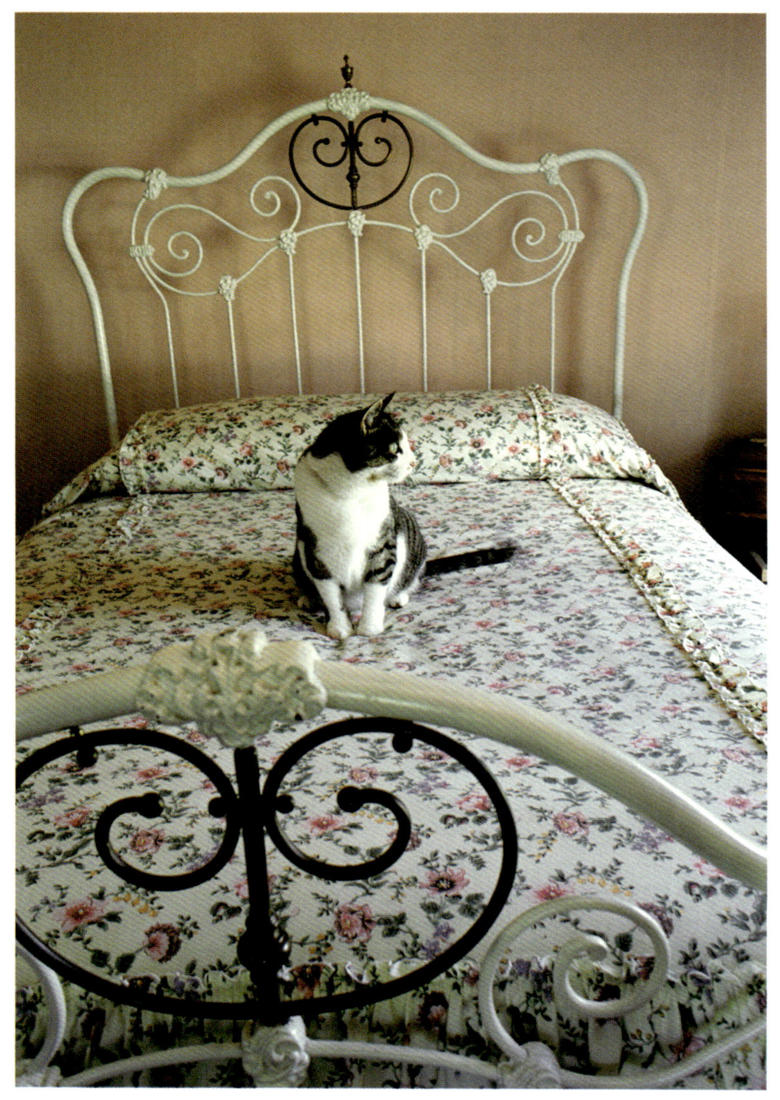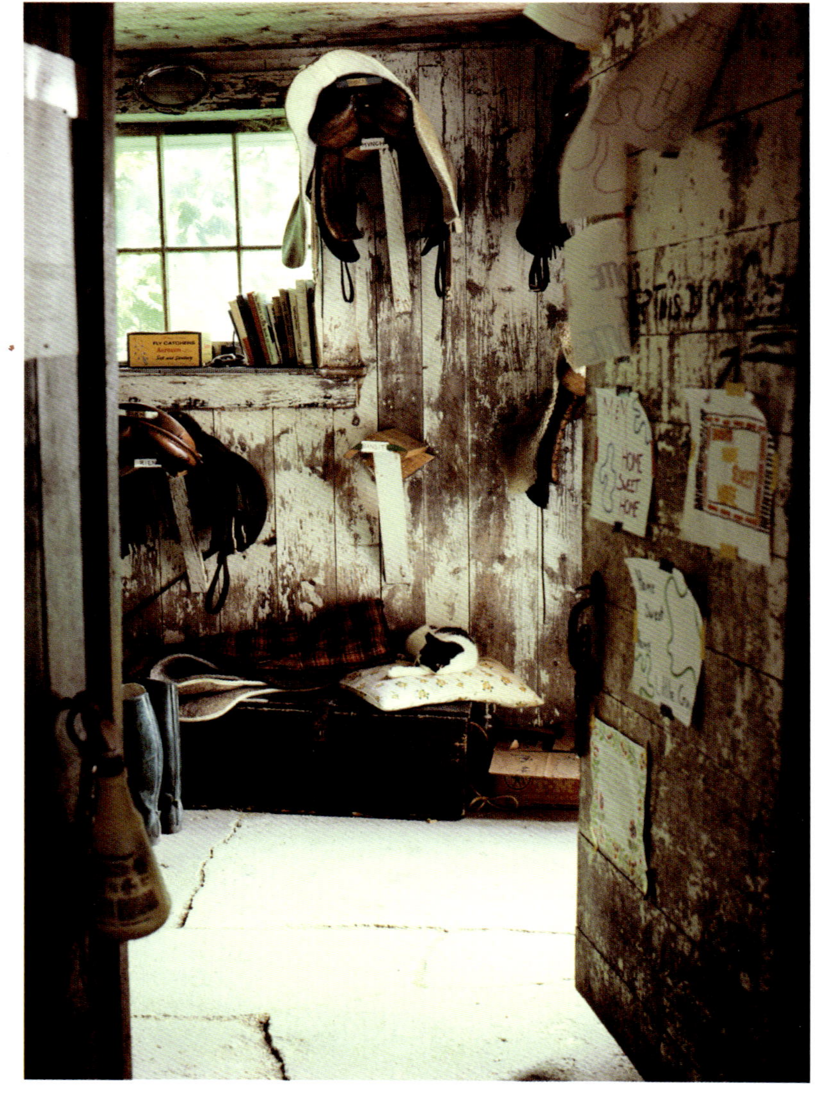

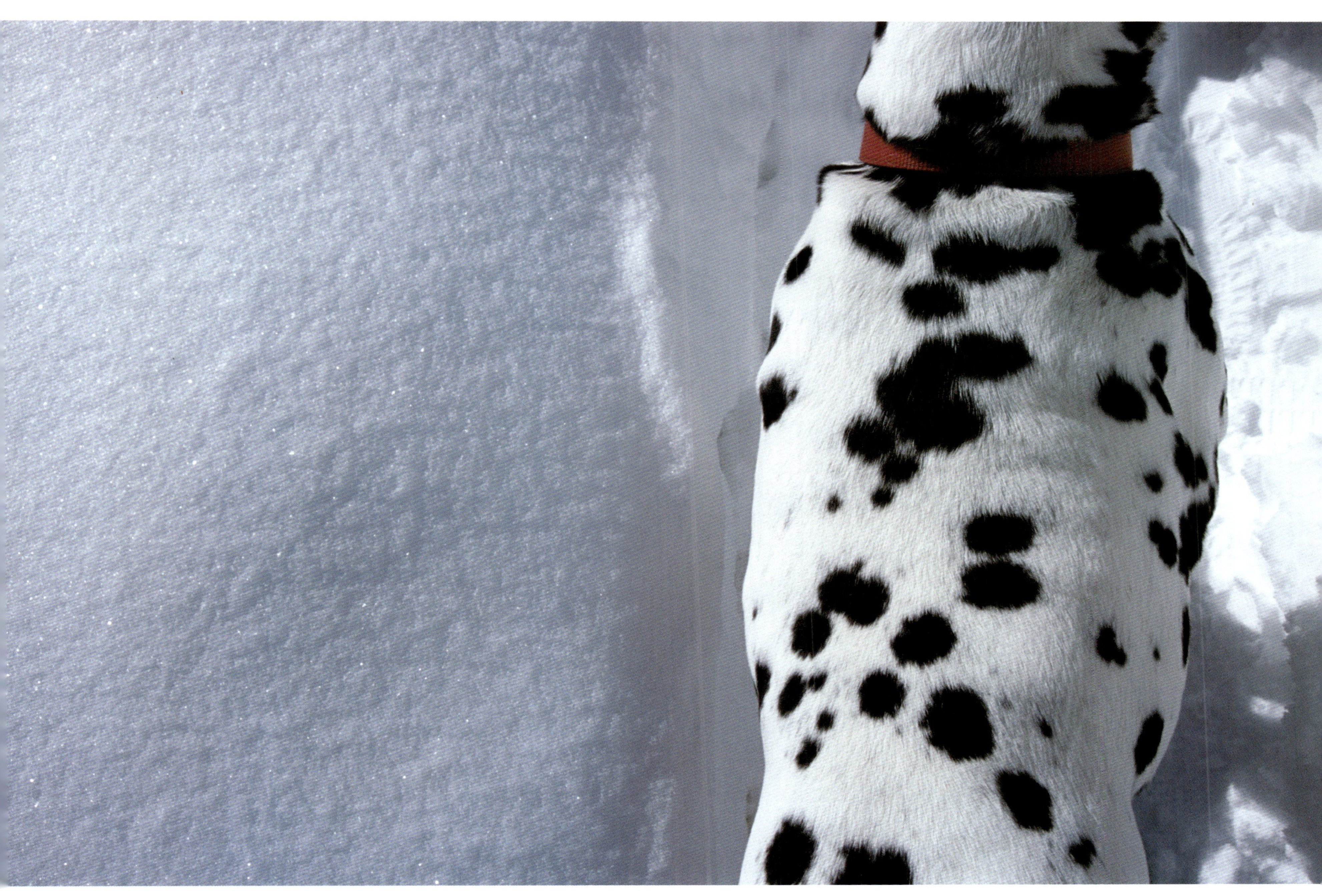

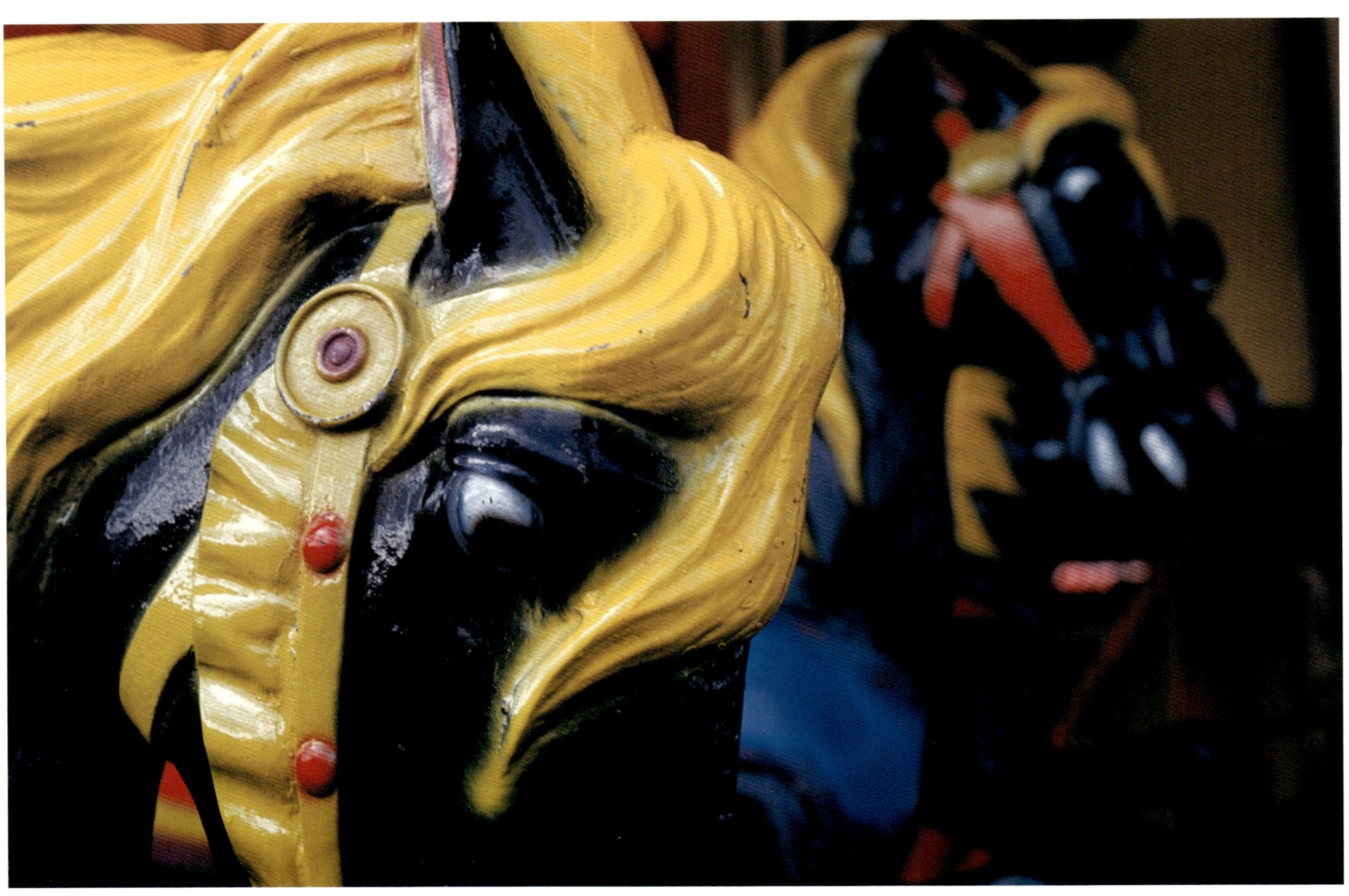

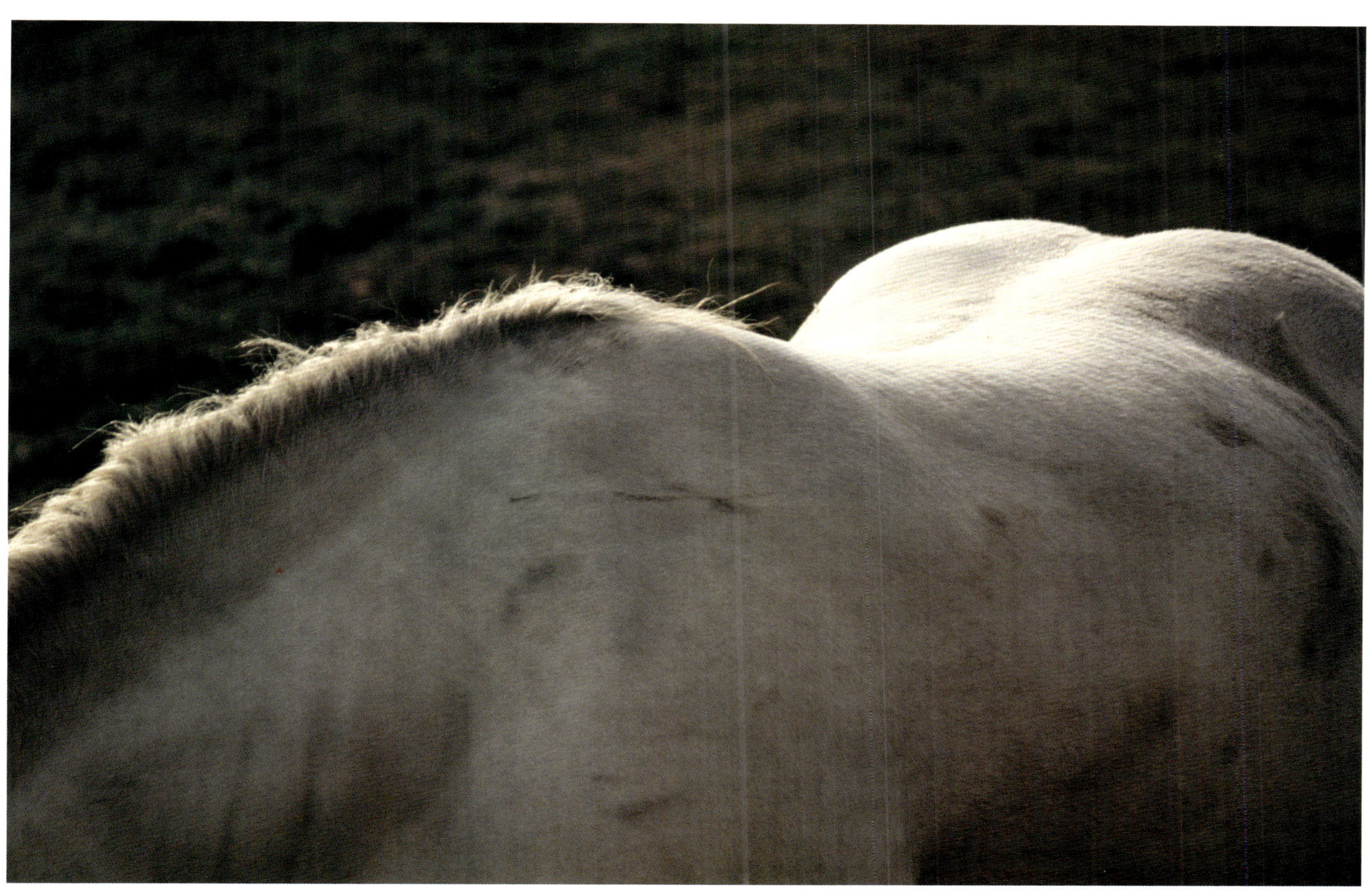

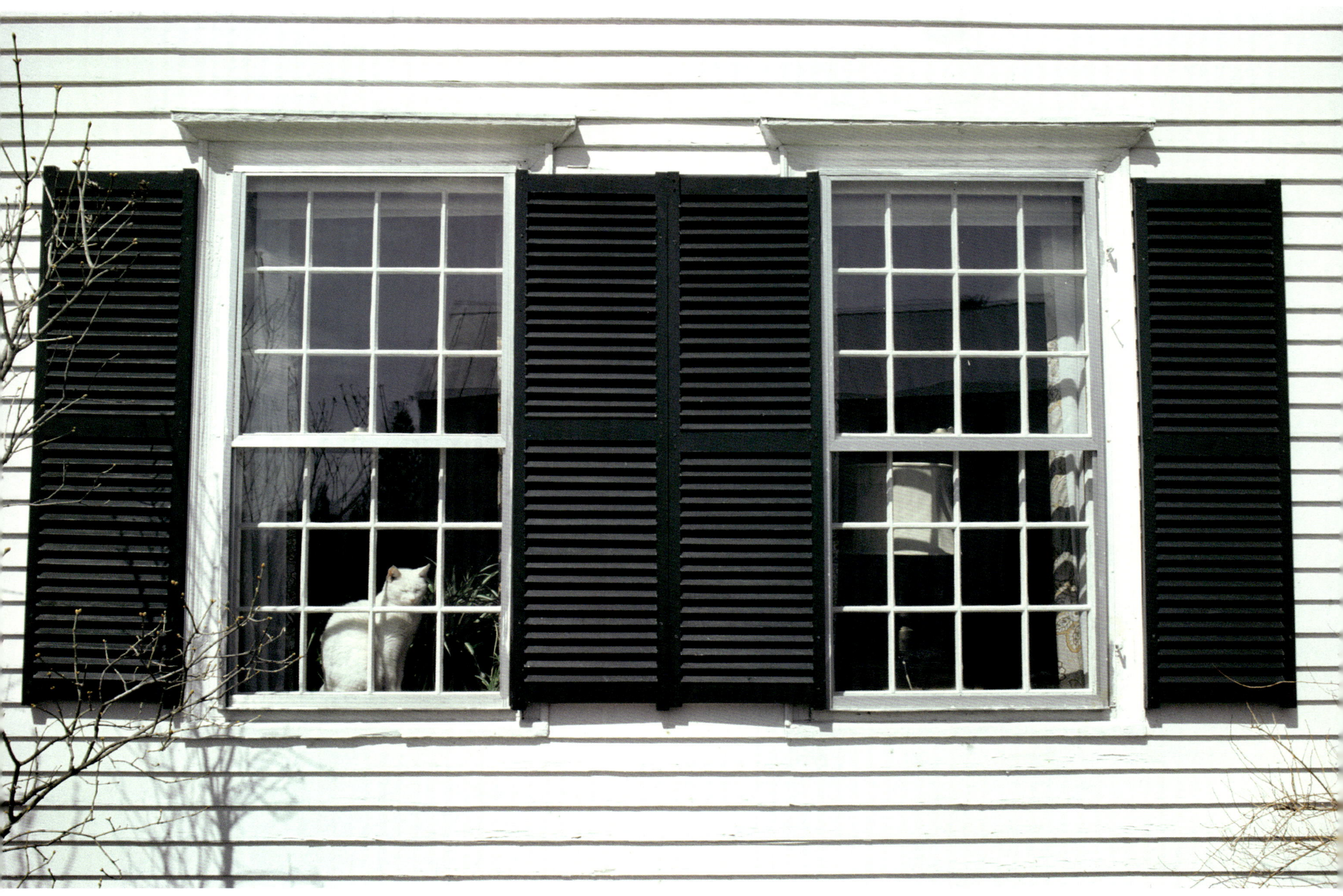

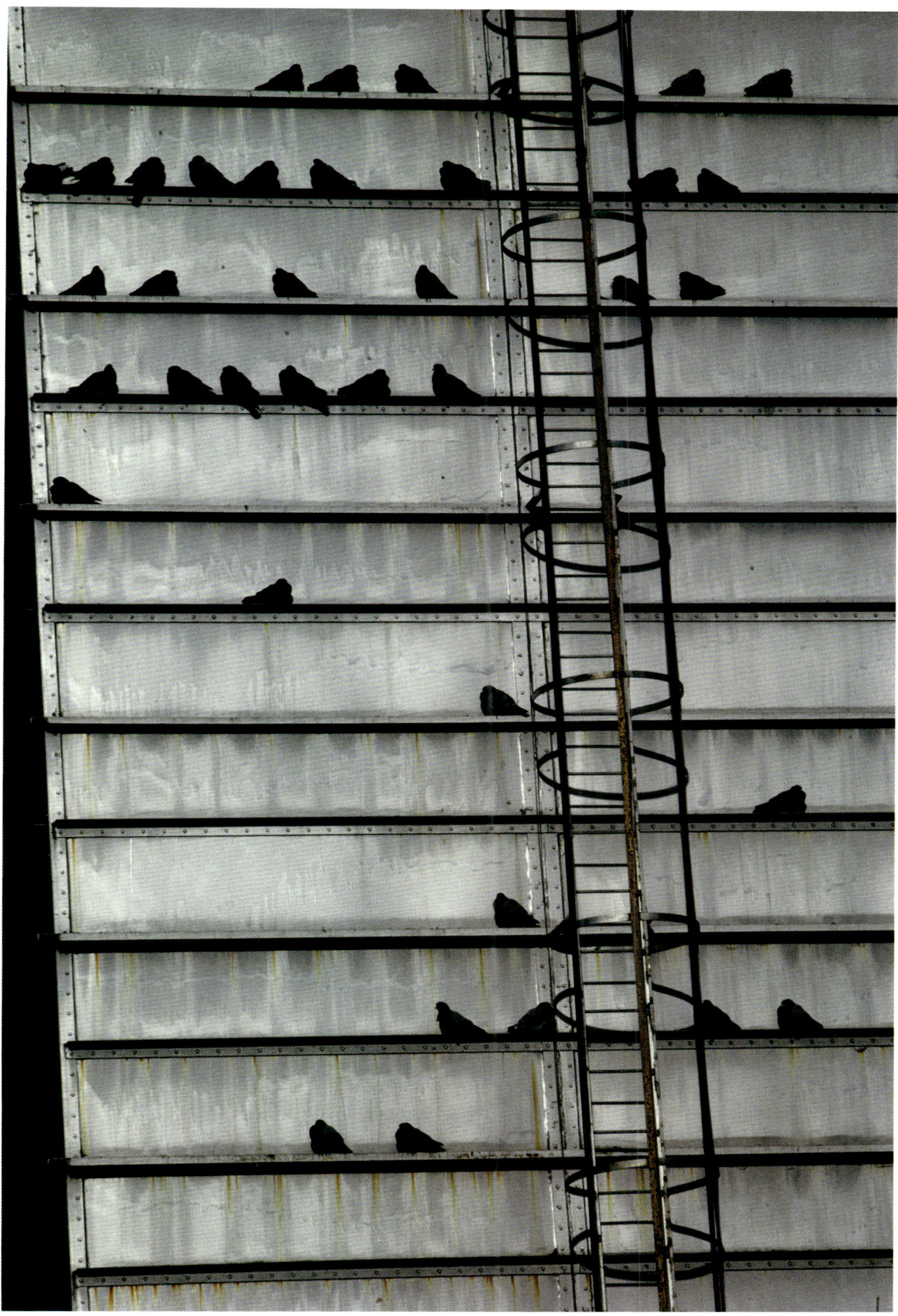

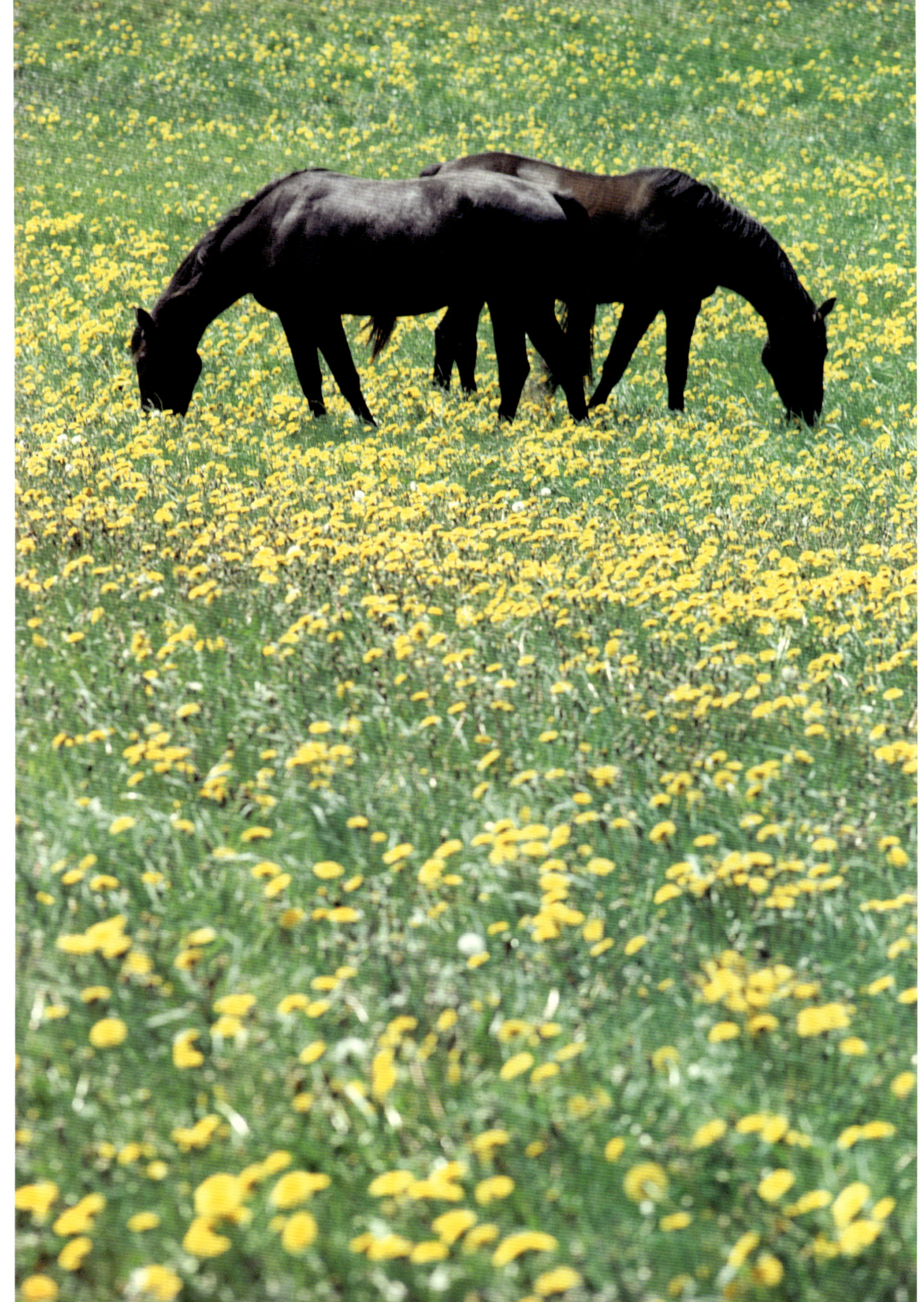

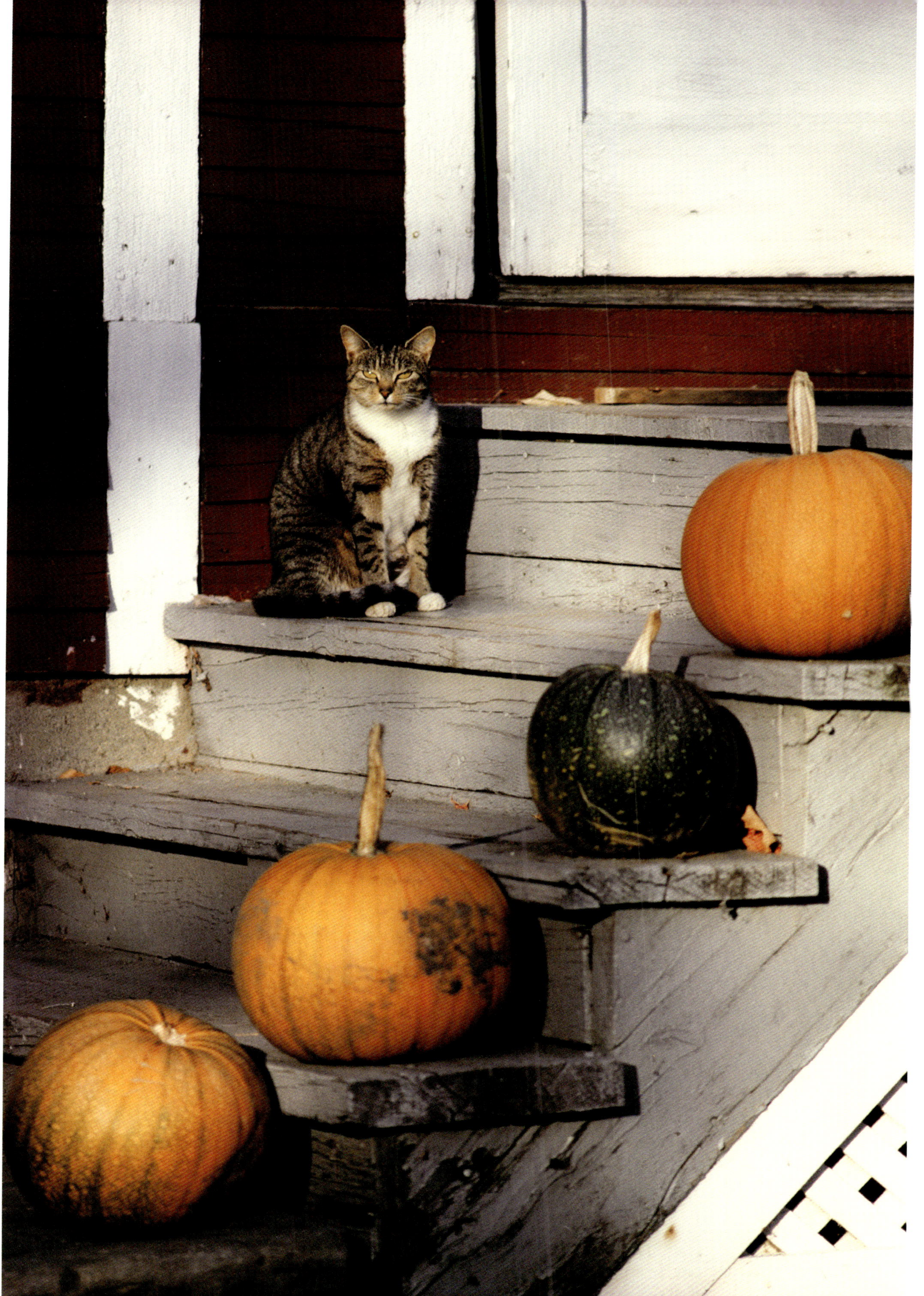

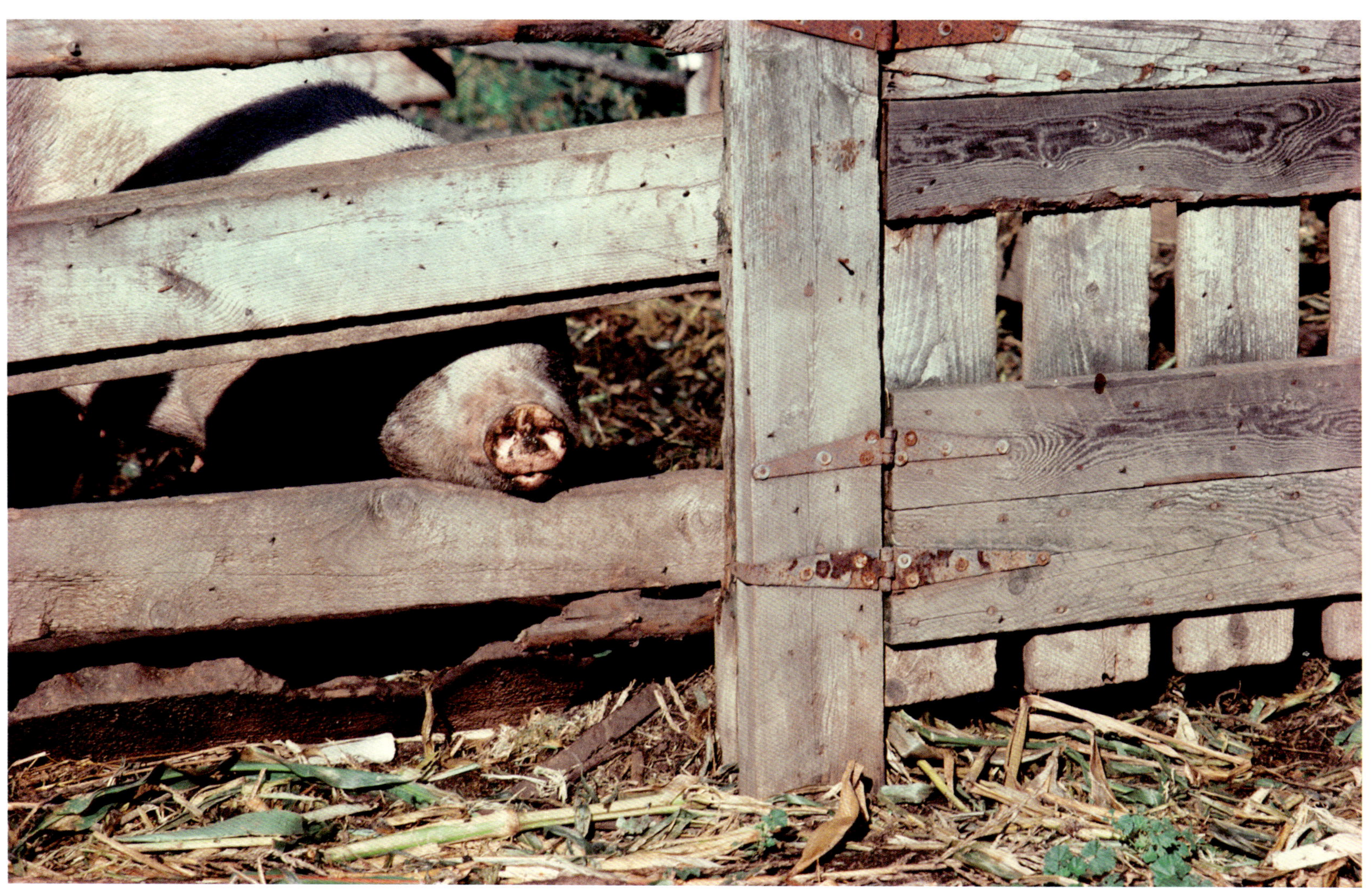

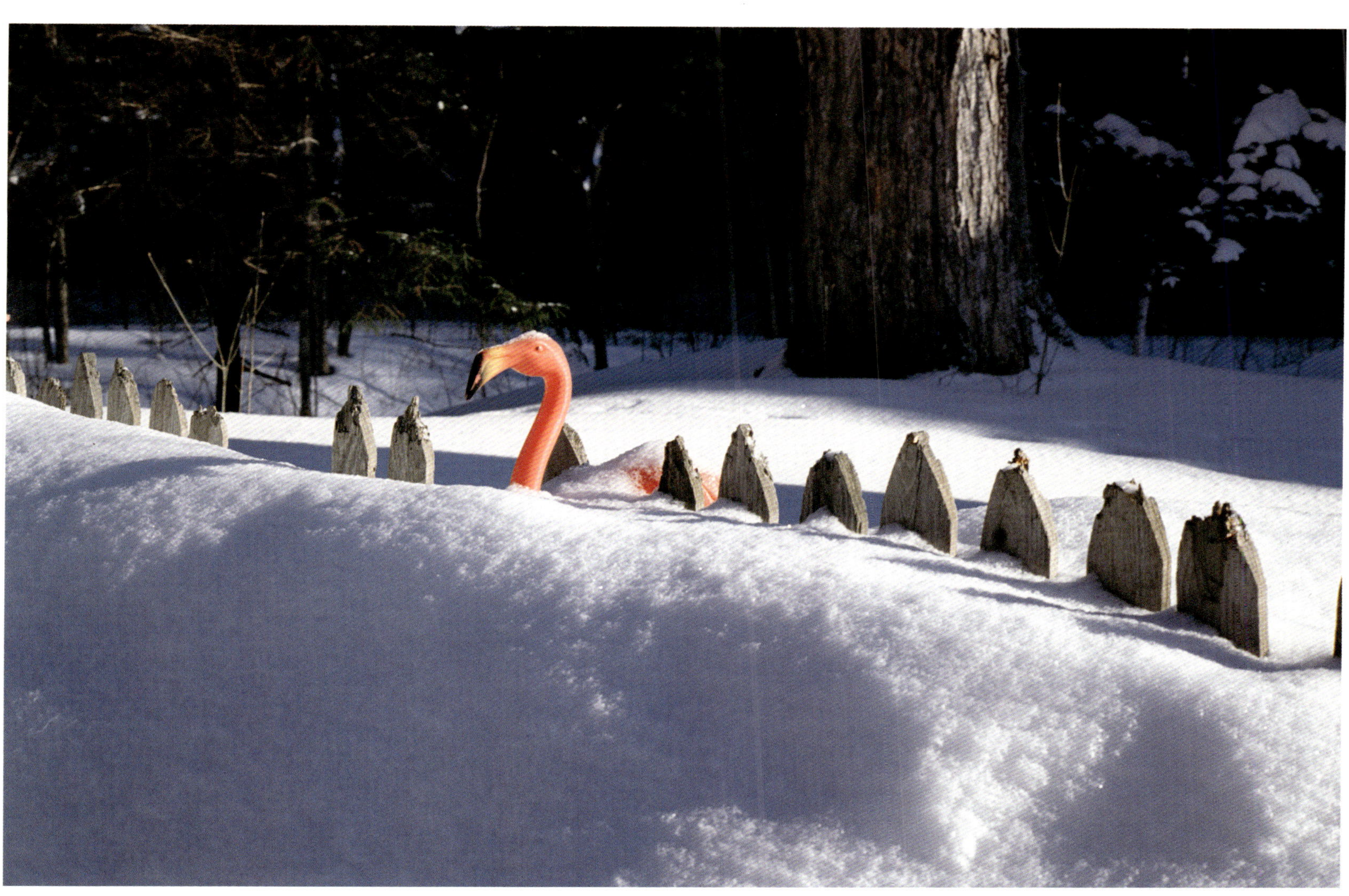

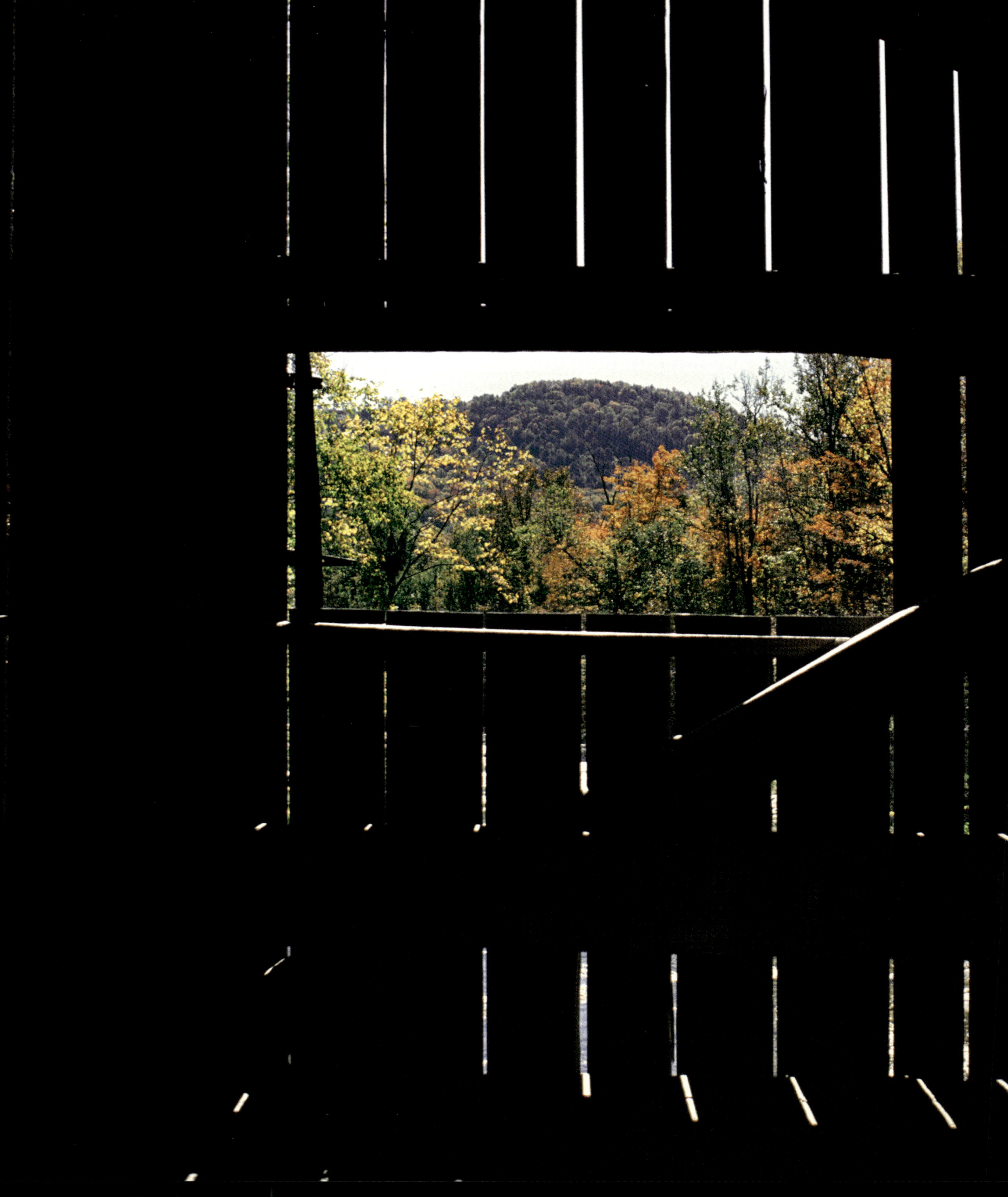

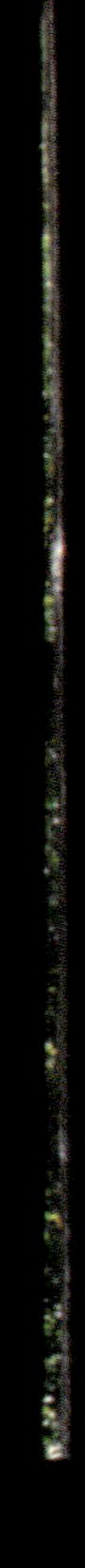

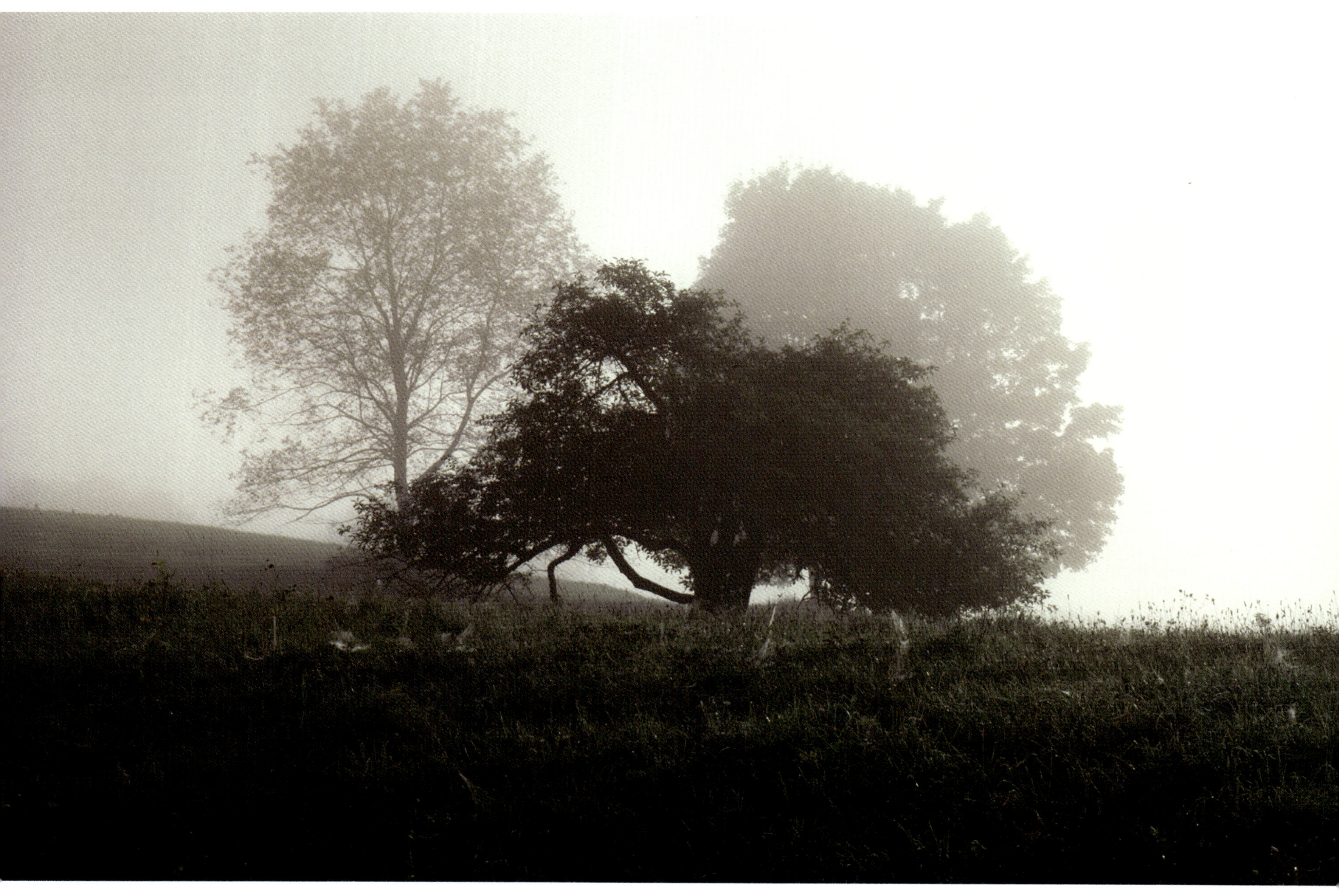

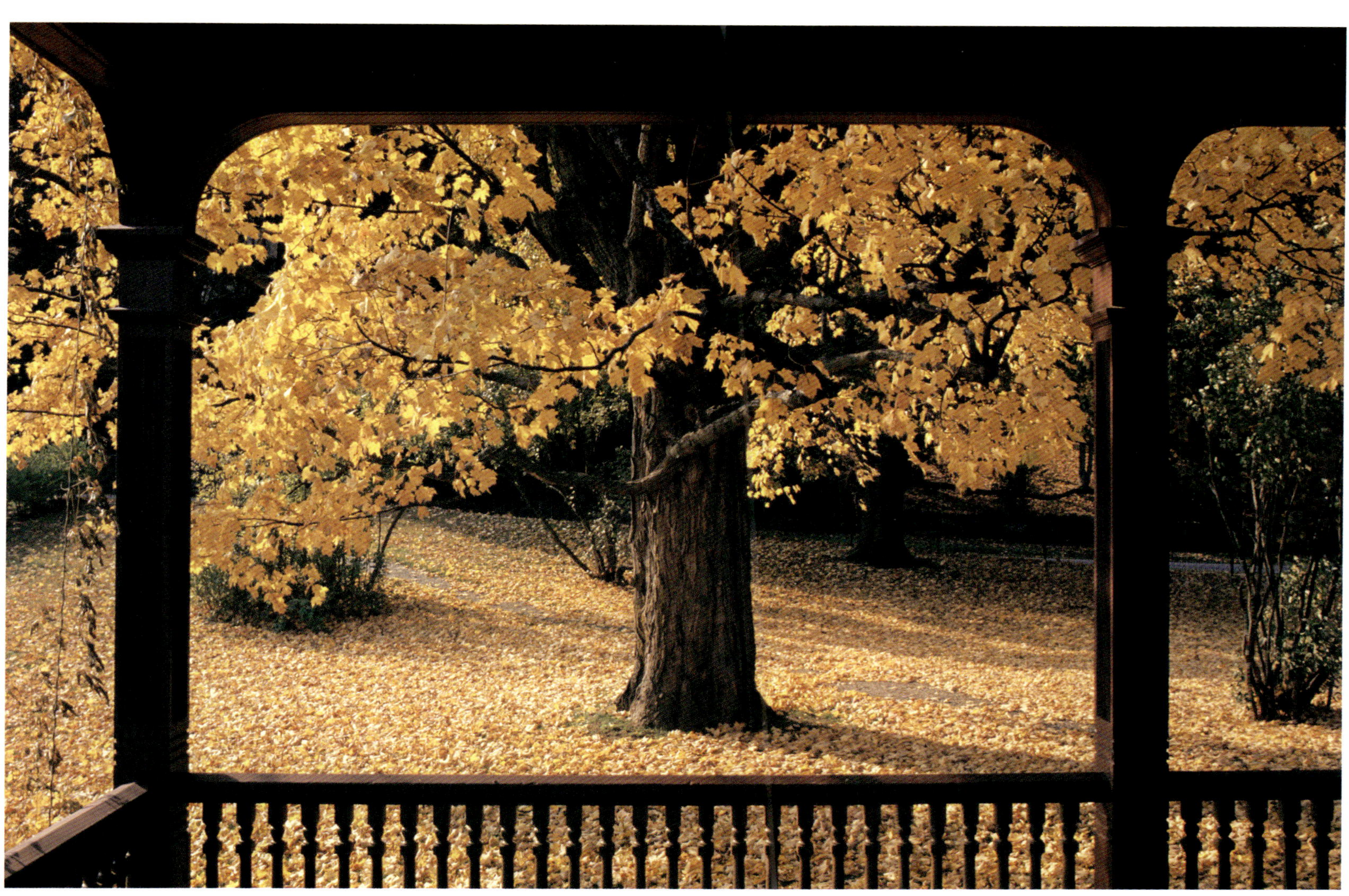

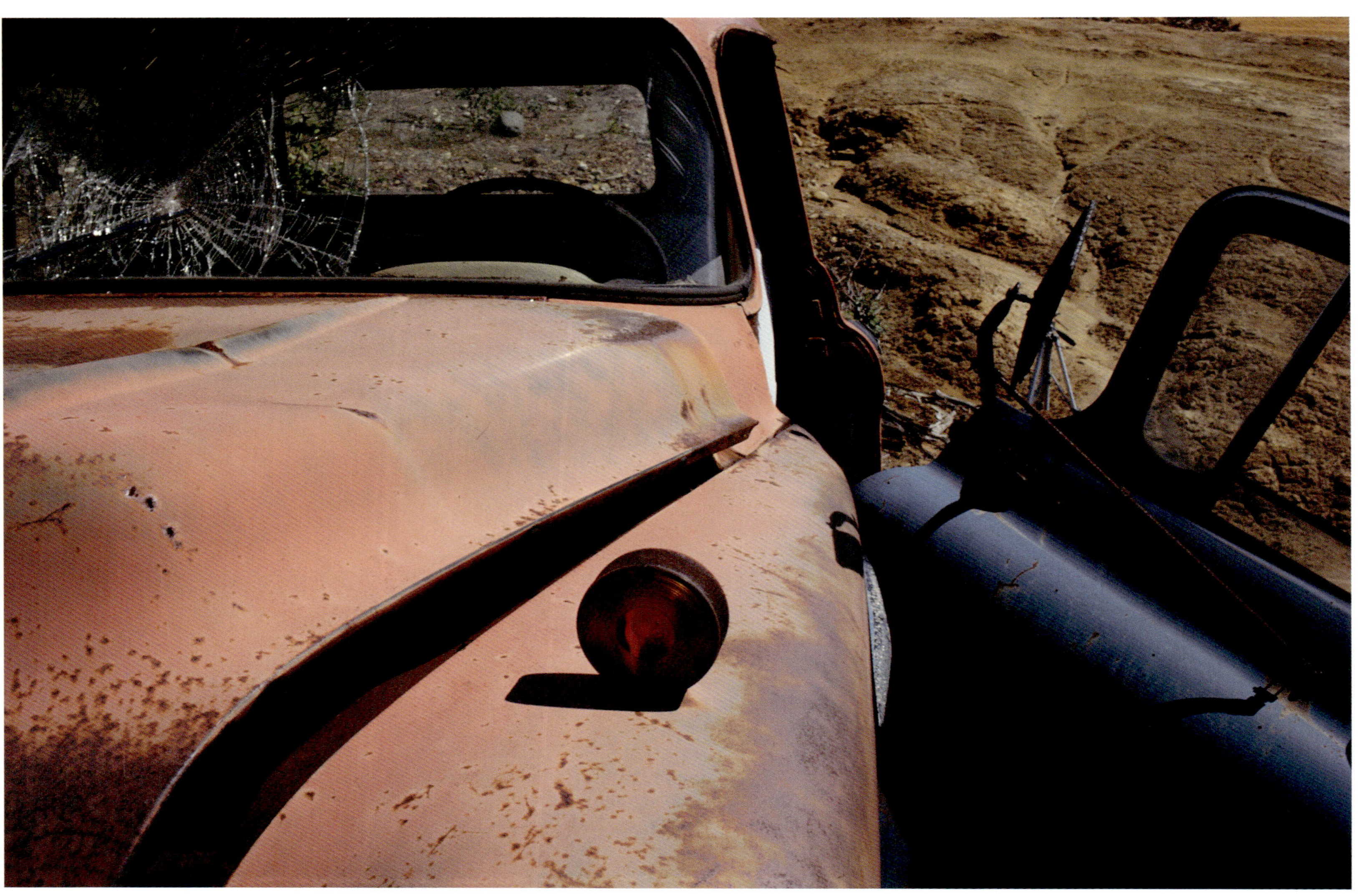

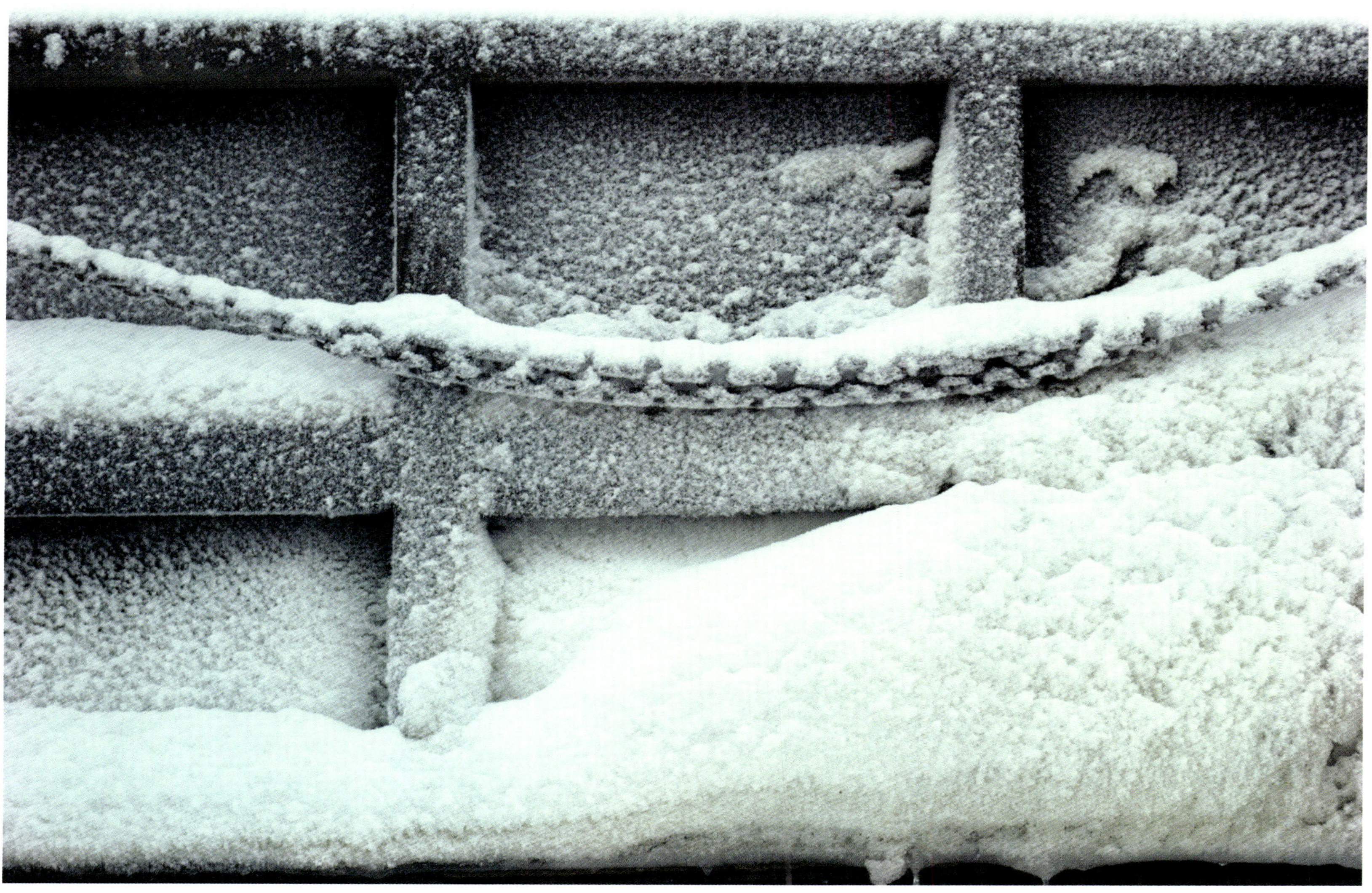

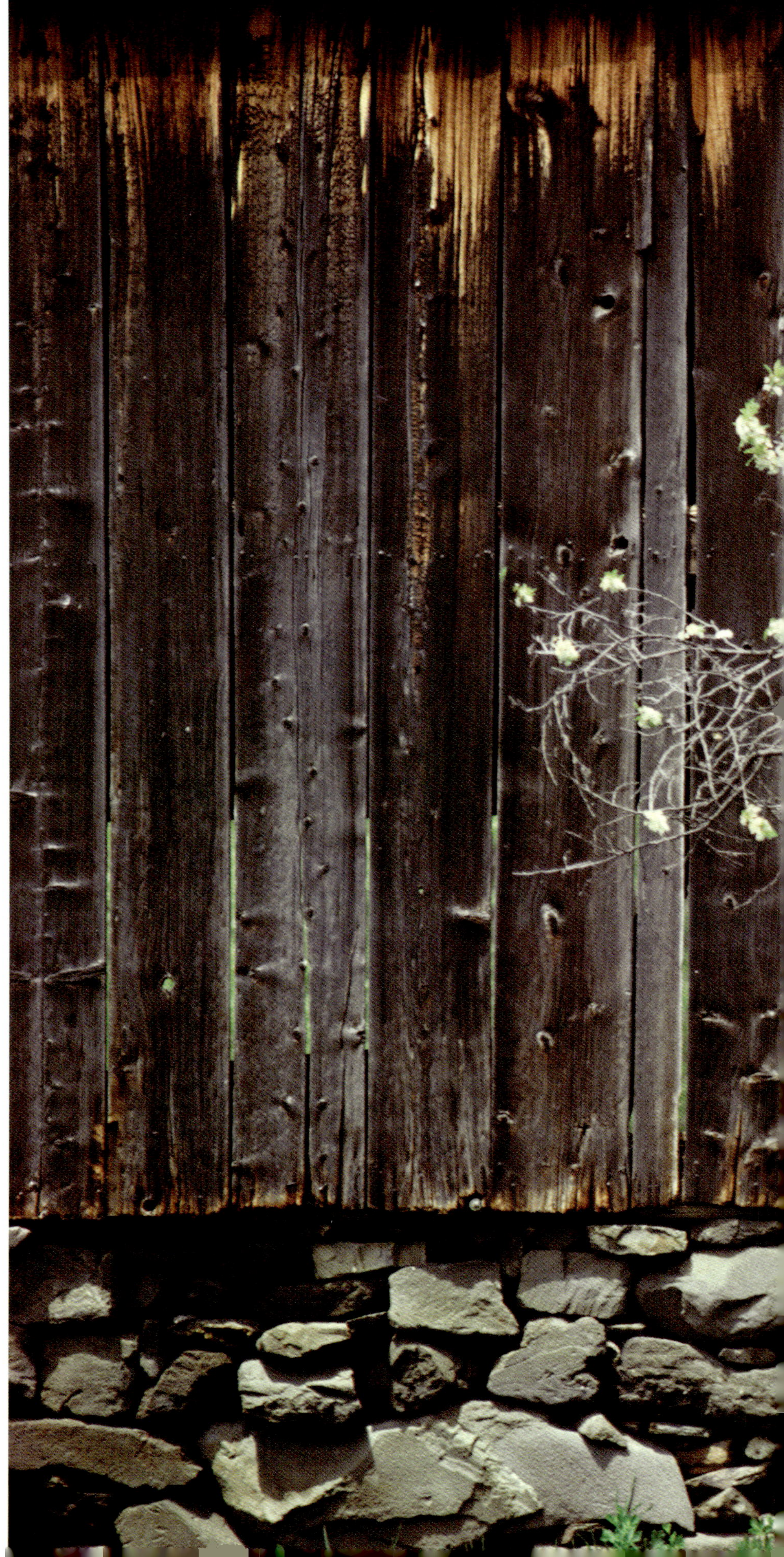

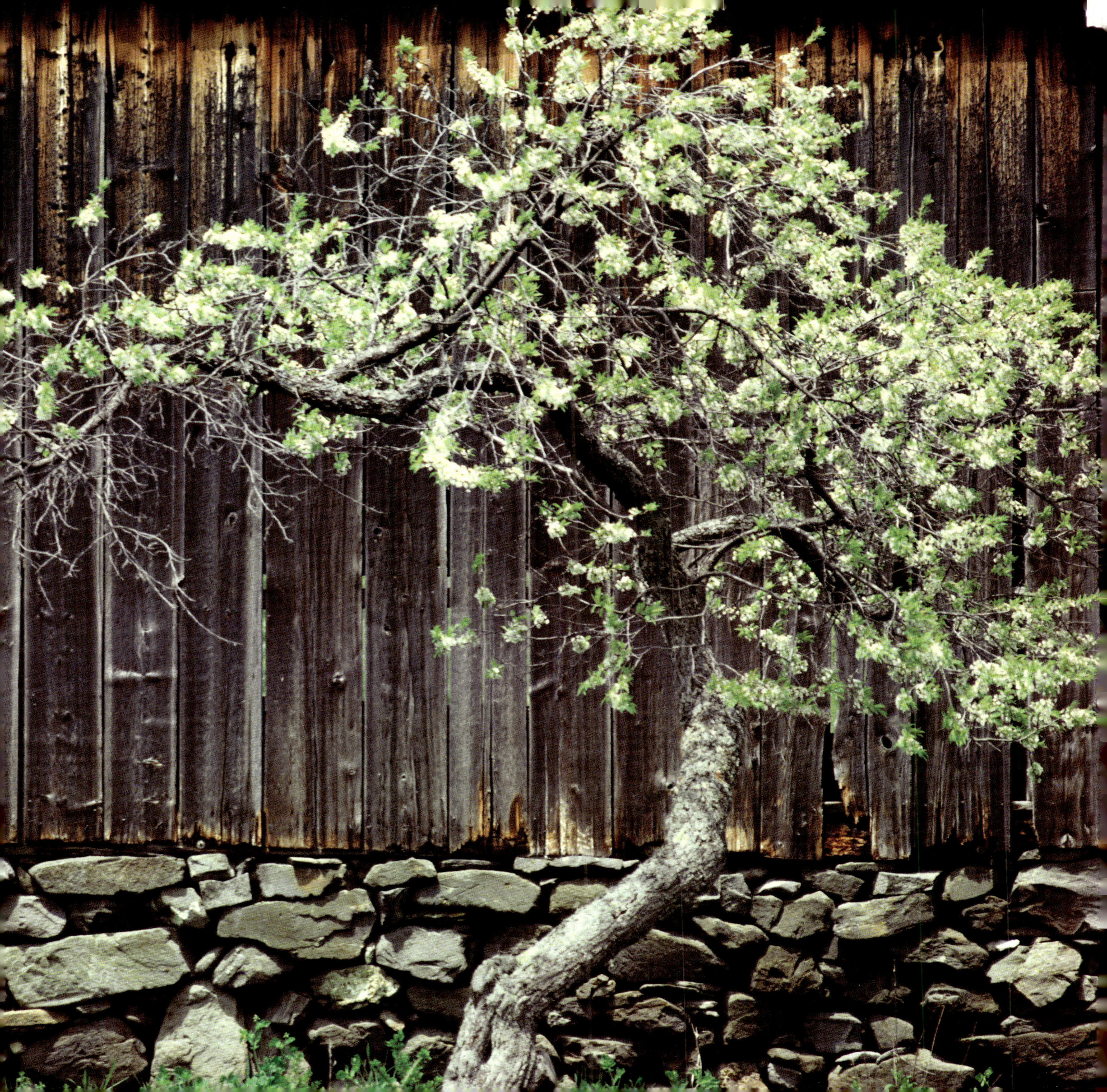

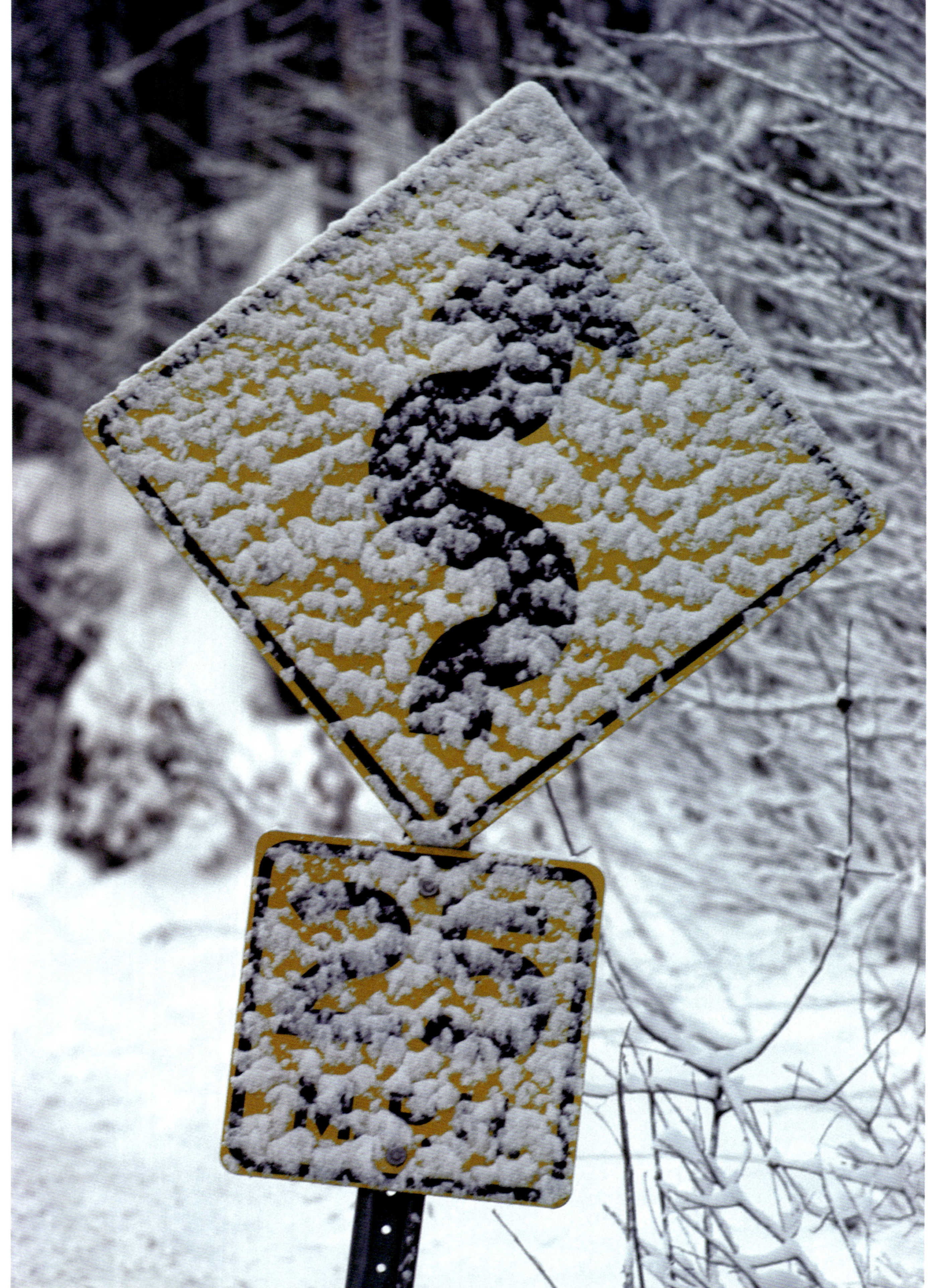

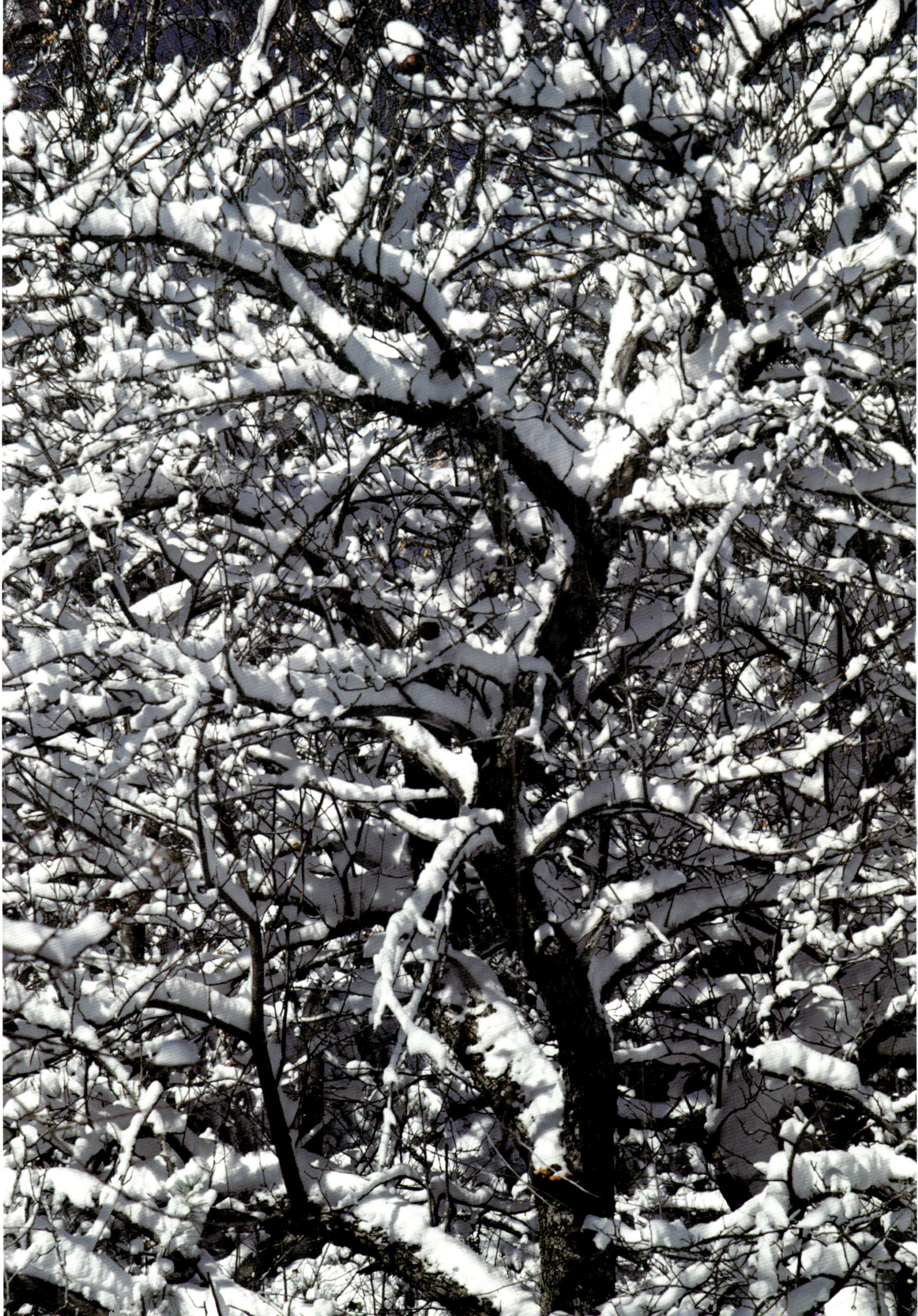

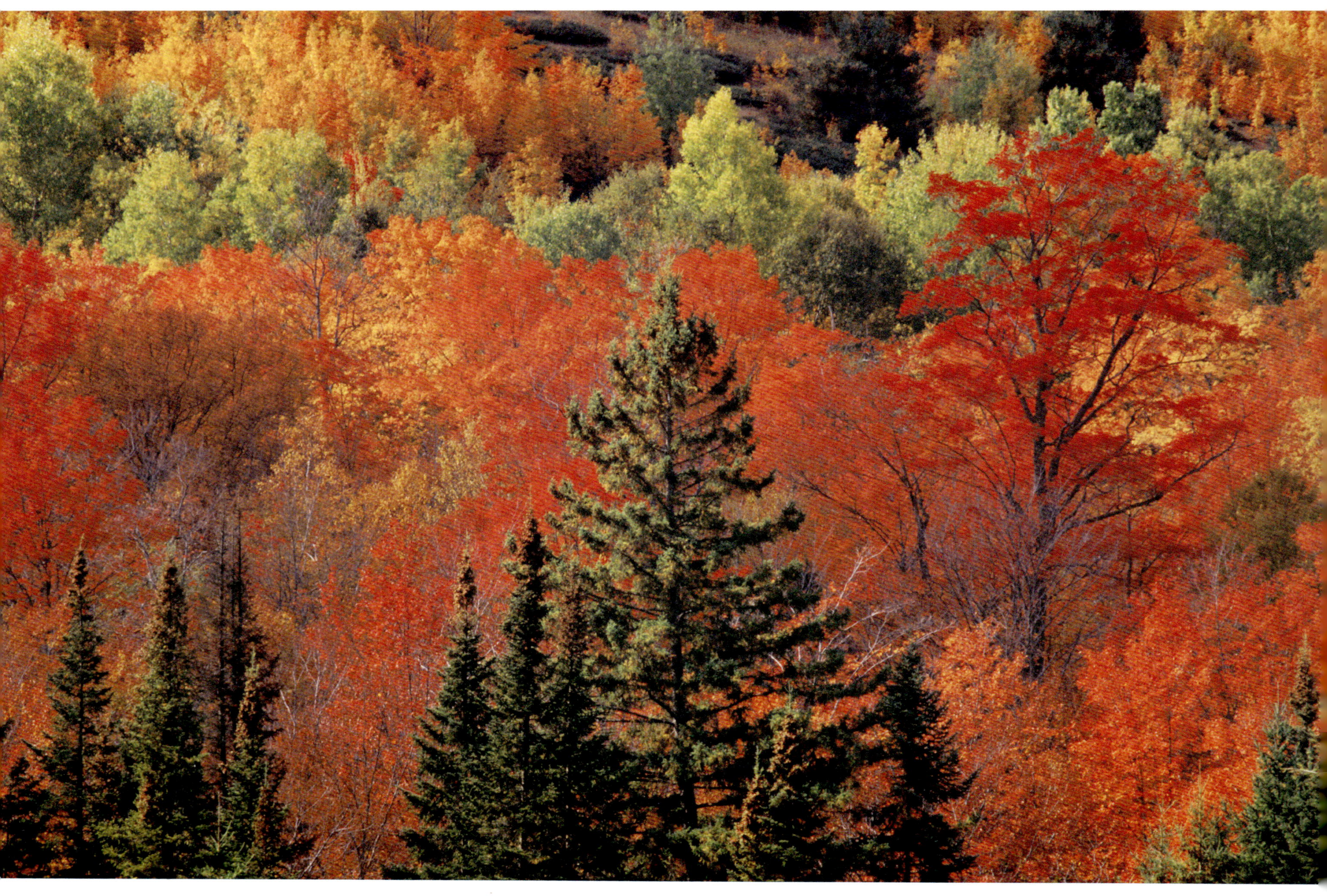

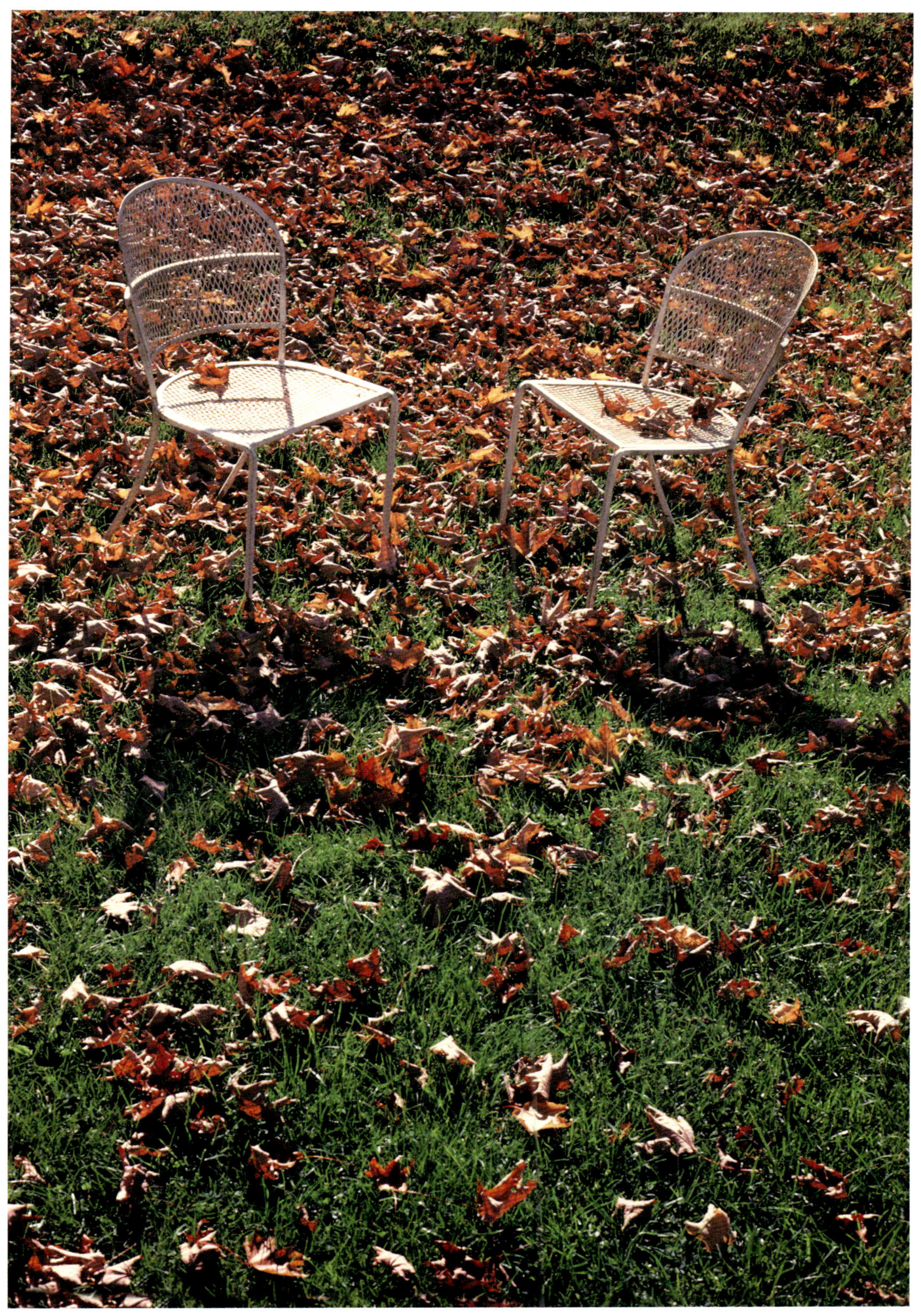

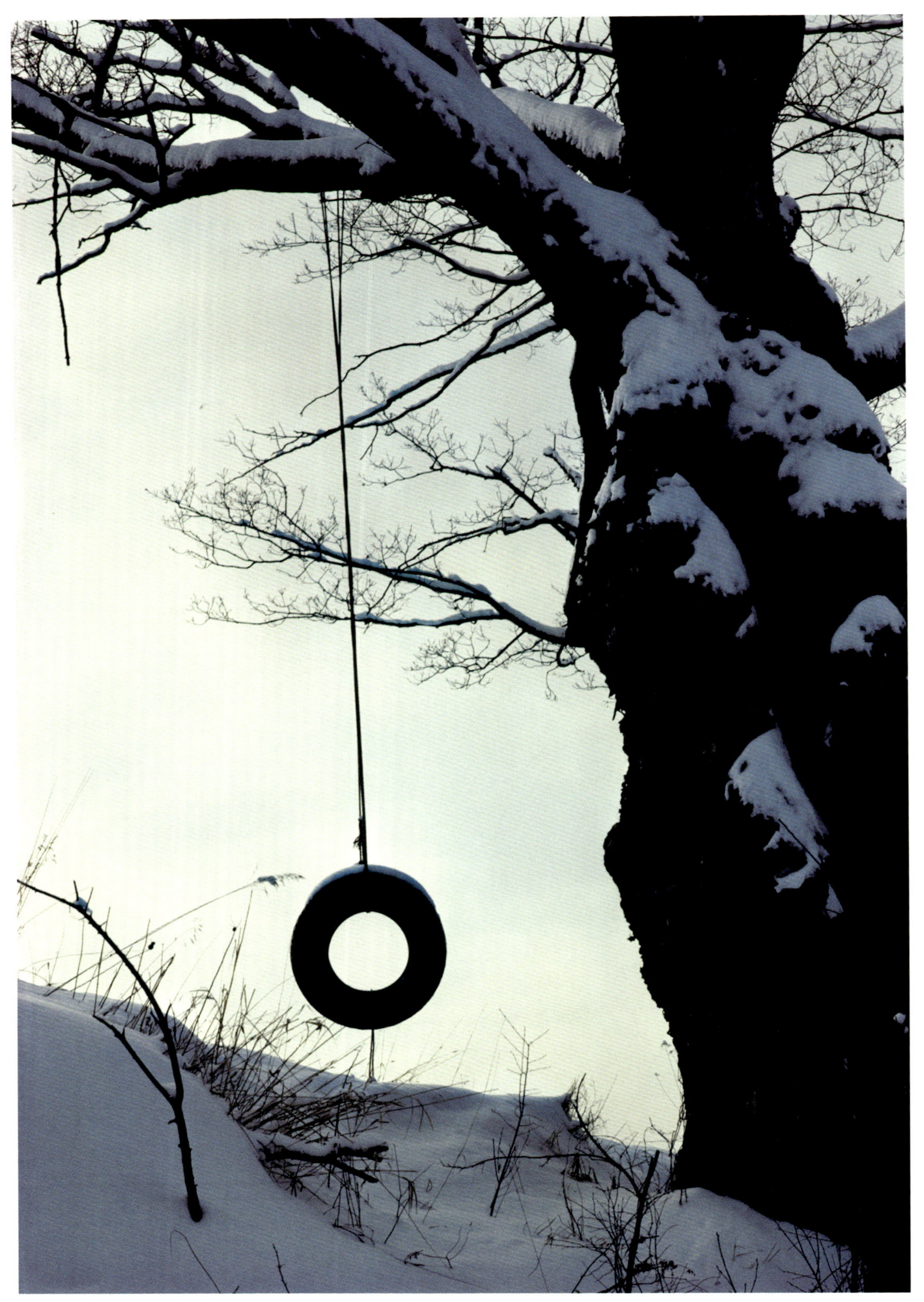

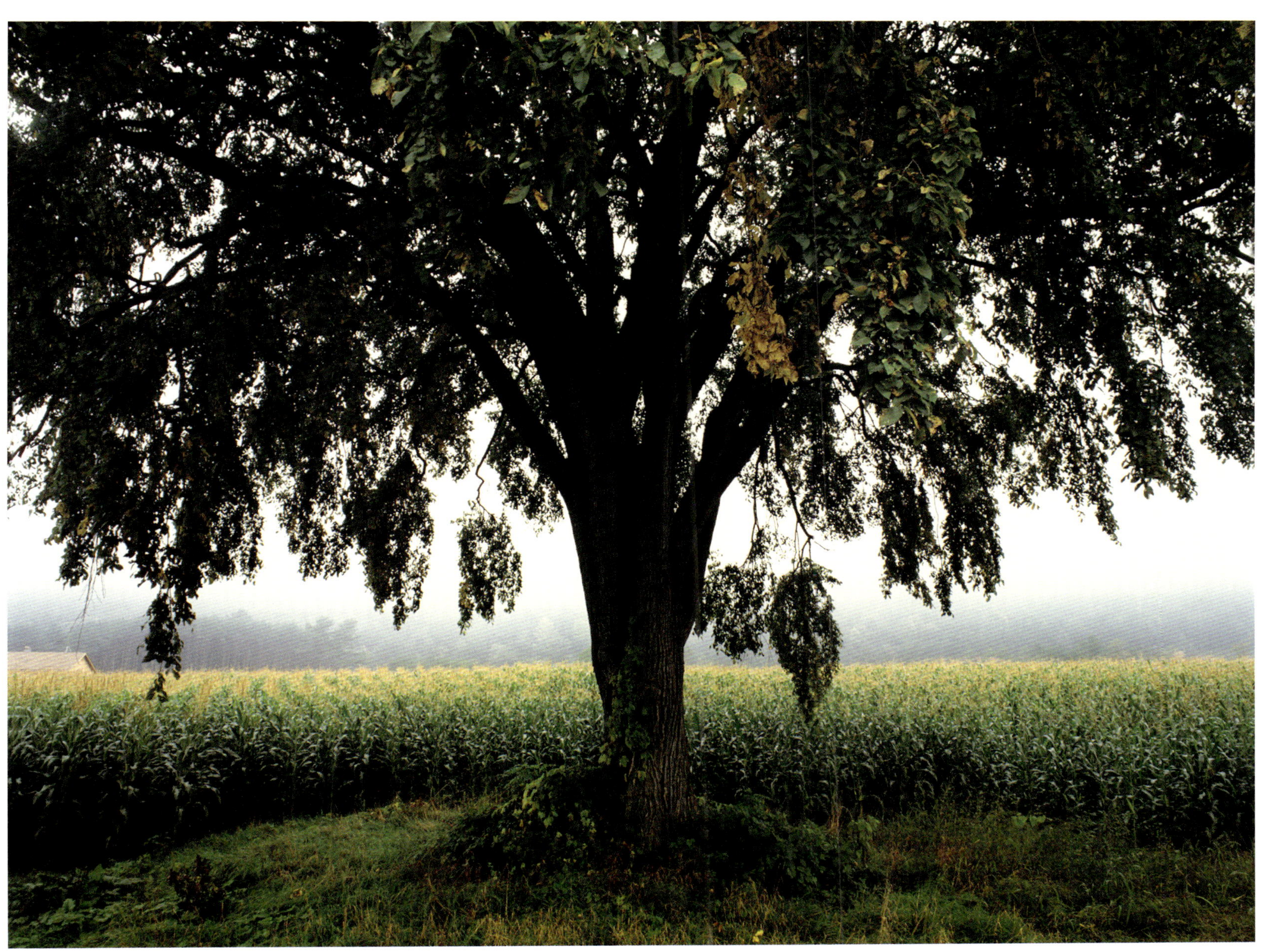

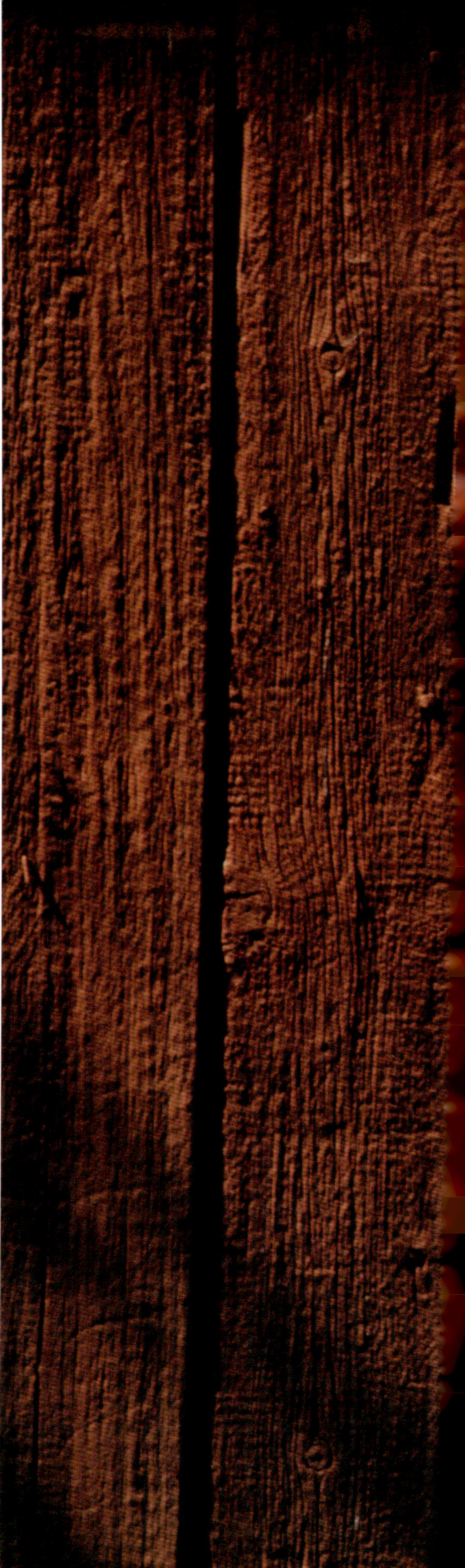

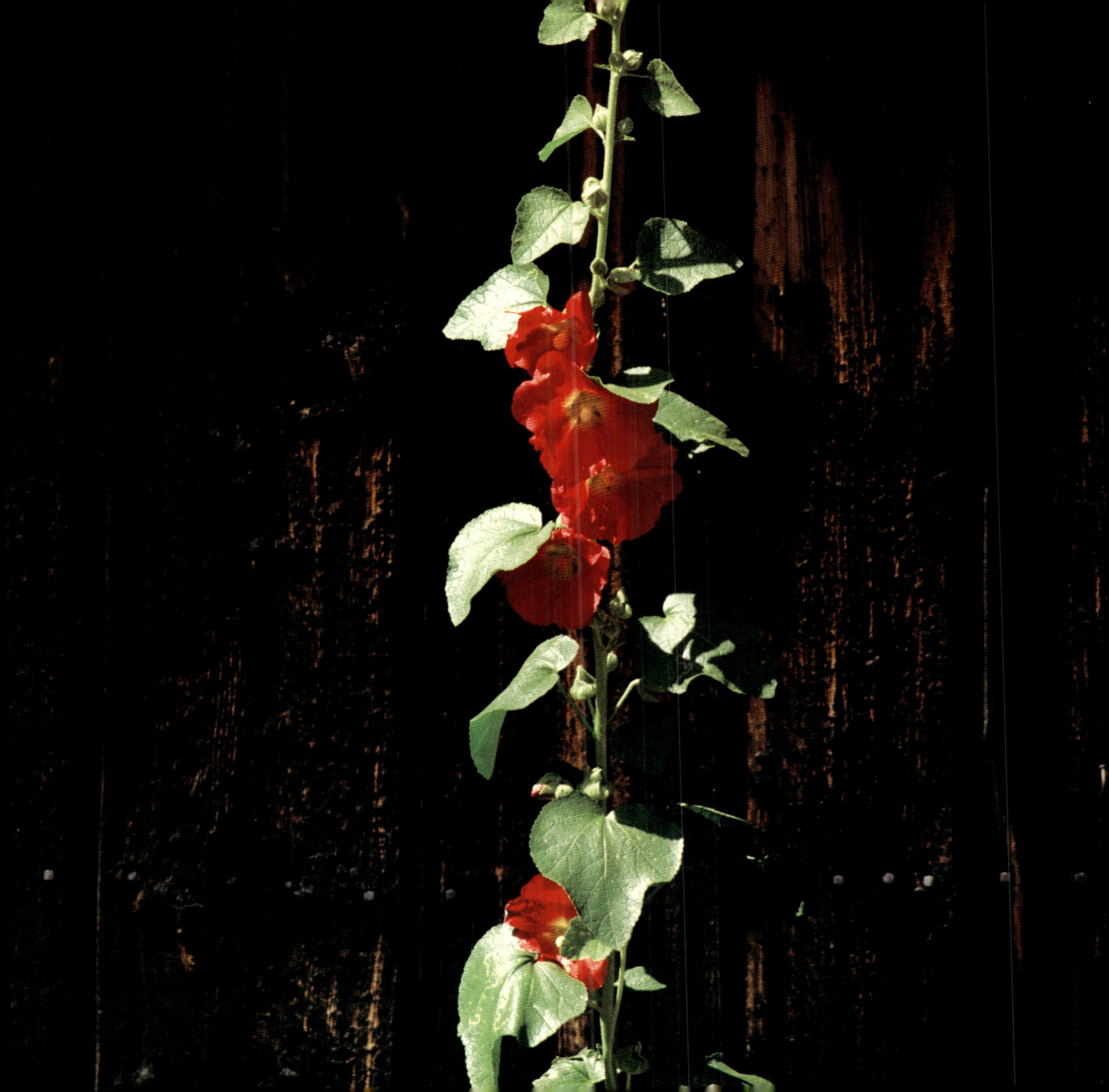

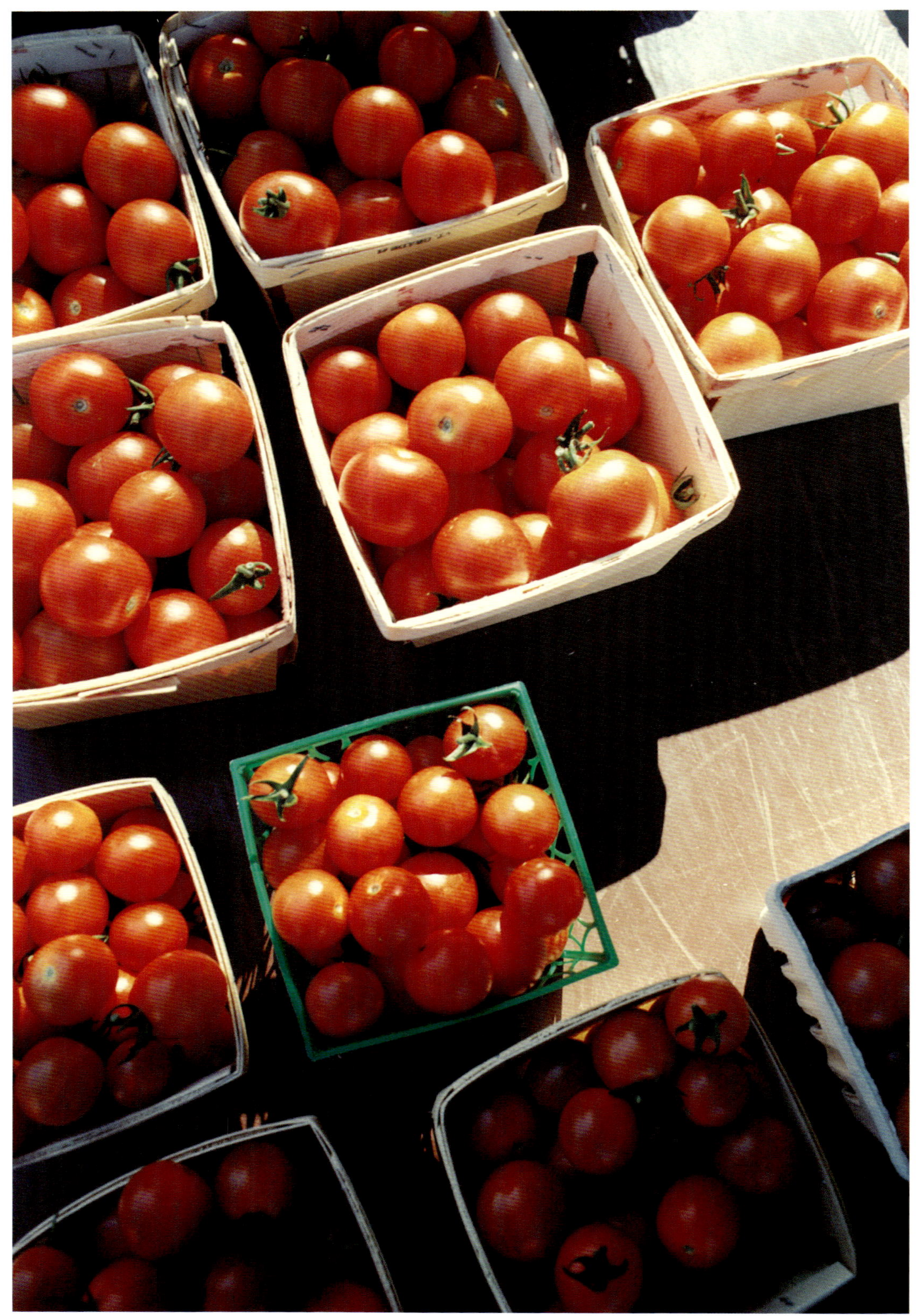

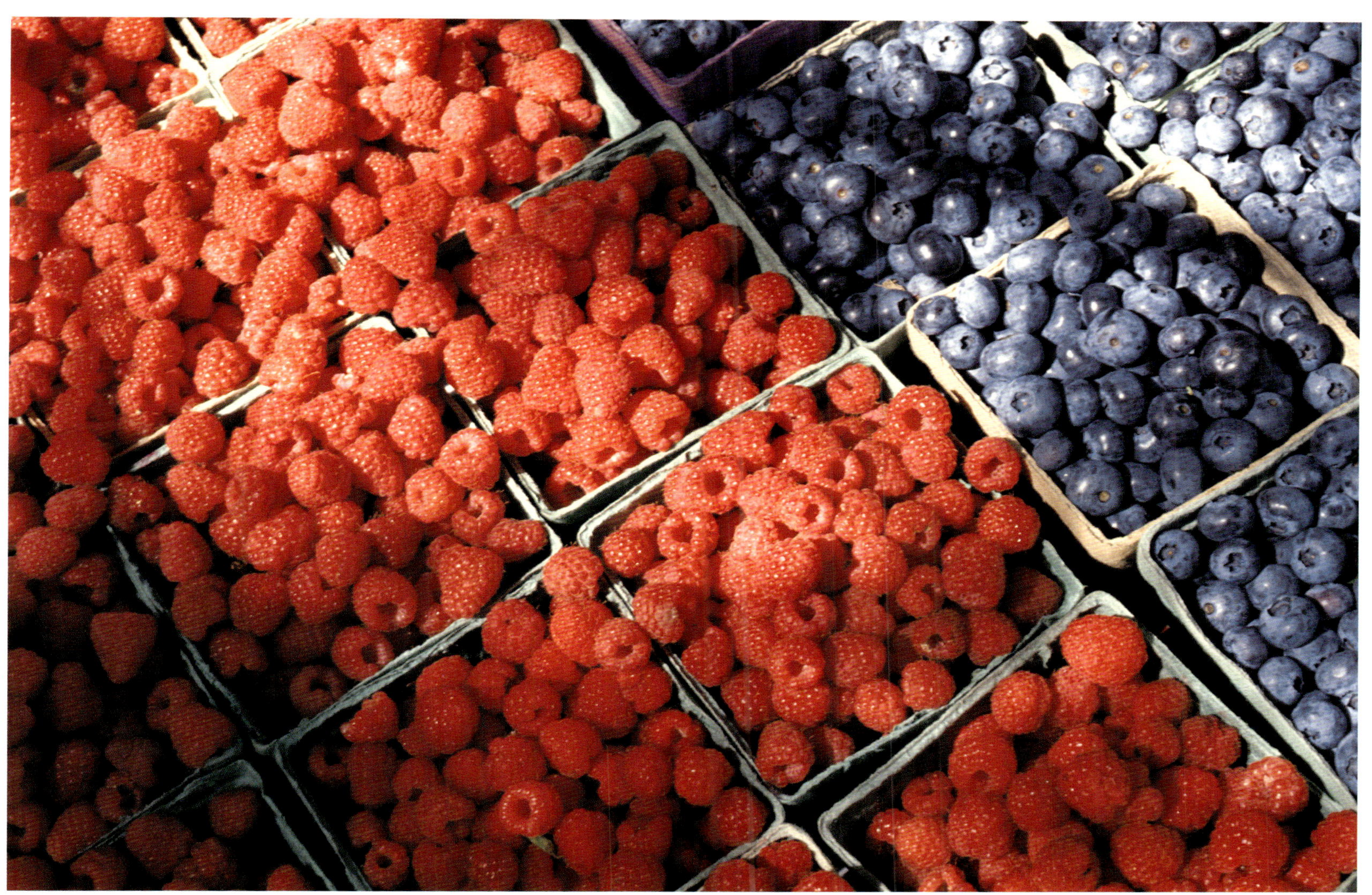

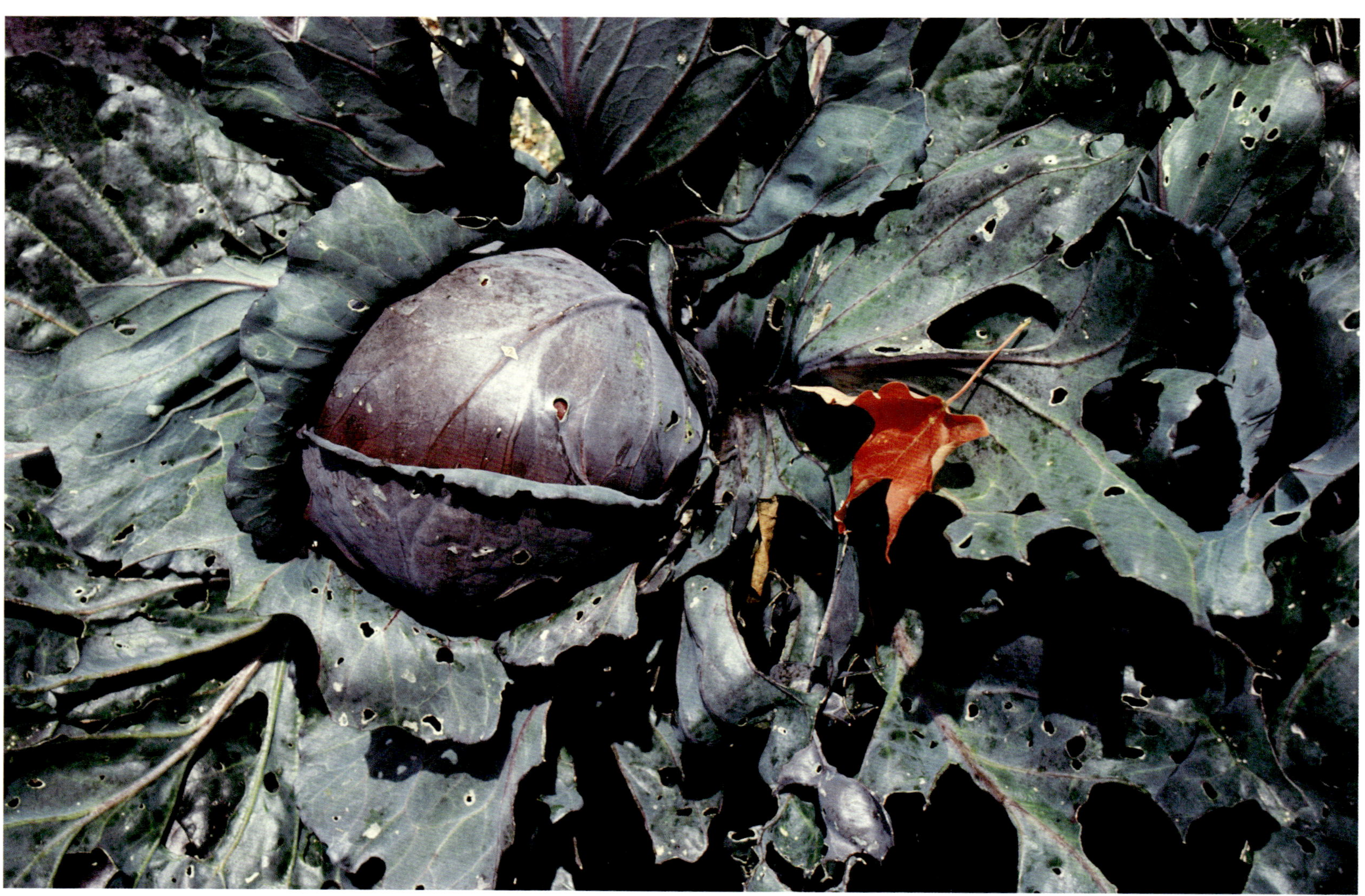

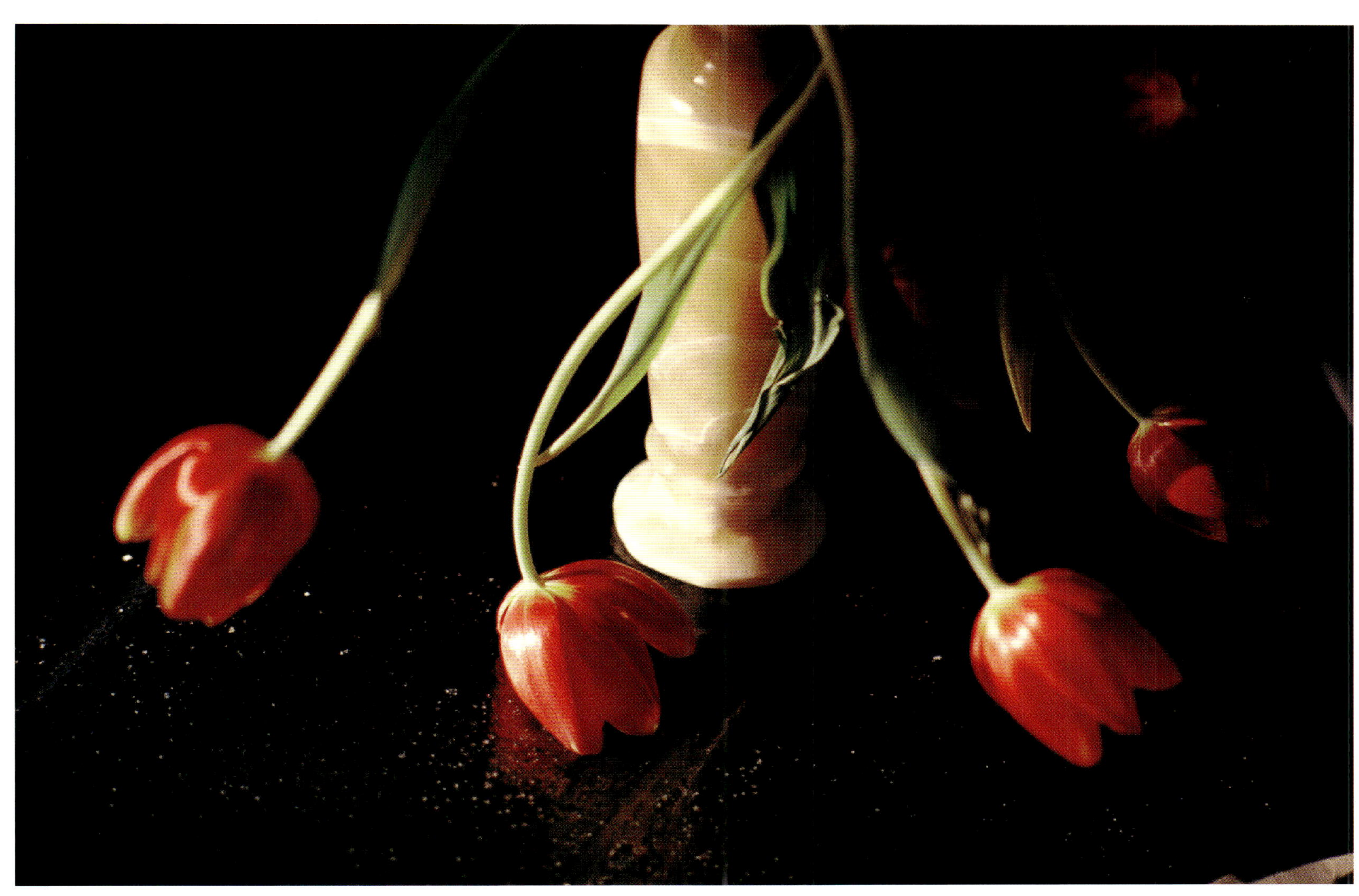

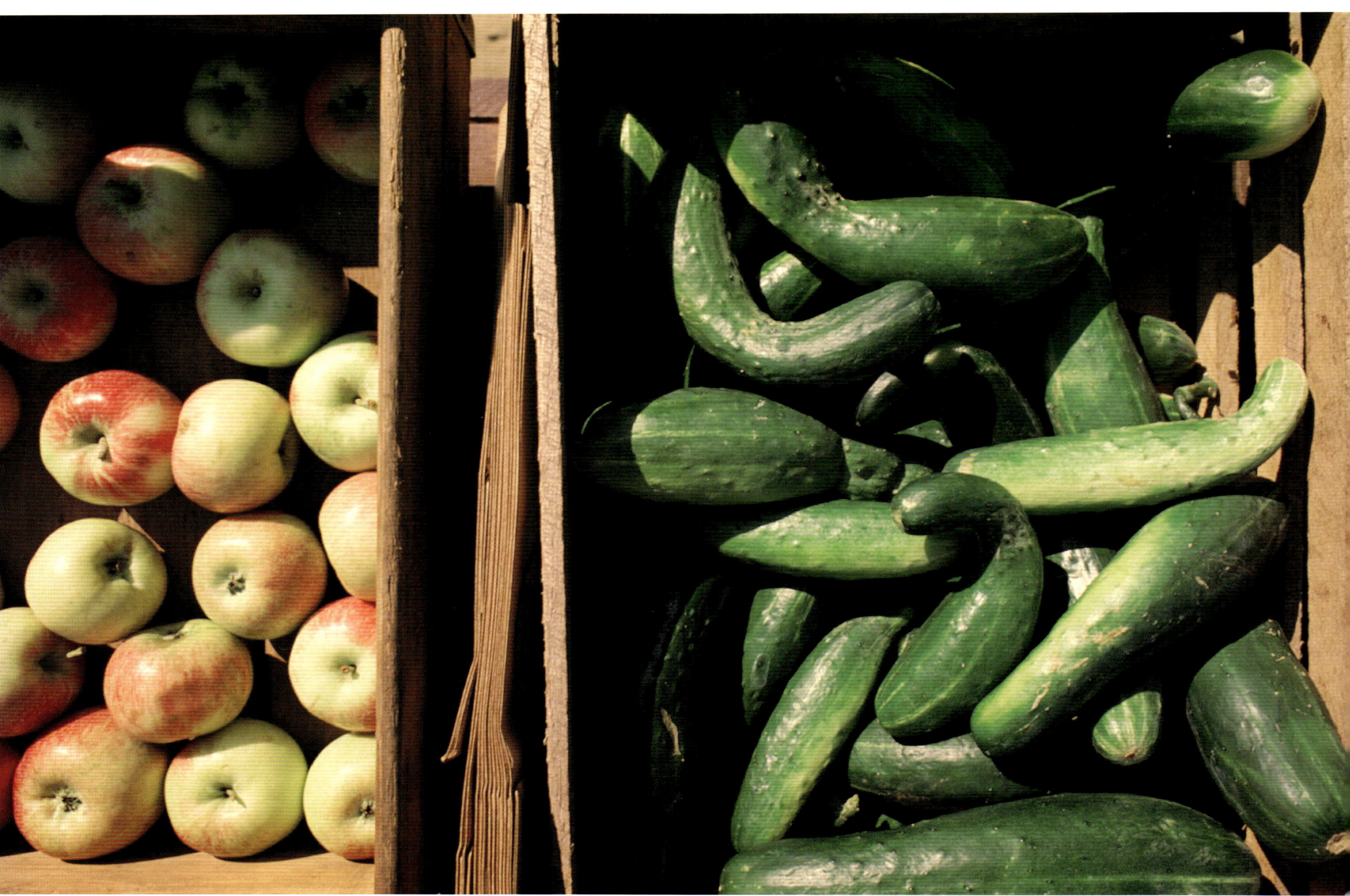

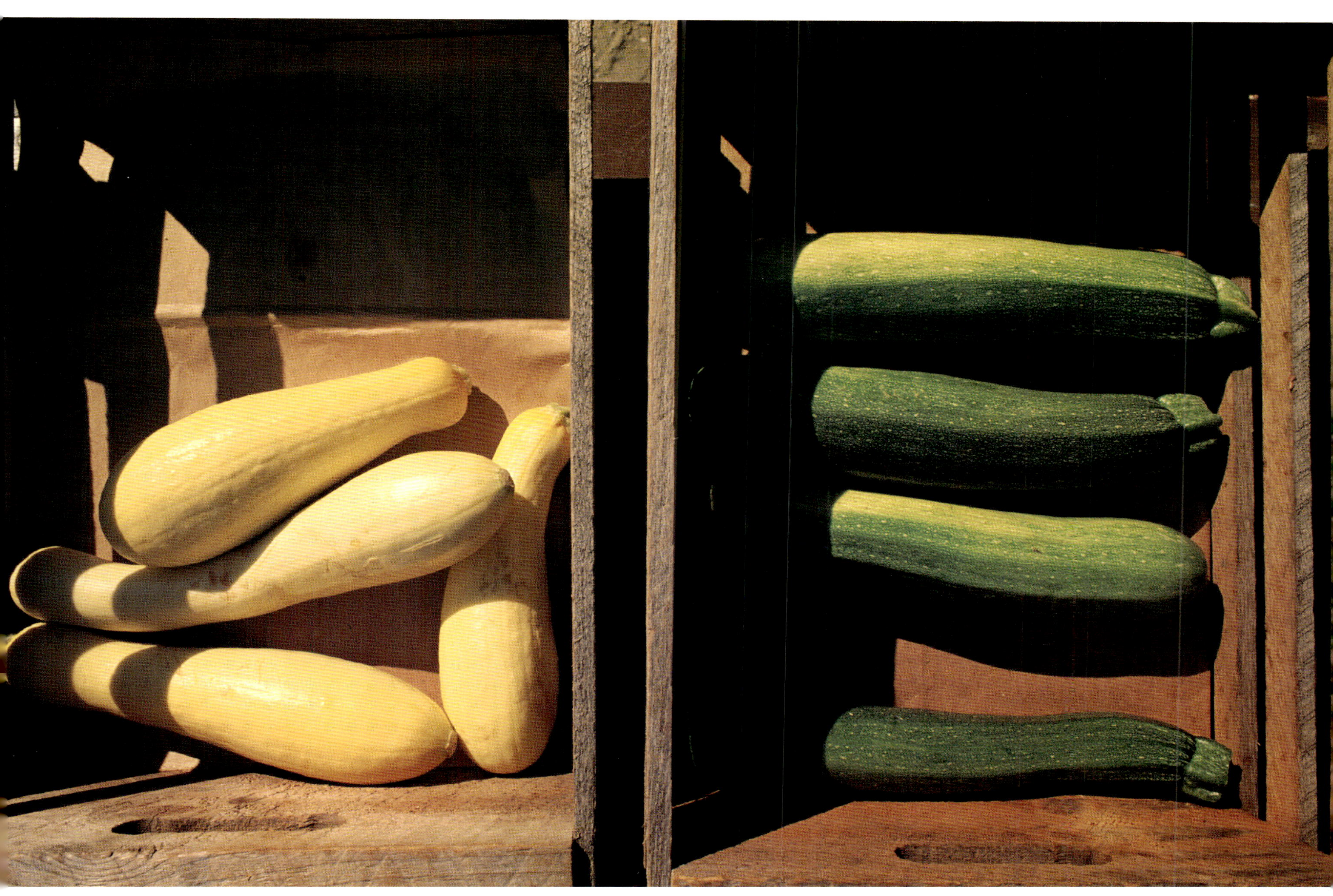

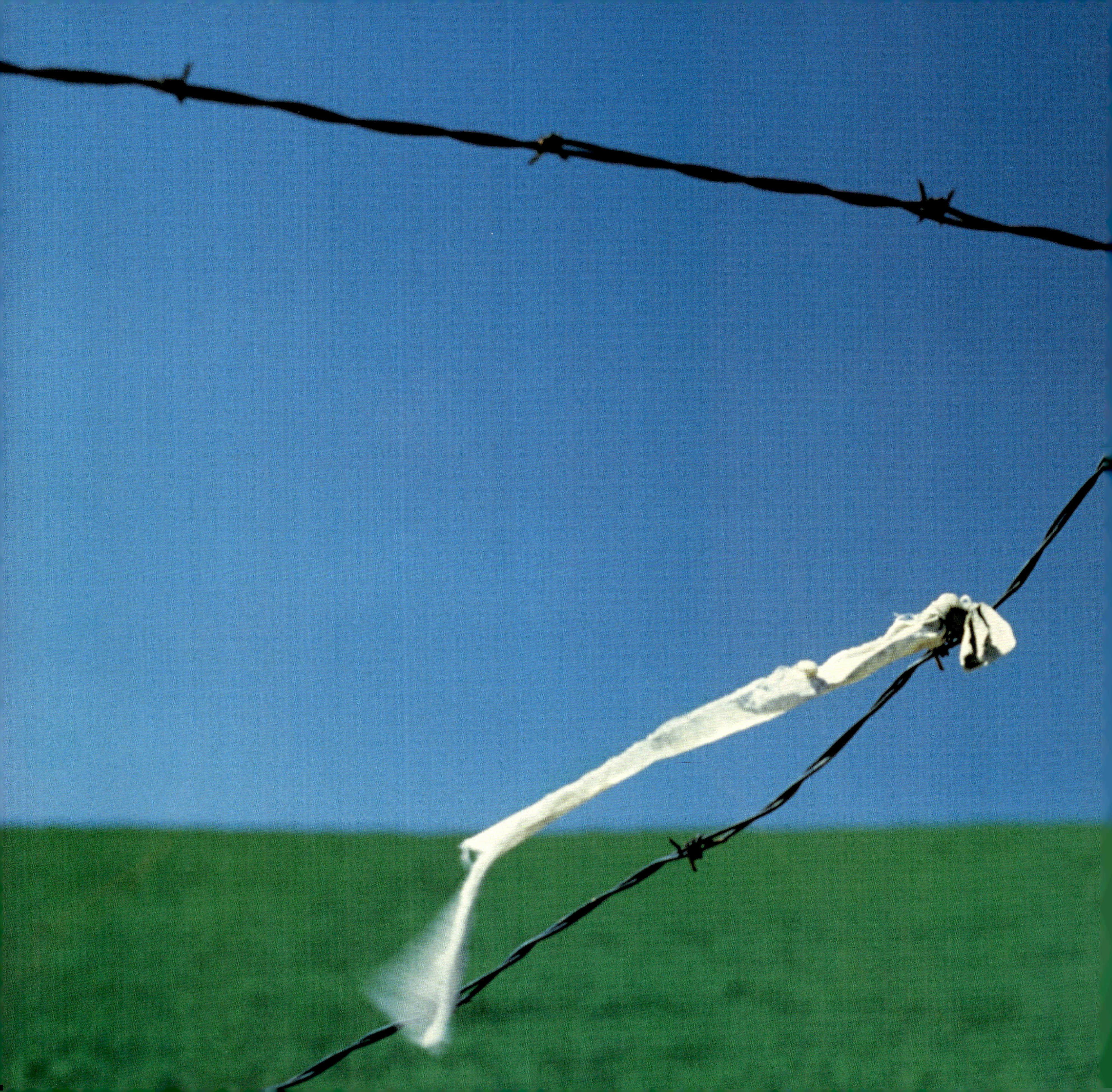

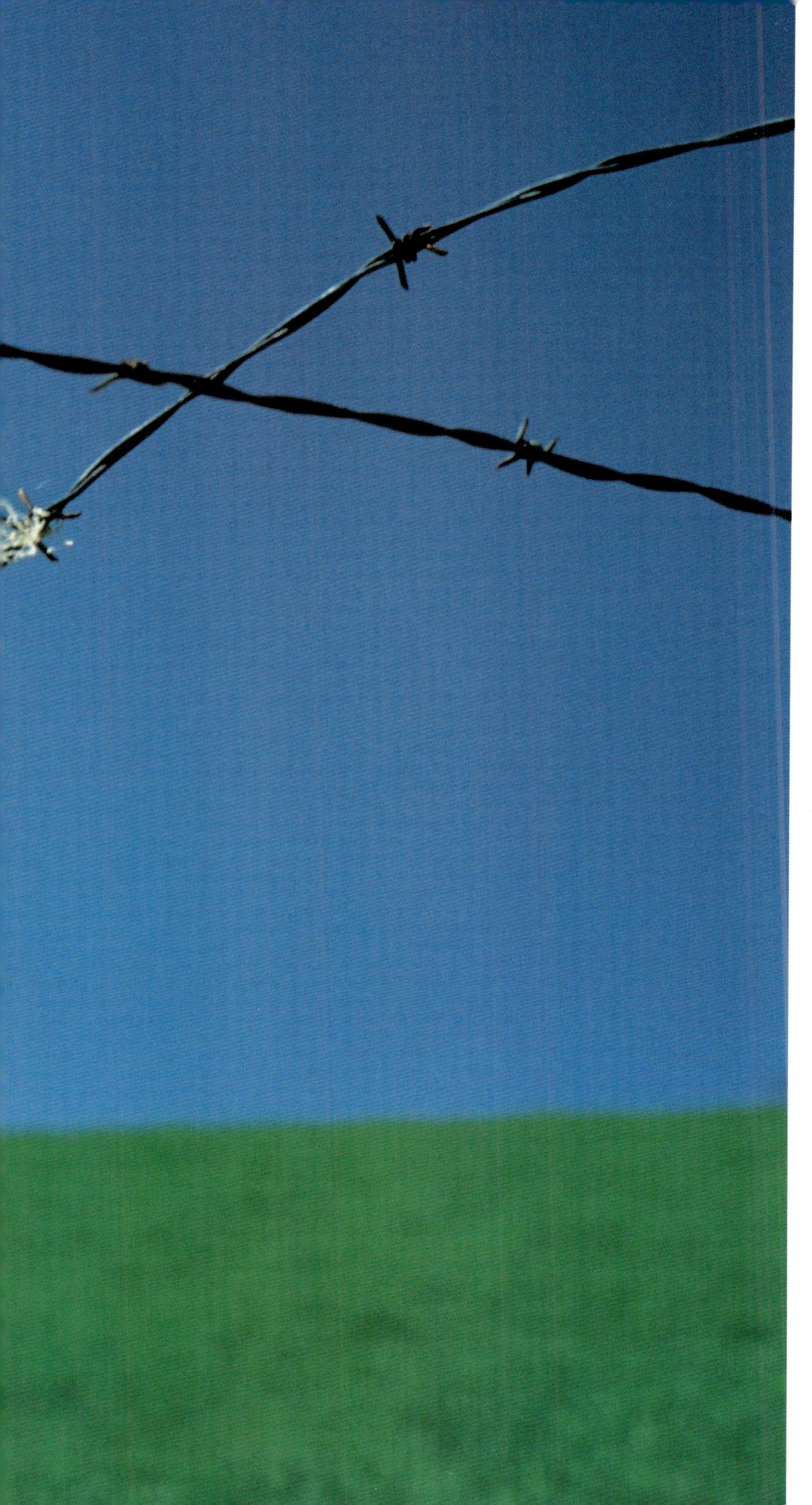

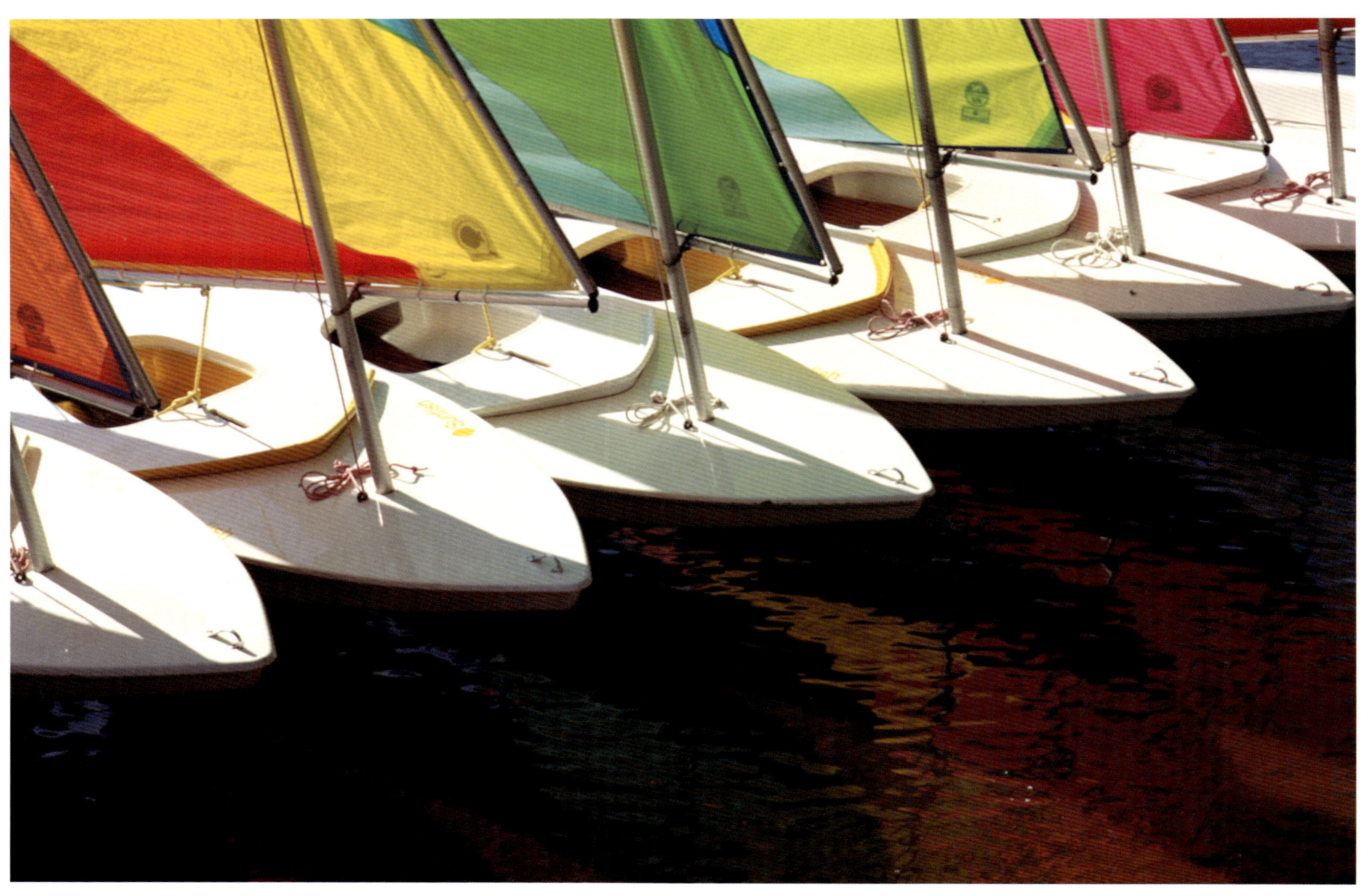

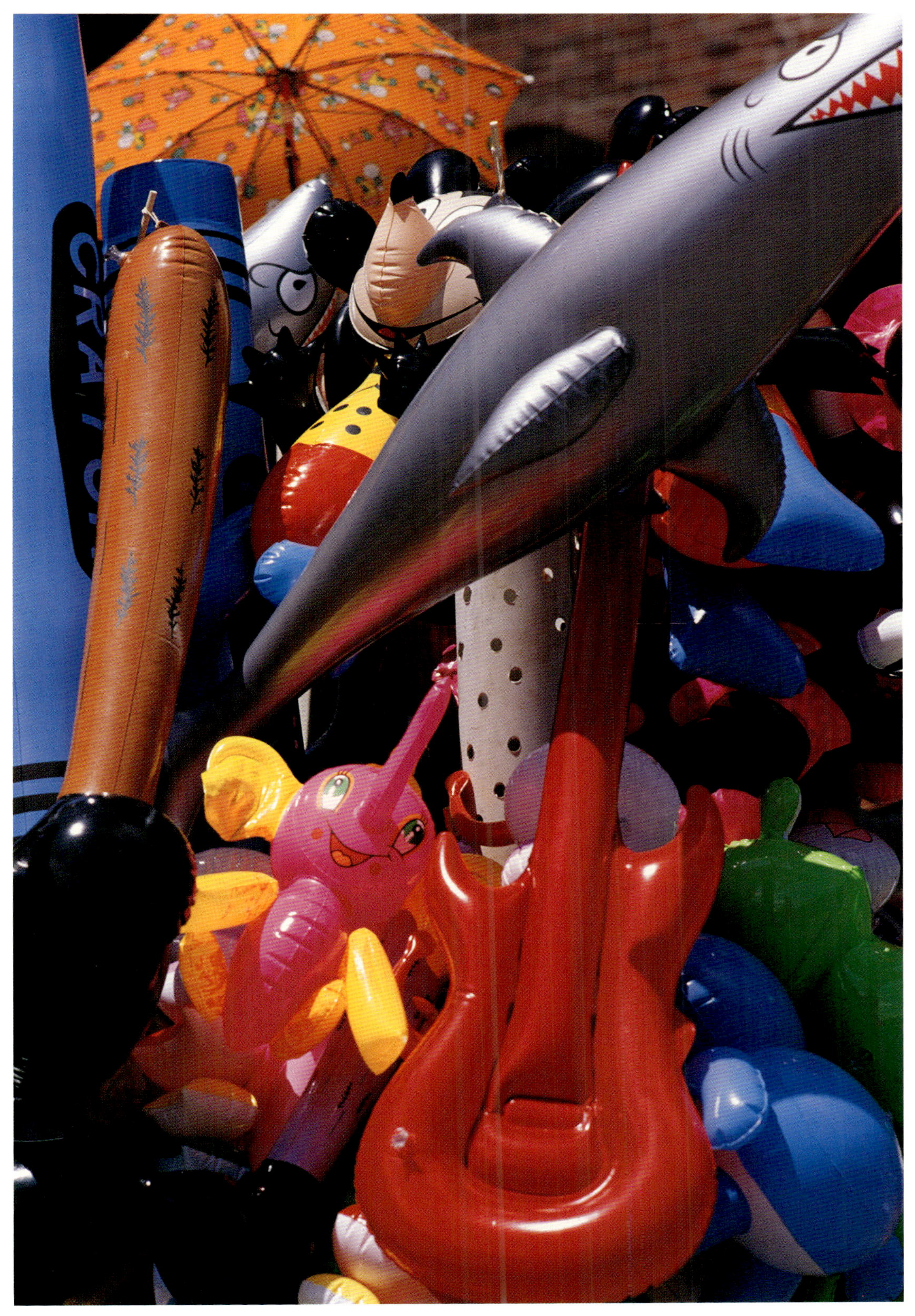

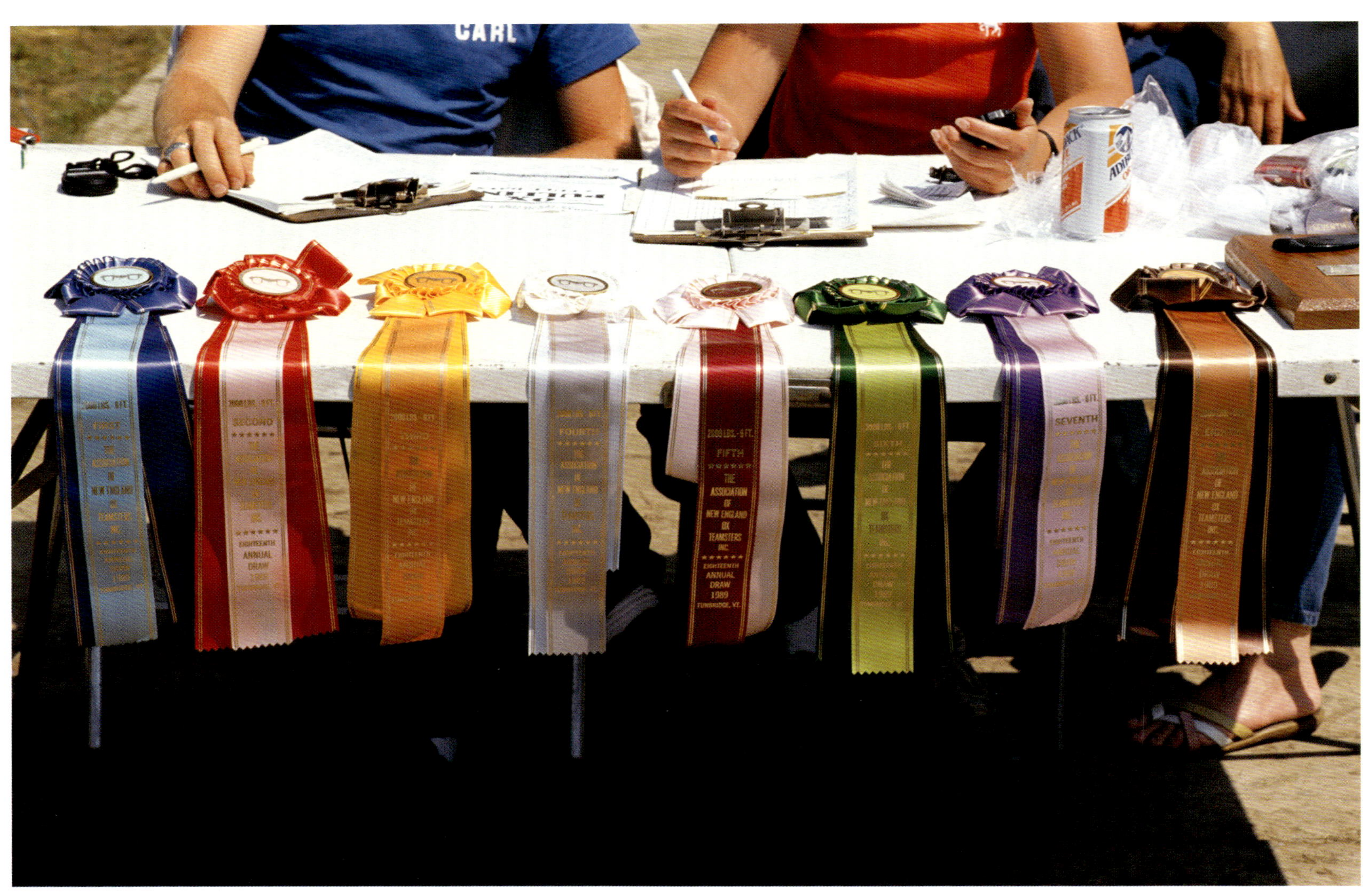

CARL

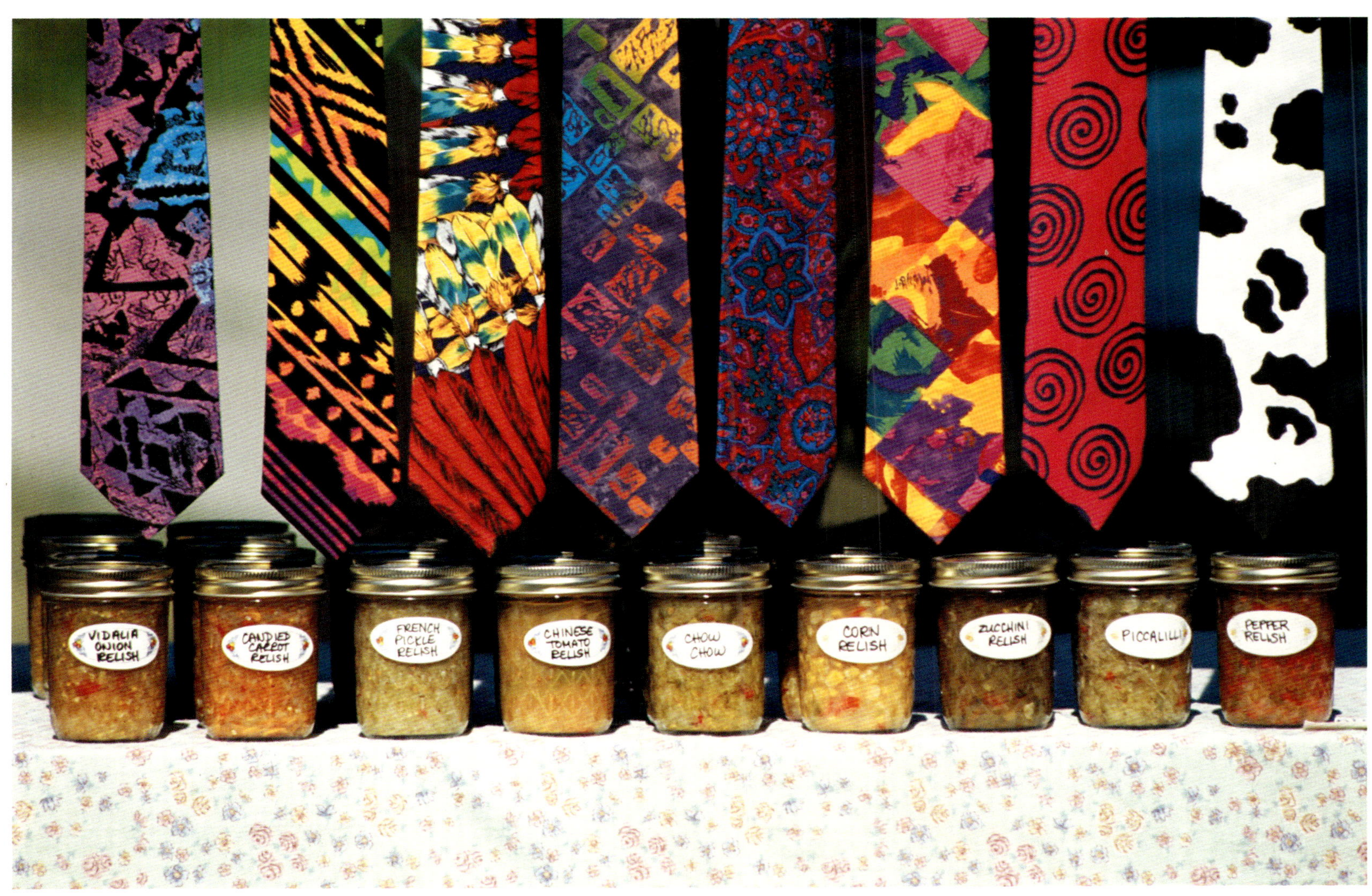

VIDALIA ONION RELISH
CANDIED CARROT RELISH
FRENCH PICKLE RELISH
CHINESE TOMATO RELISH
CHOW CHOW
CORN RELISH
ZUCCHINI RELISH
PICCALILLI
PEPPER RELISH

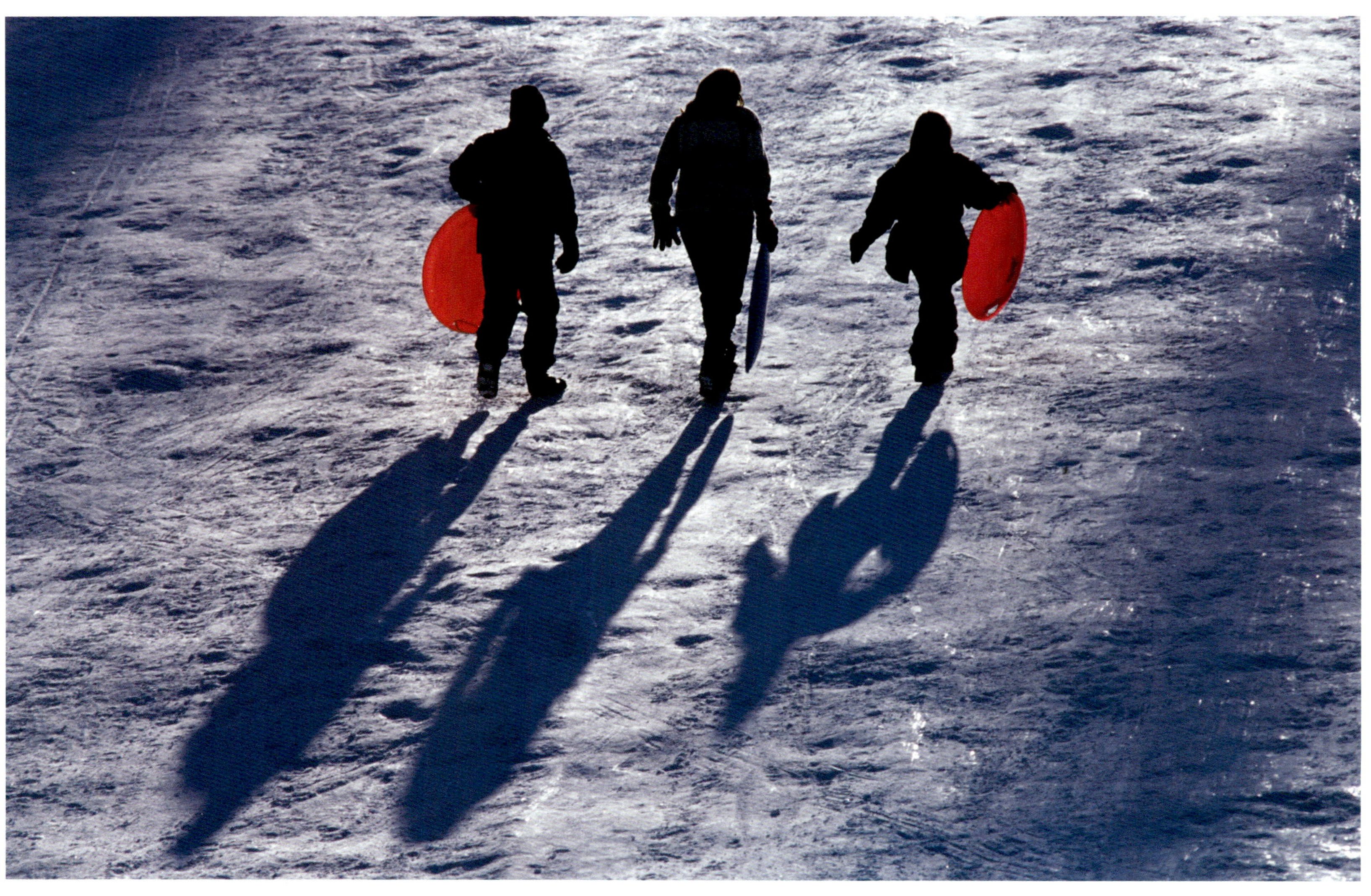

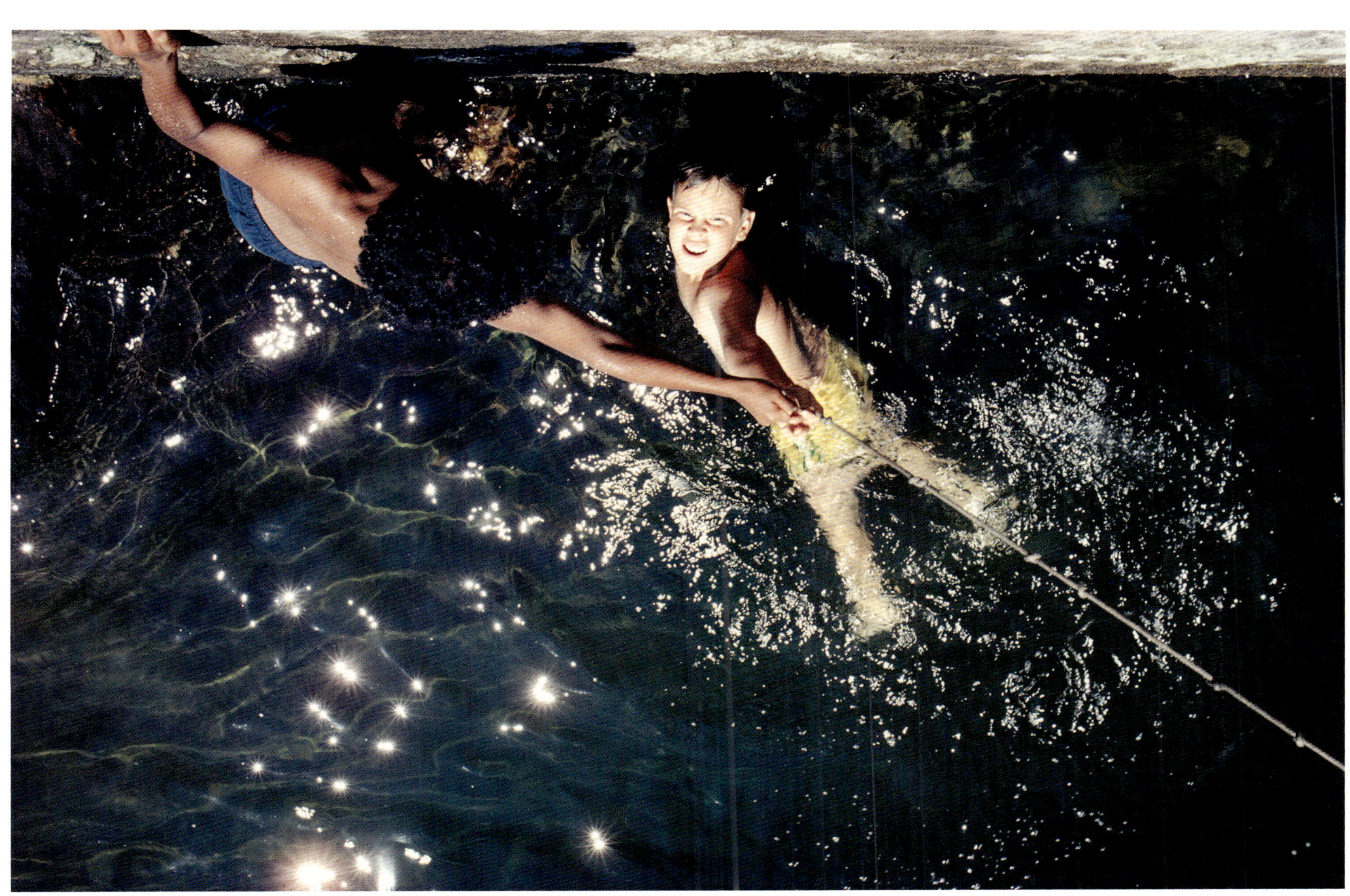

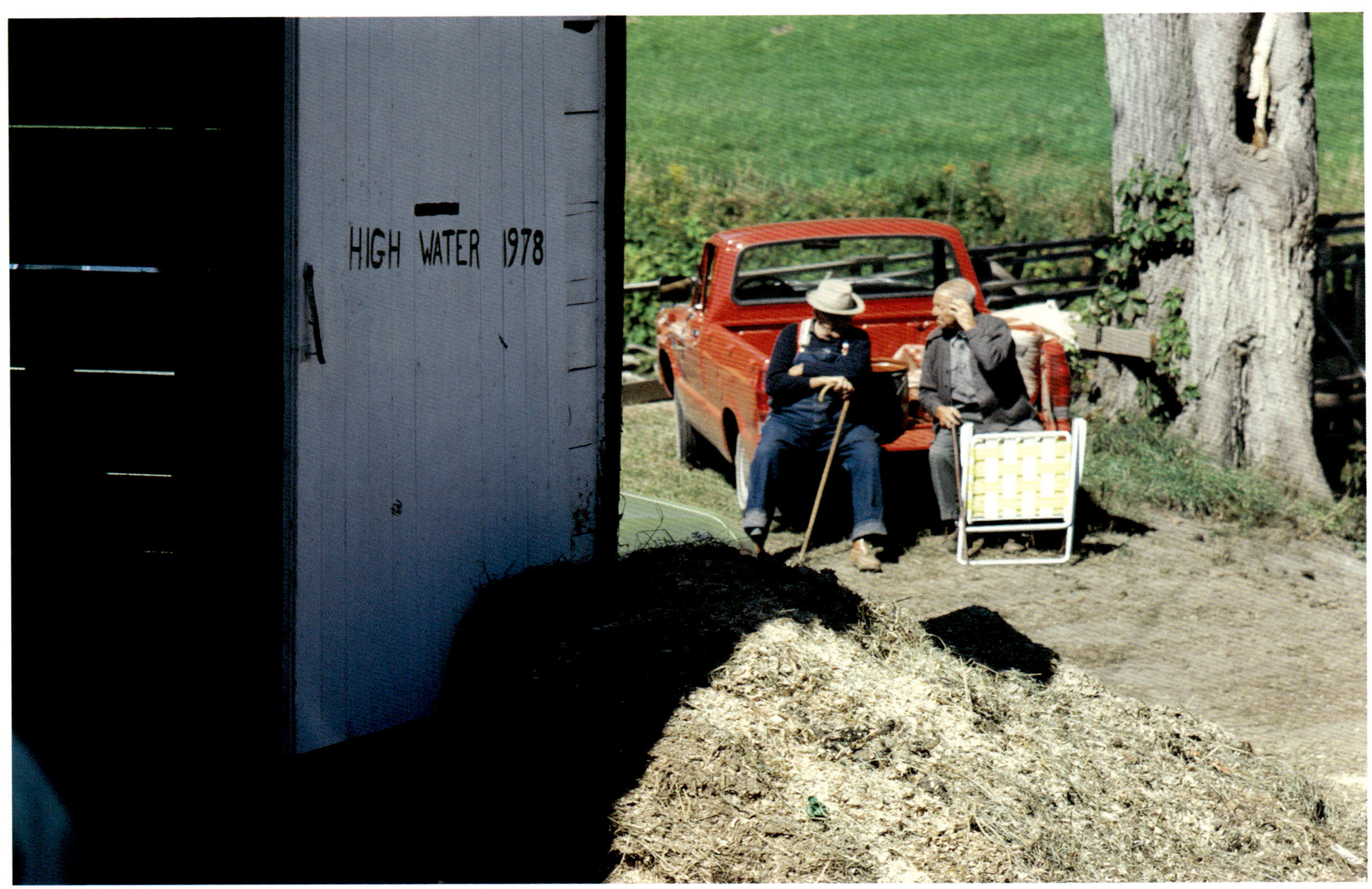
HIGH WATER 1978

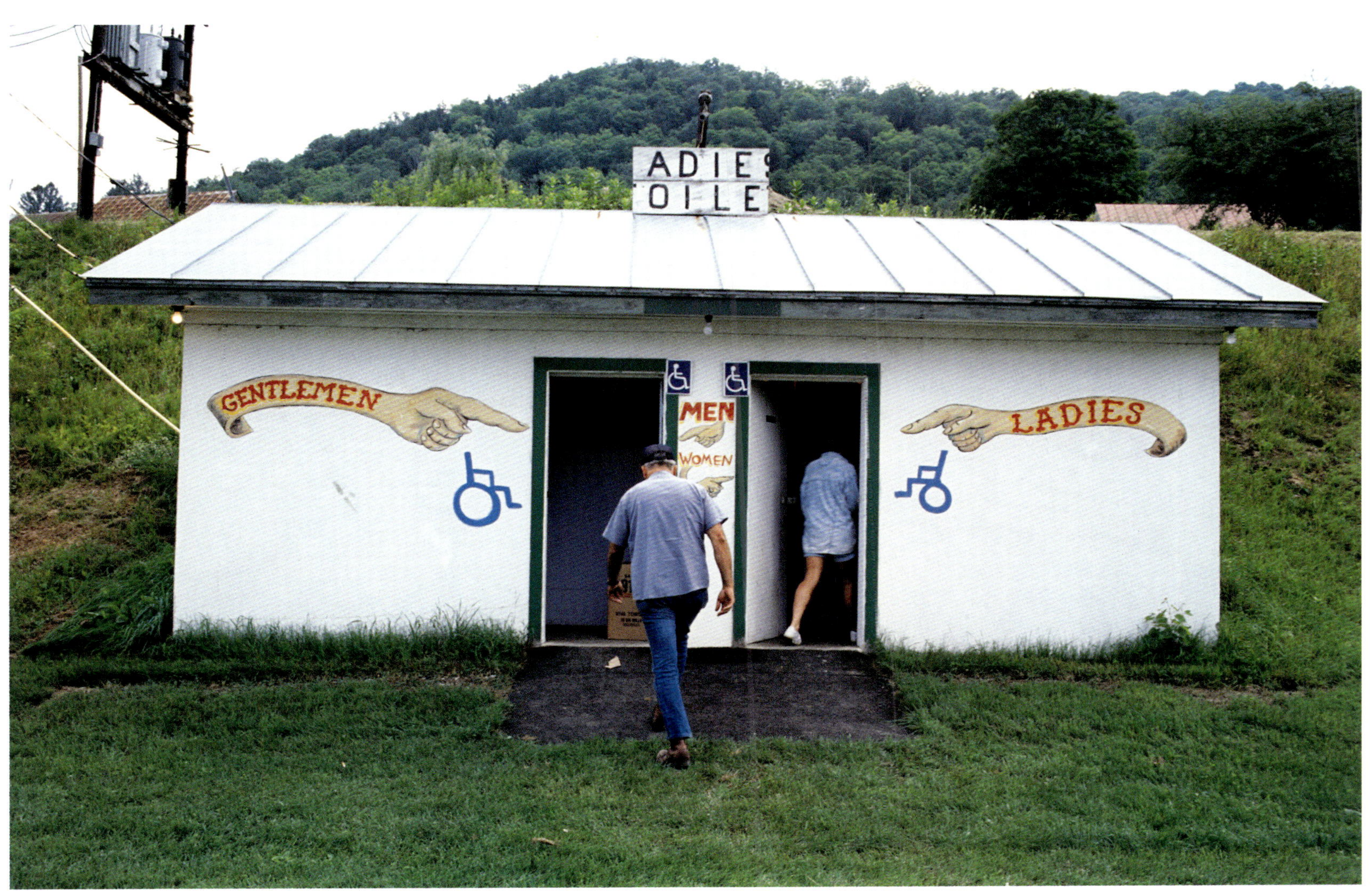

ADIES
OILE
GENTLEMEN
MEN
WOMEN
LADIES

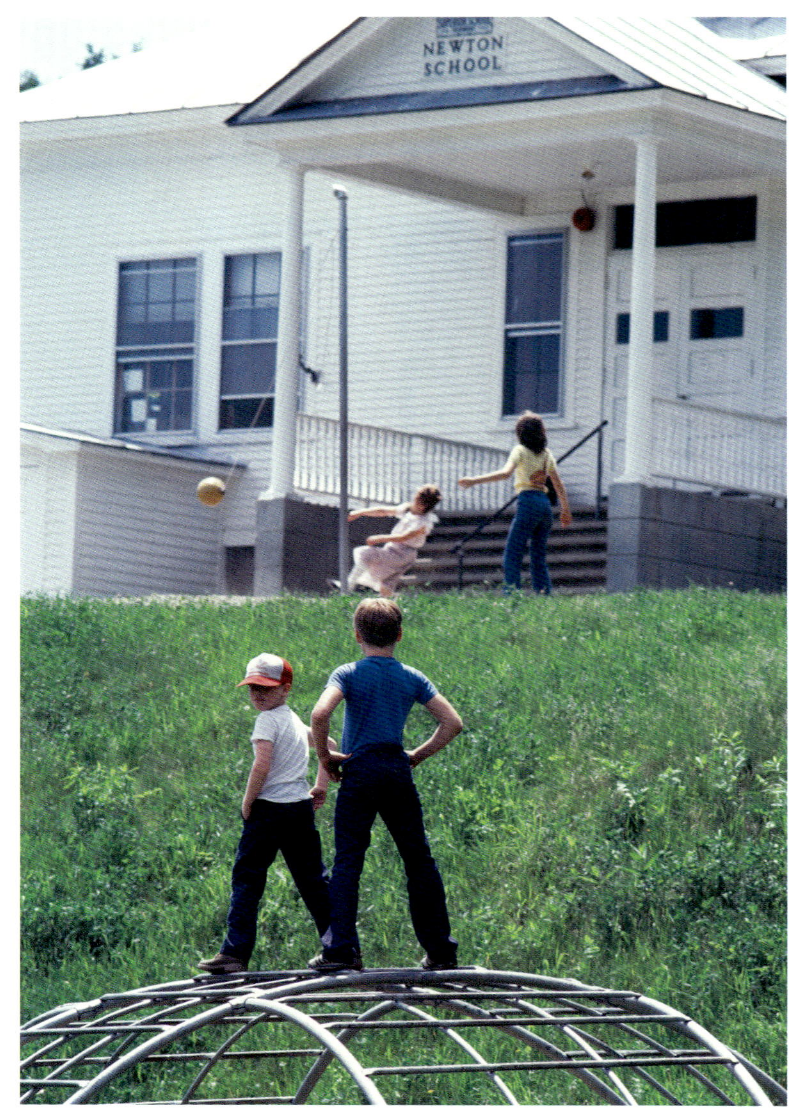

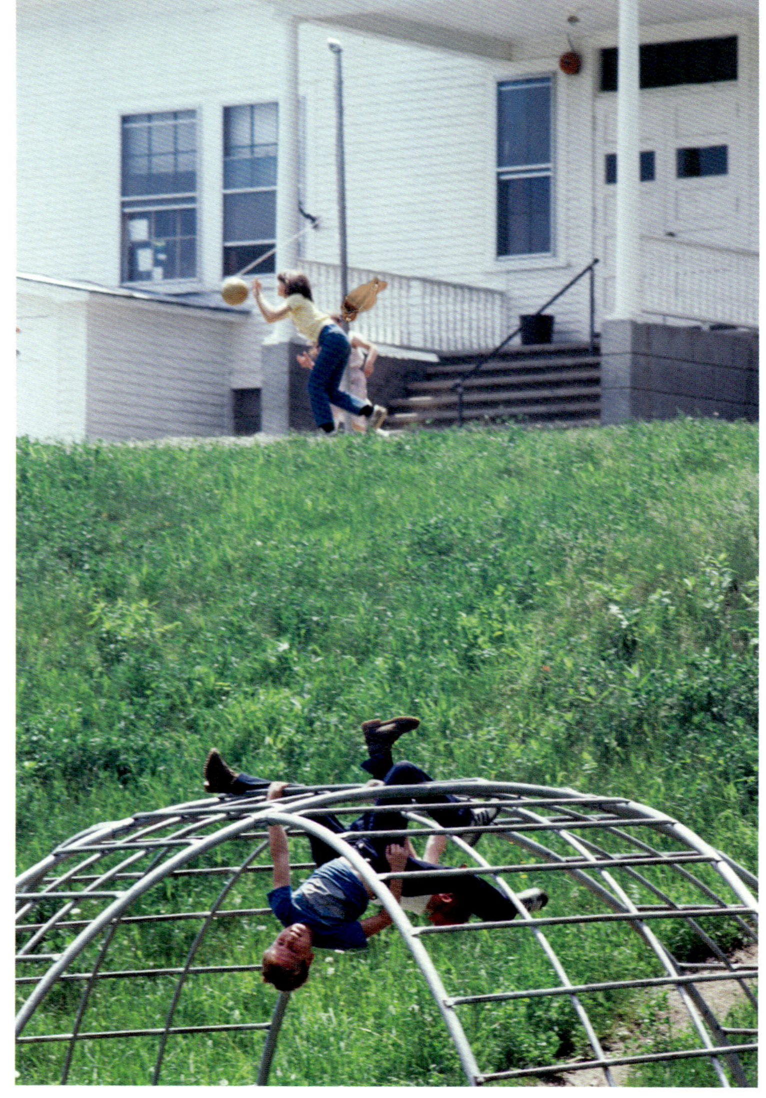

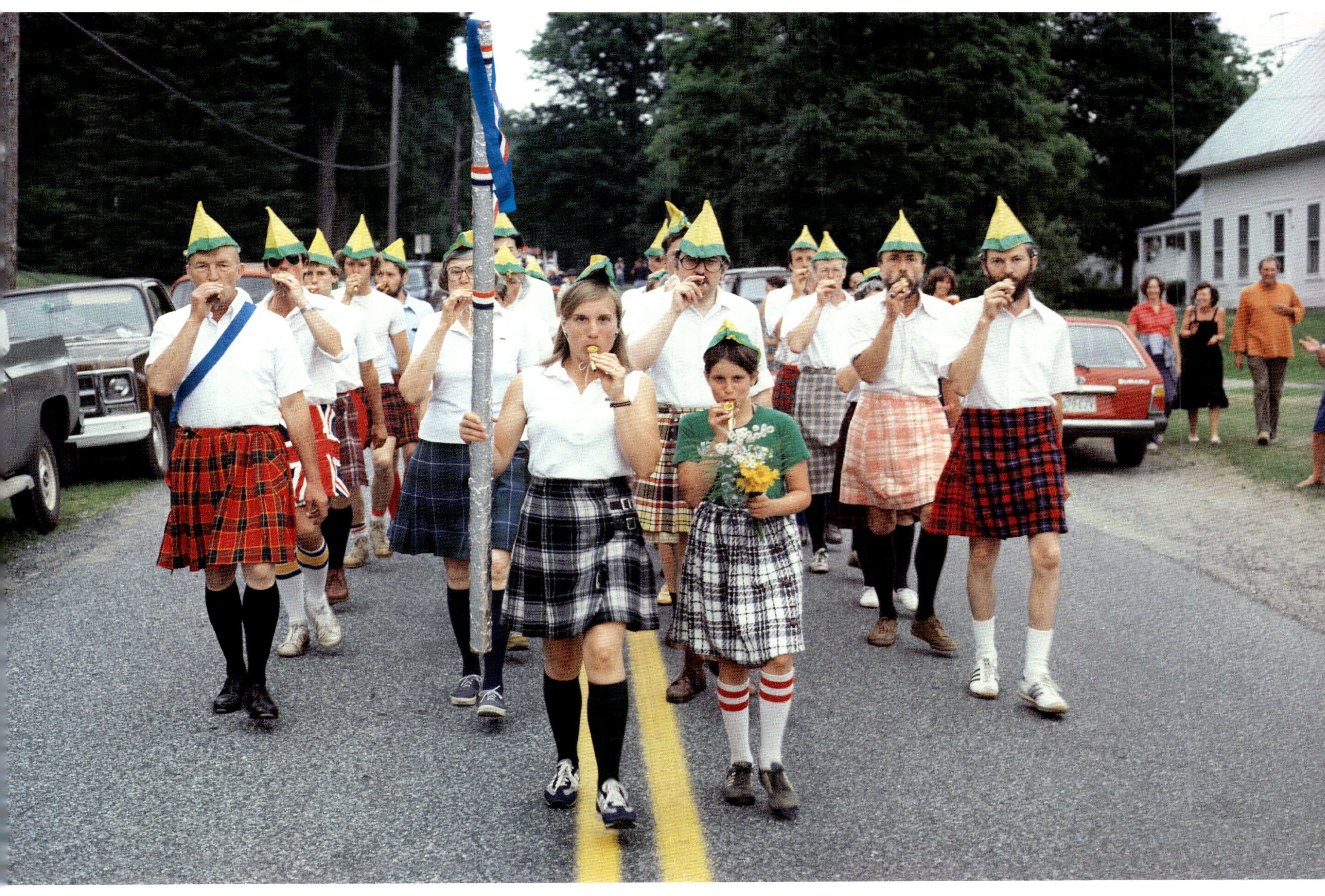

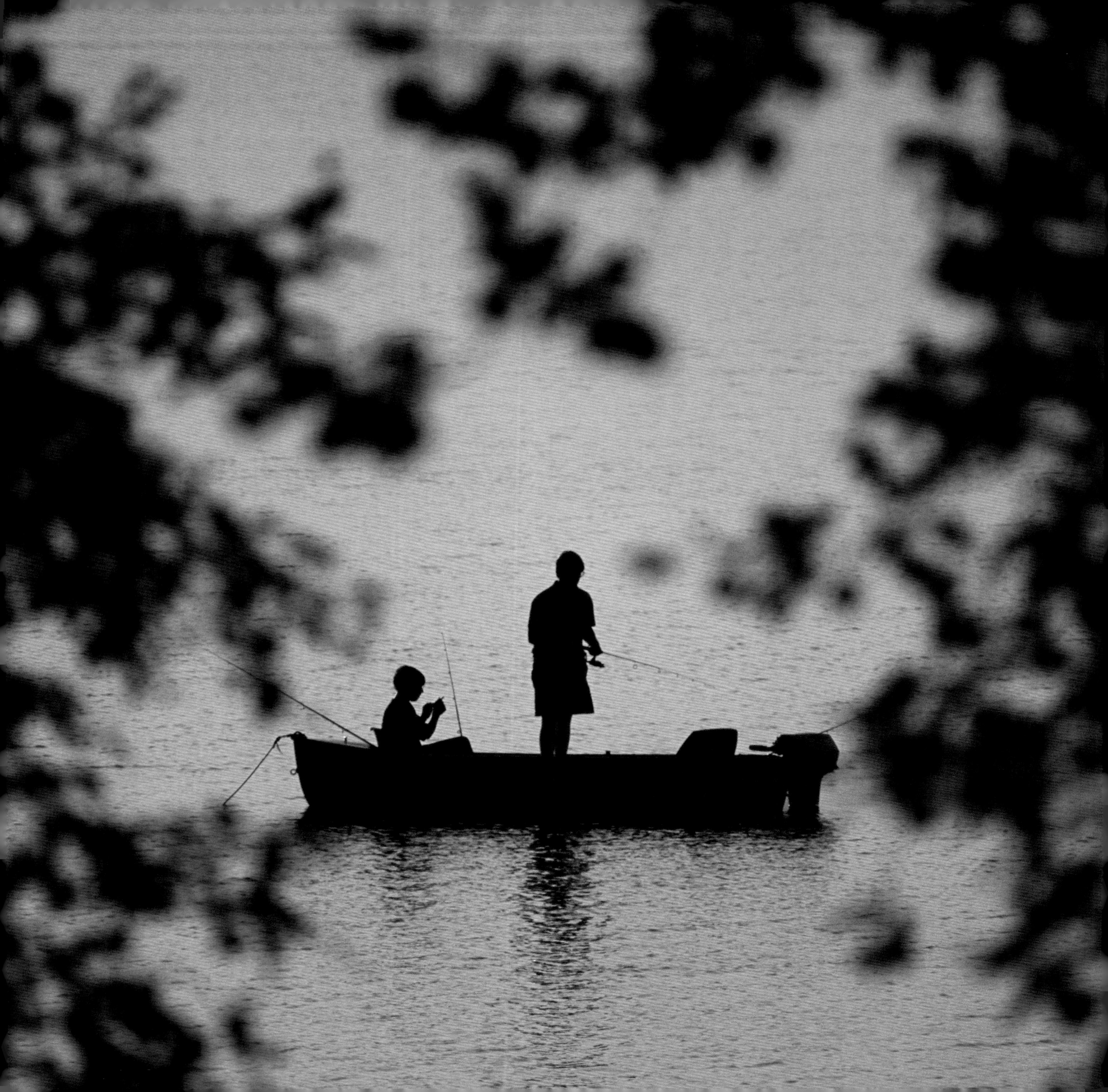

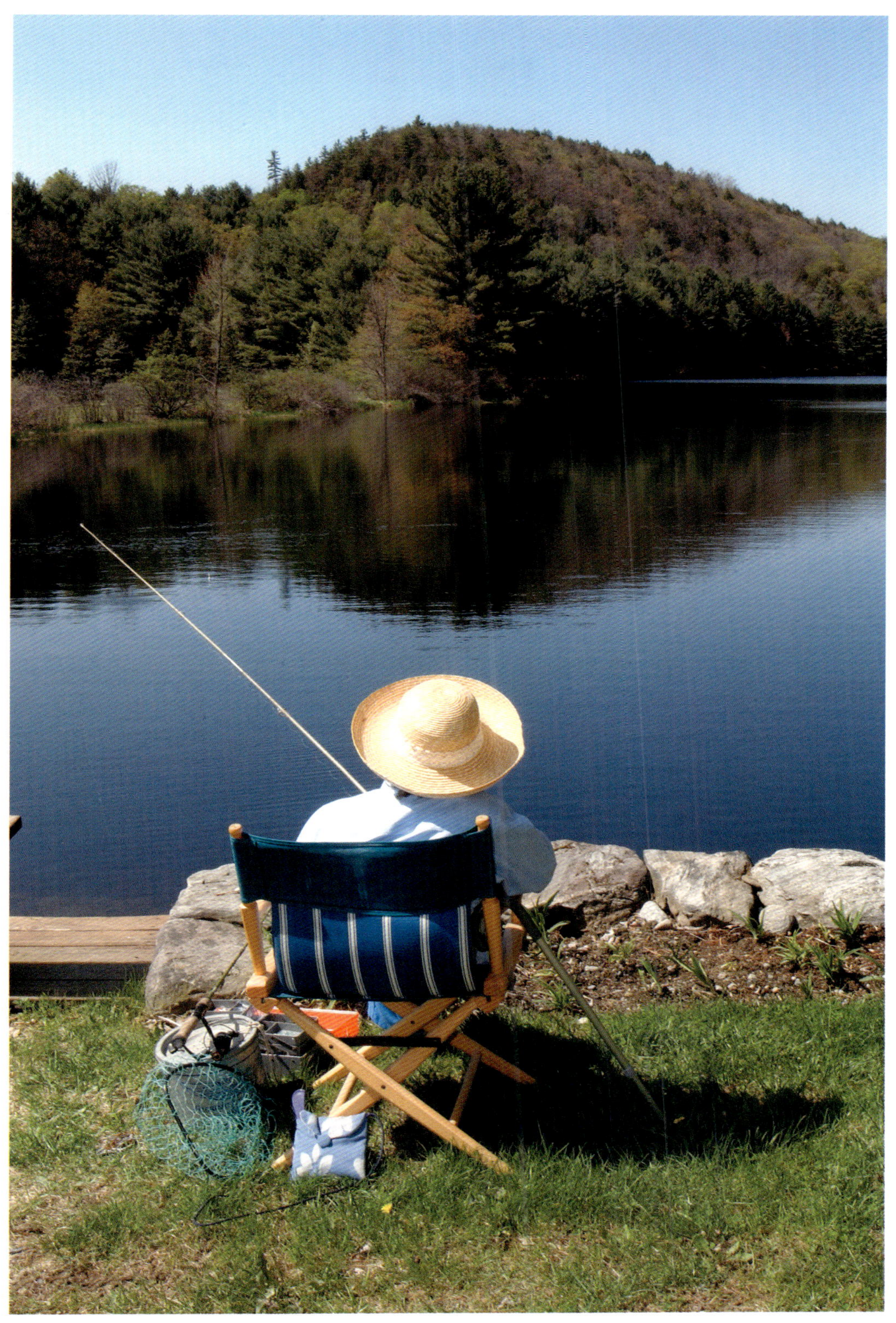

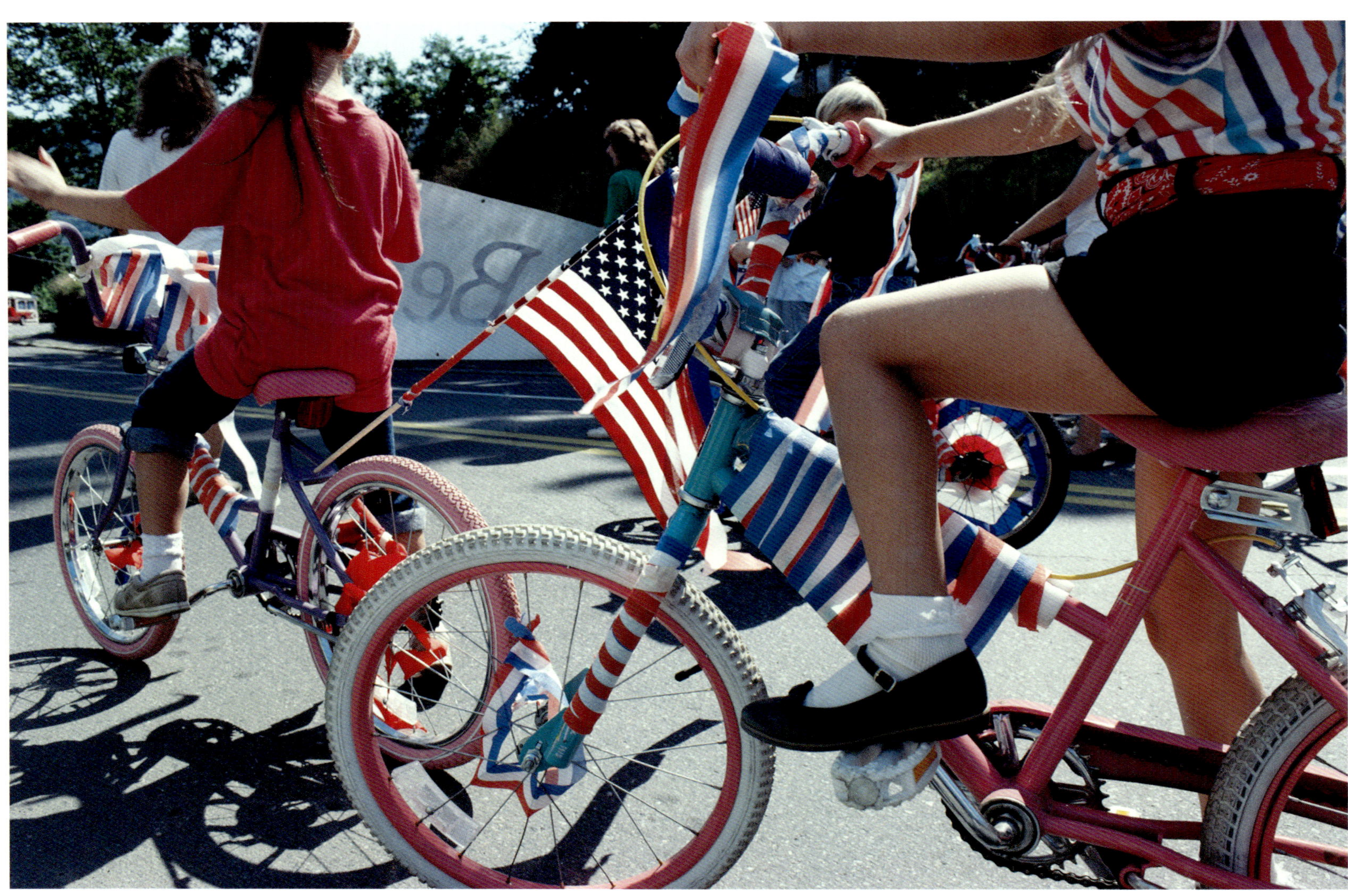

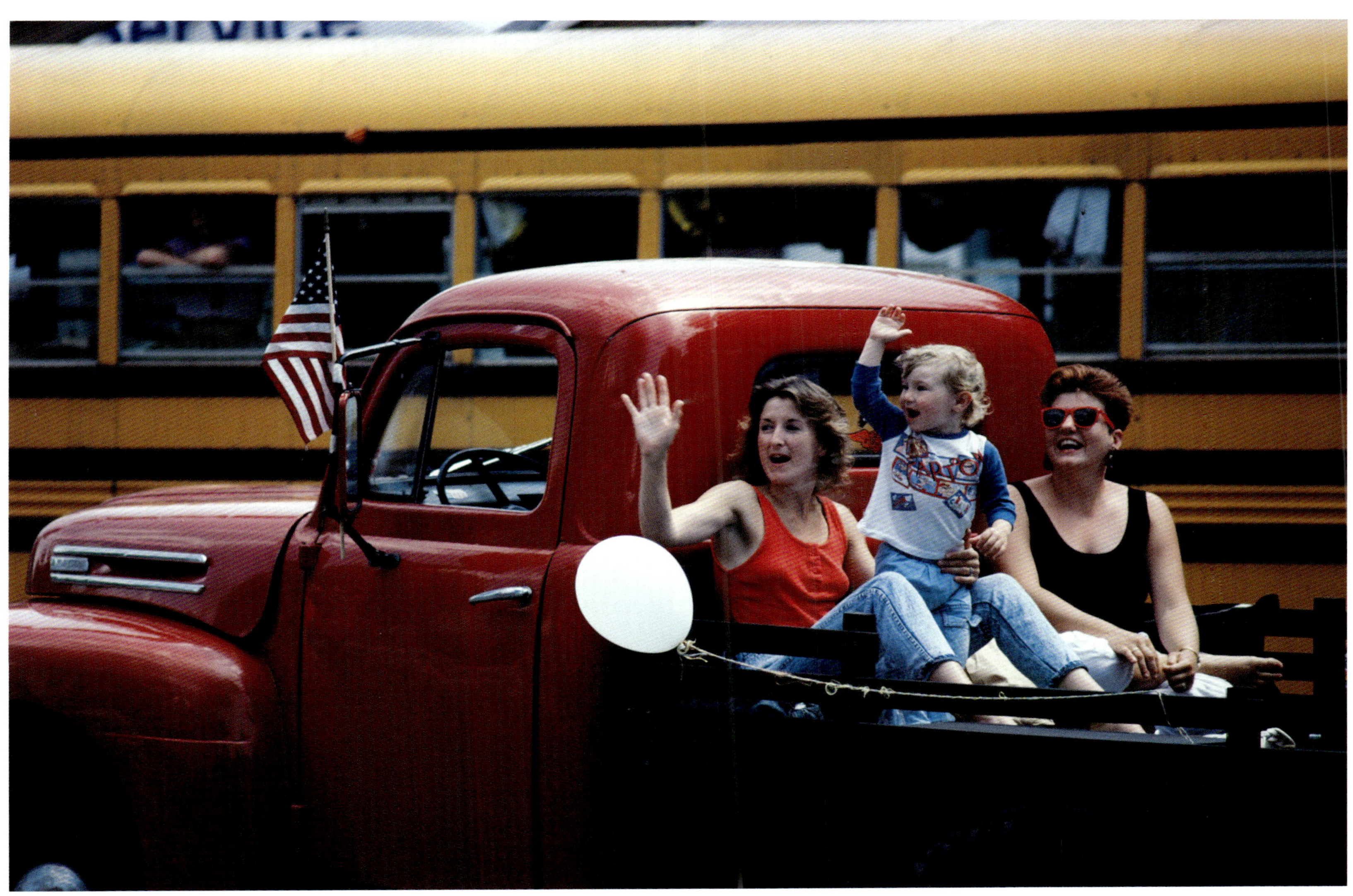

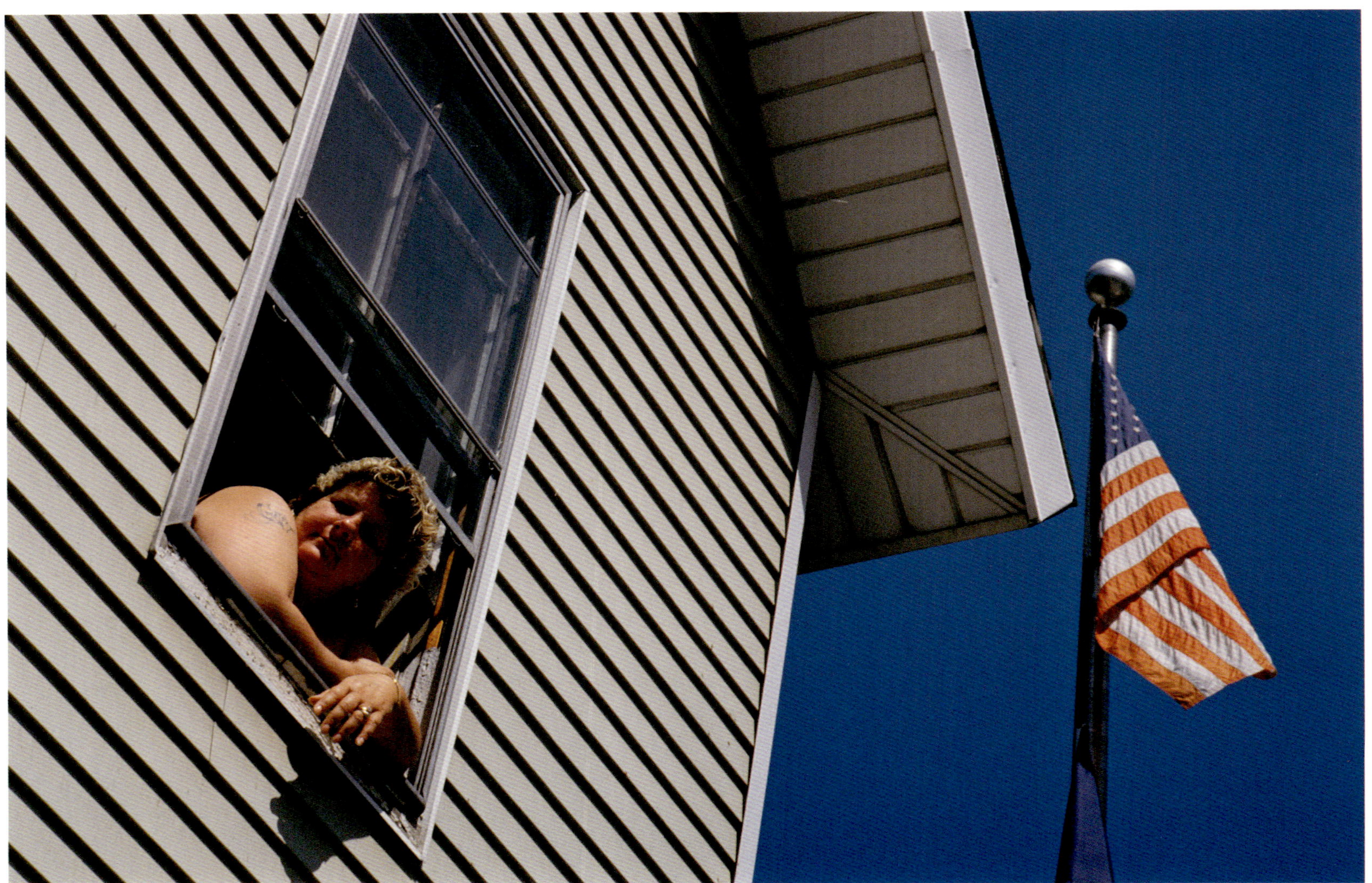

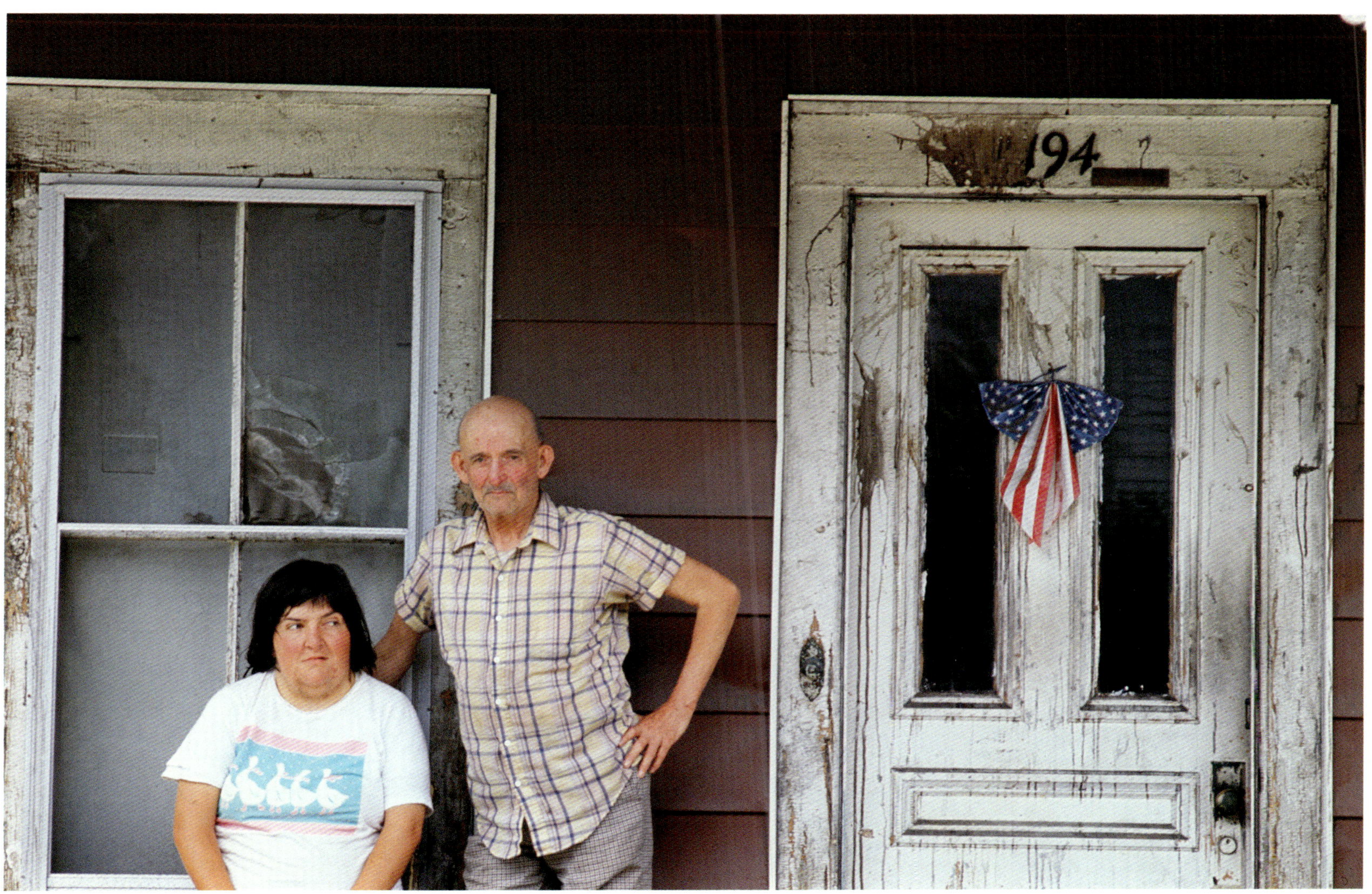

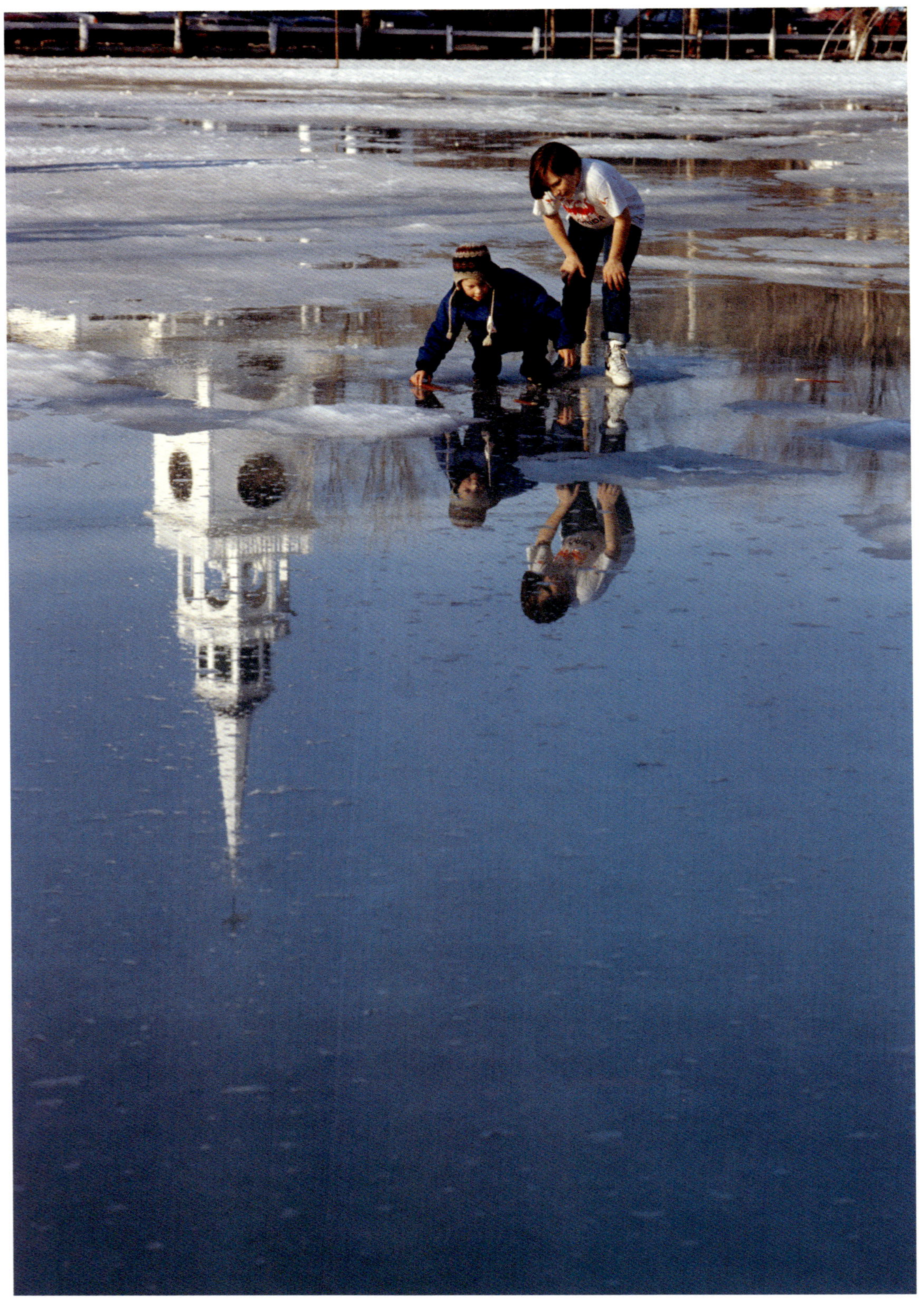

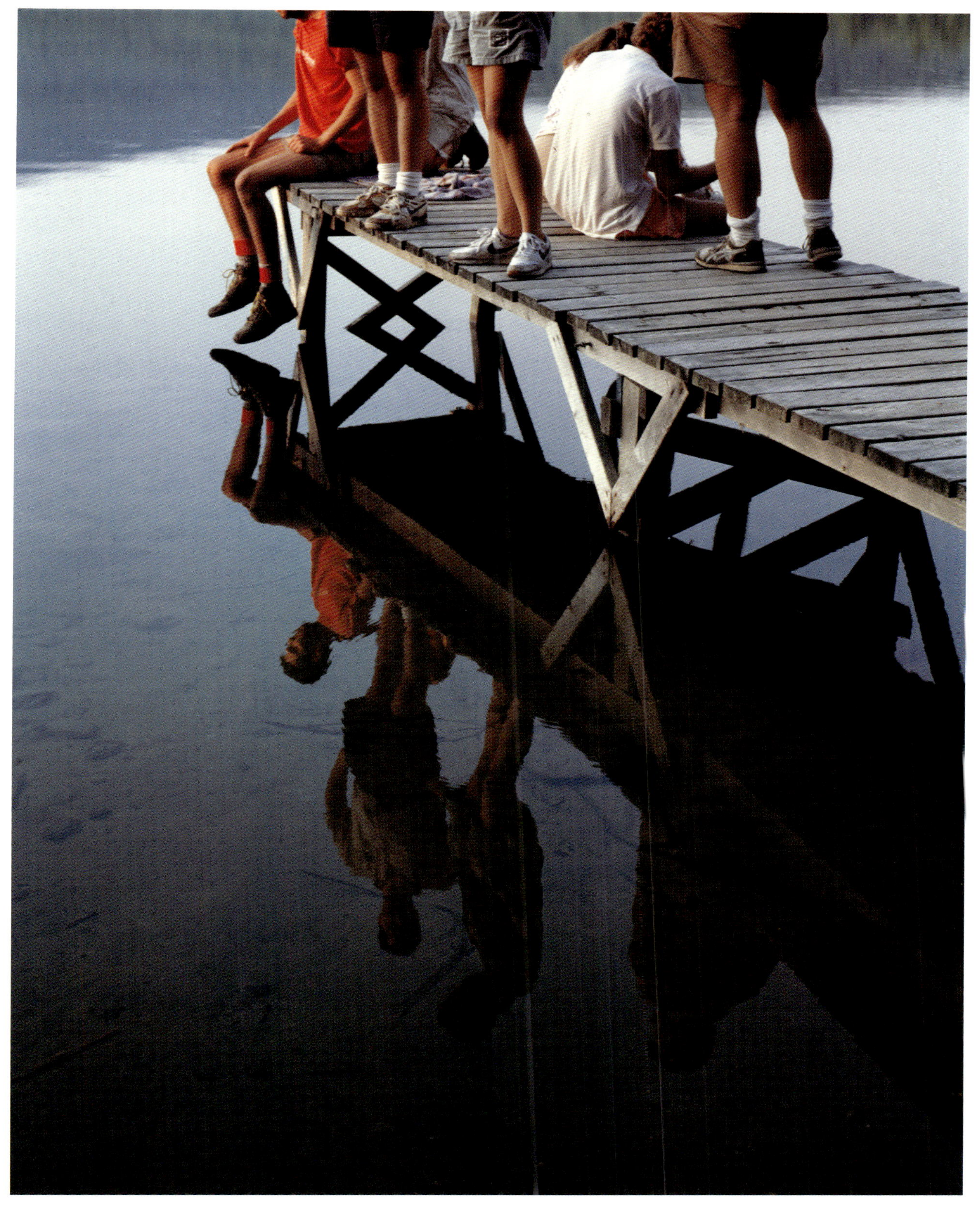

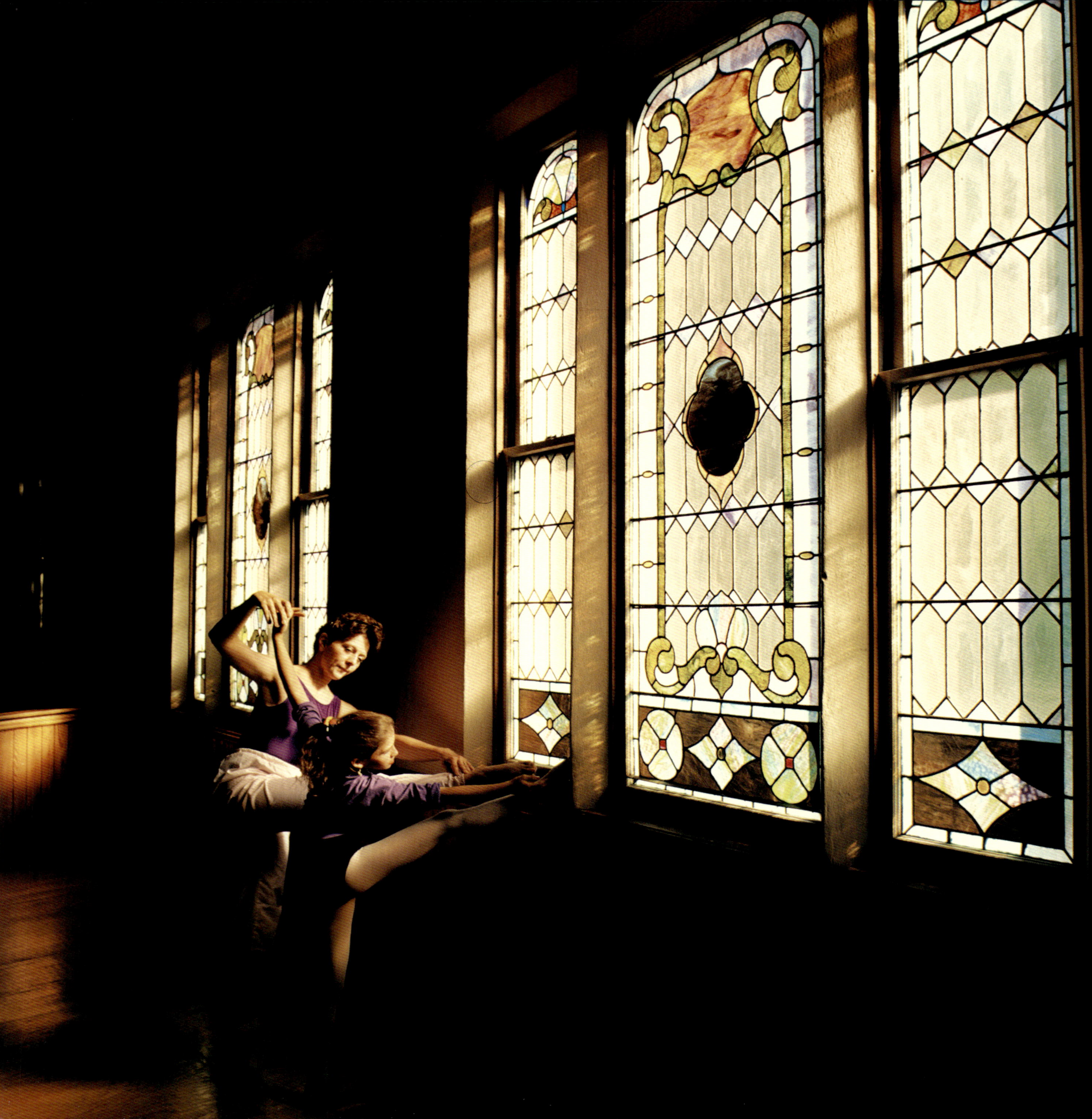

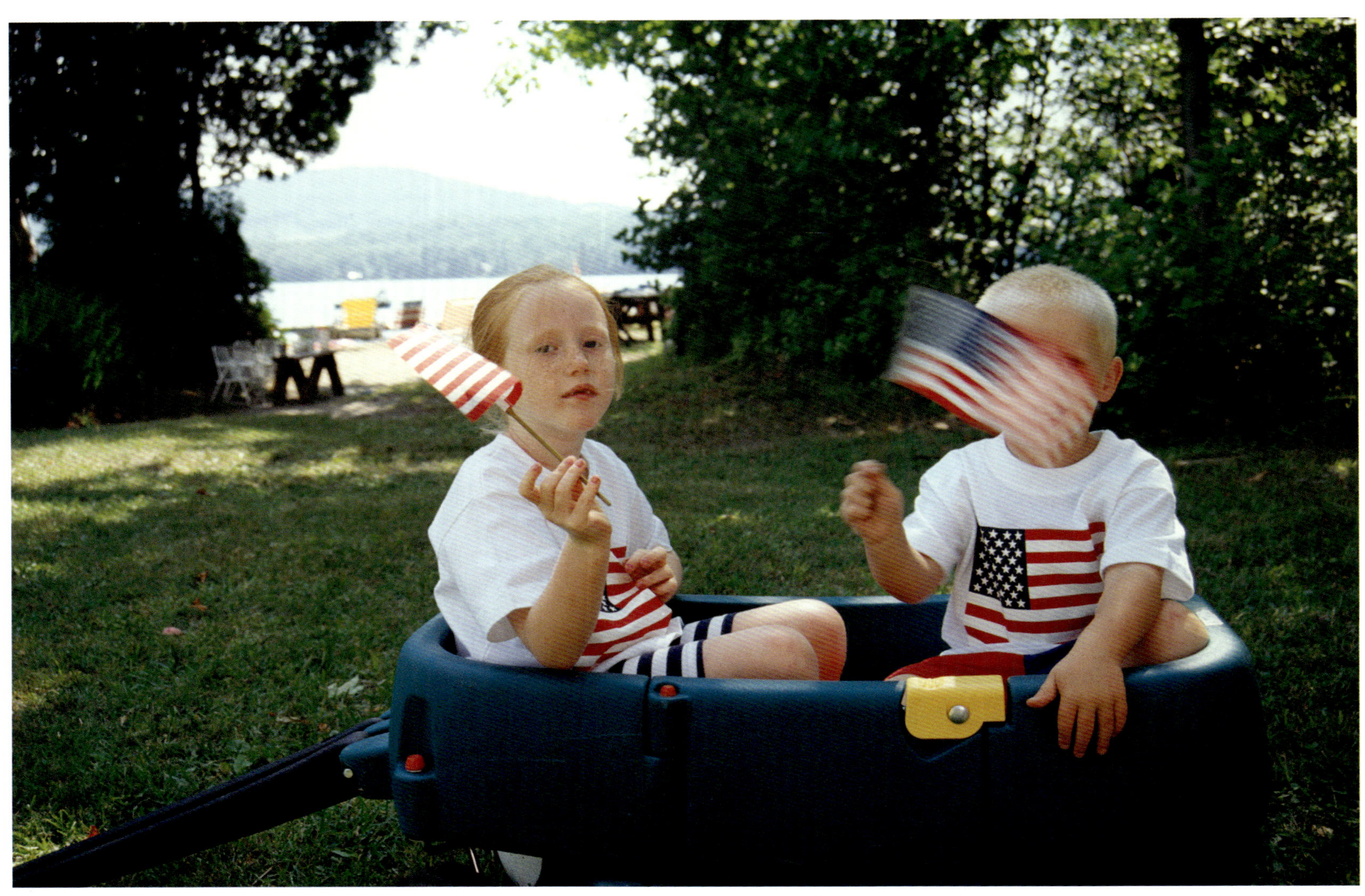

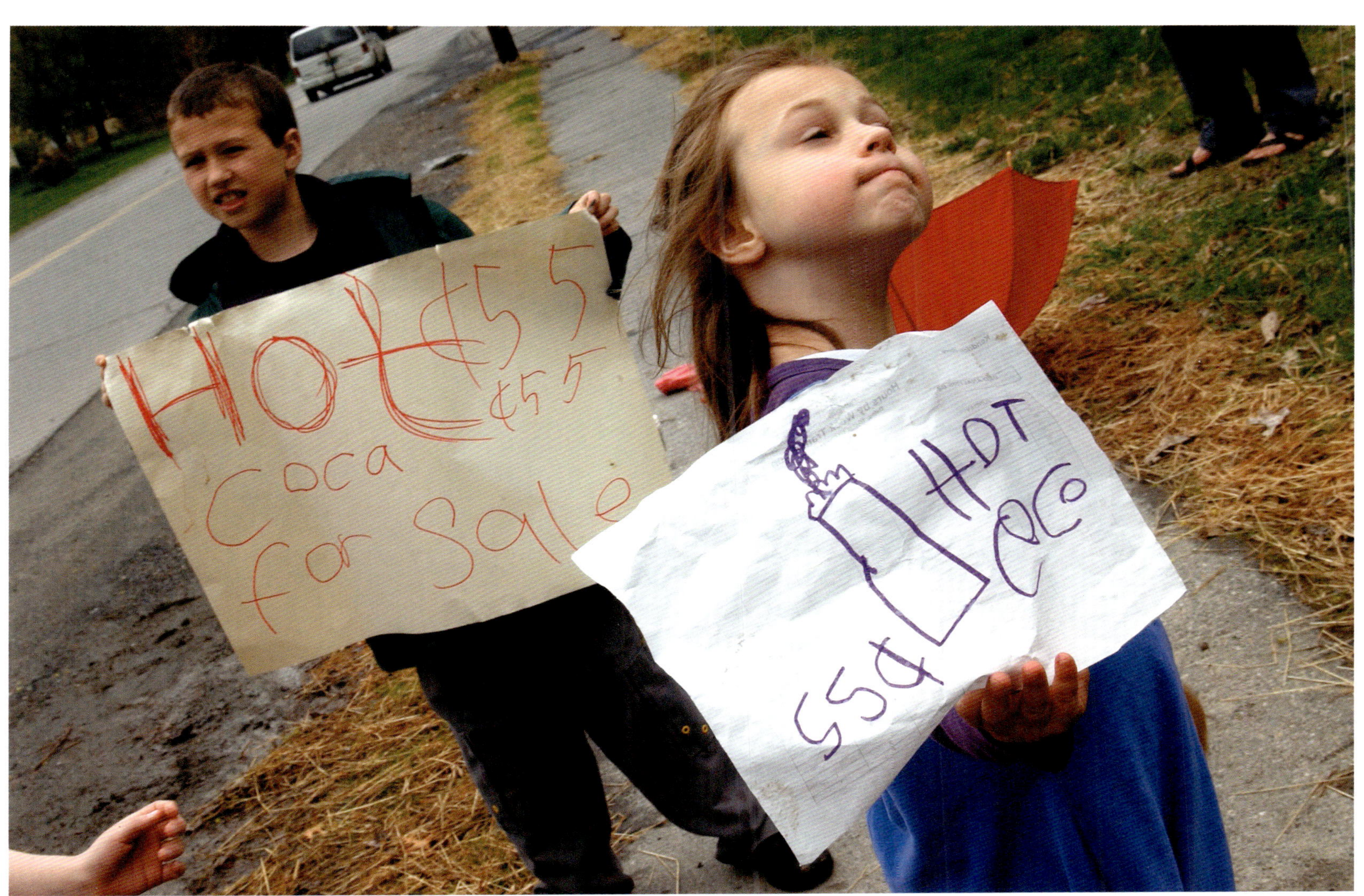

HOT $5 5
$5 5
Coca
for Sale
HOT
Coco
55¢

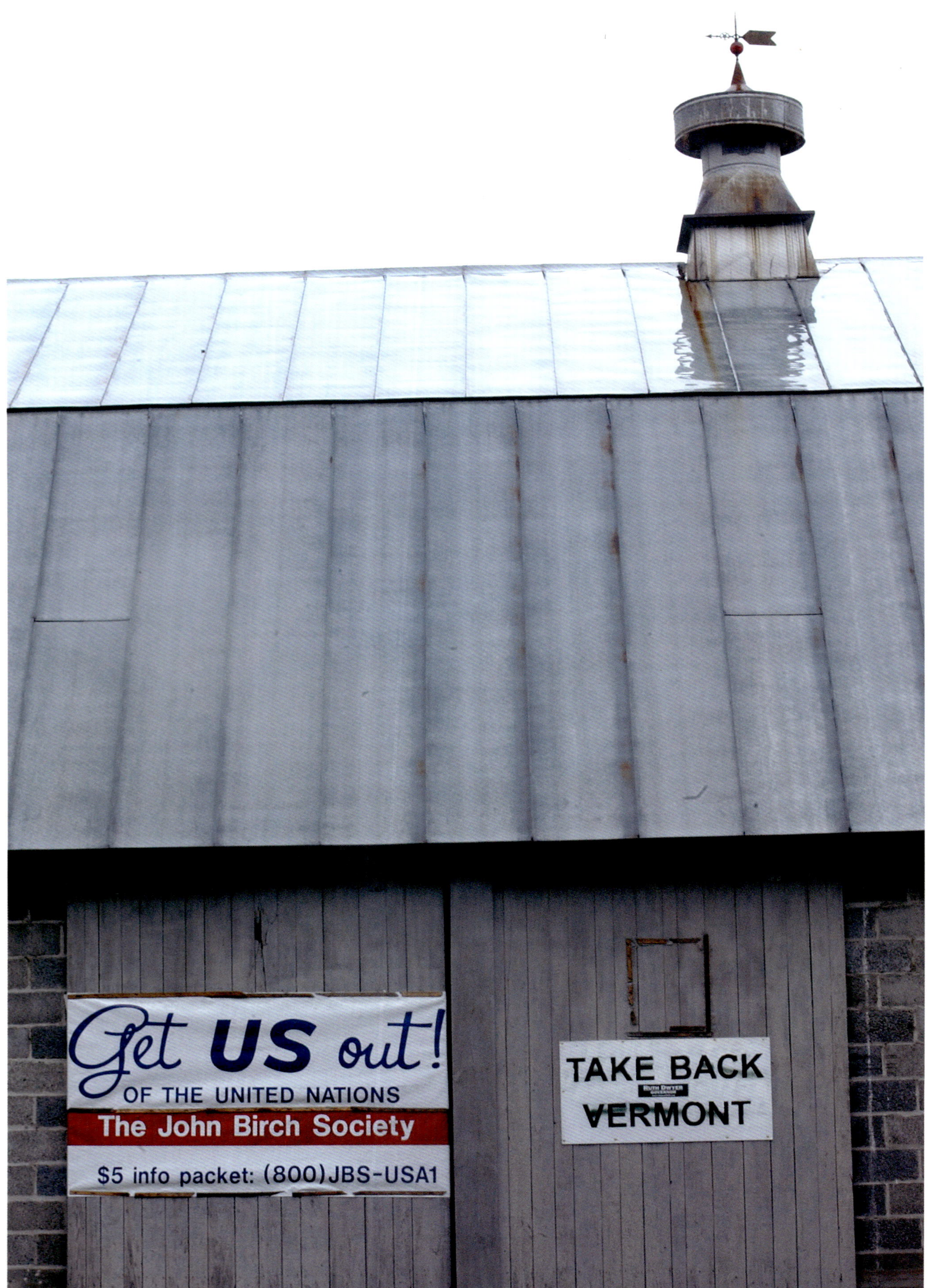
Get US out!
OF THE UNITED NATIONS
The John Birch Society
$5 info packet: (800)JBS-USA1
TAKE BACK
VERMONT

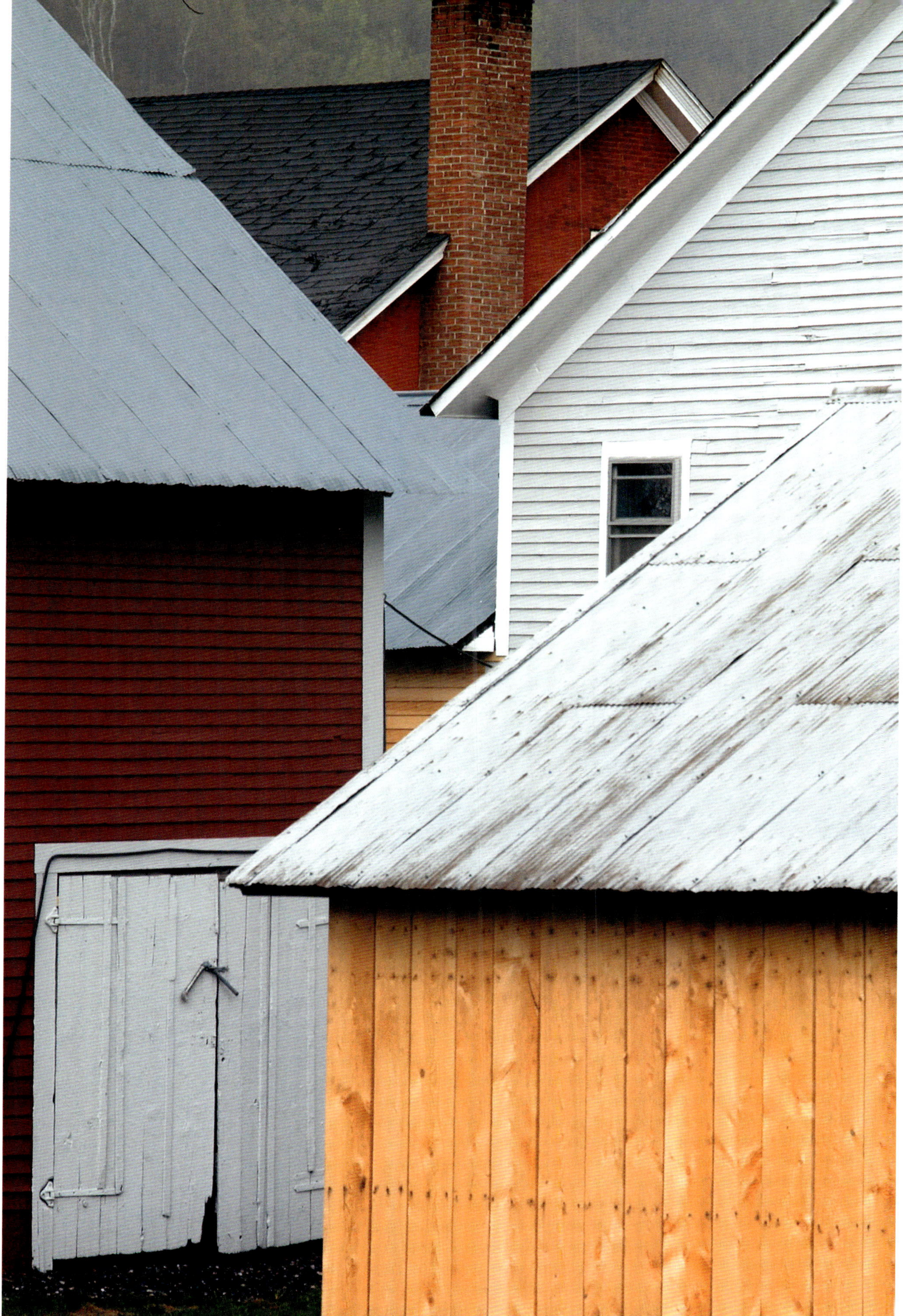

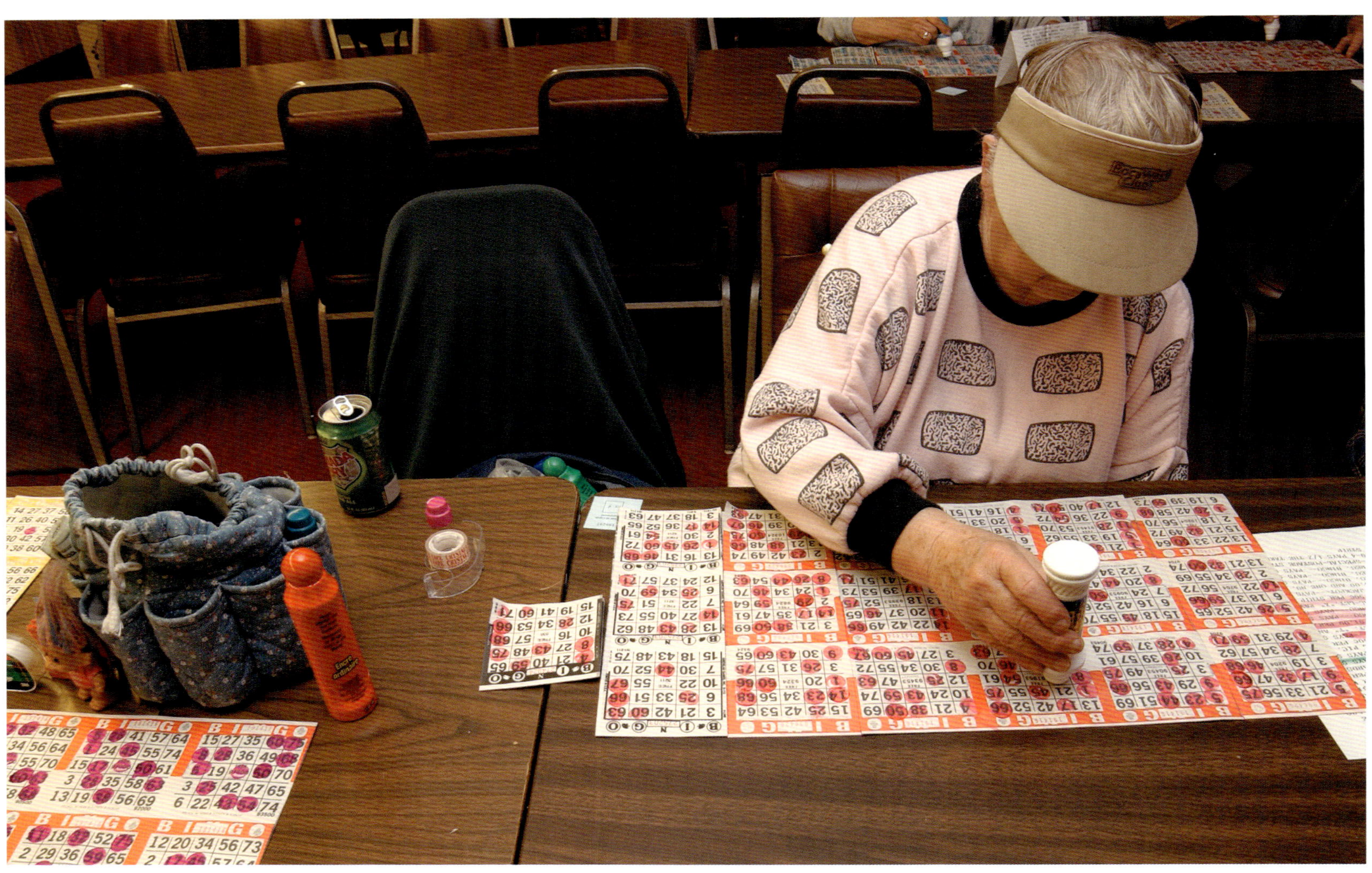

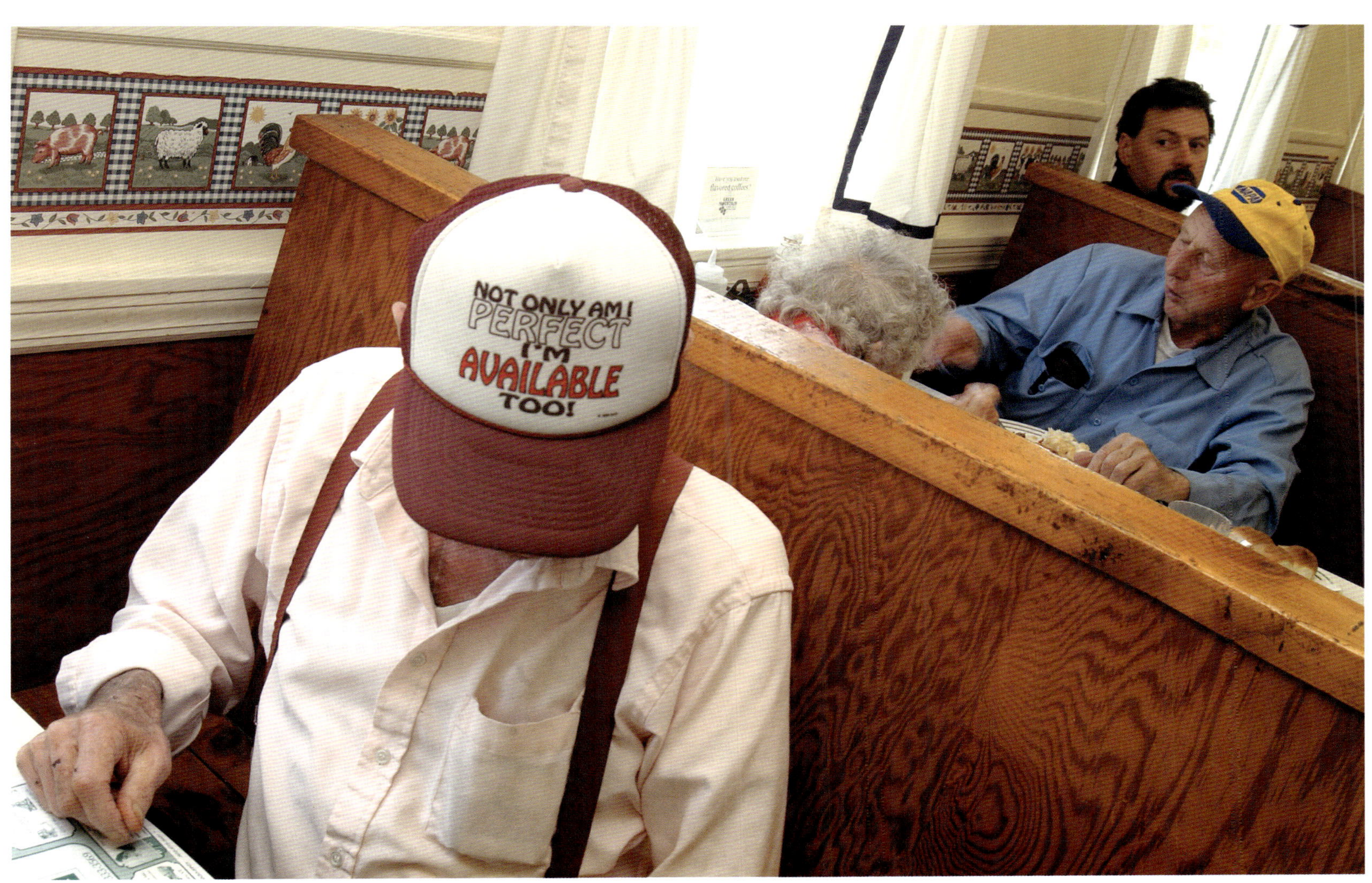
NOT ONLY AM I
PERFECT
I'M
AVAILABLE
TOO!

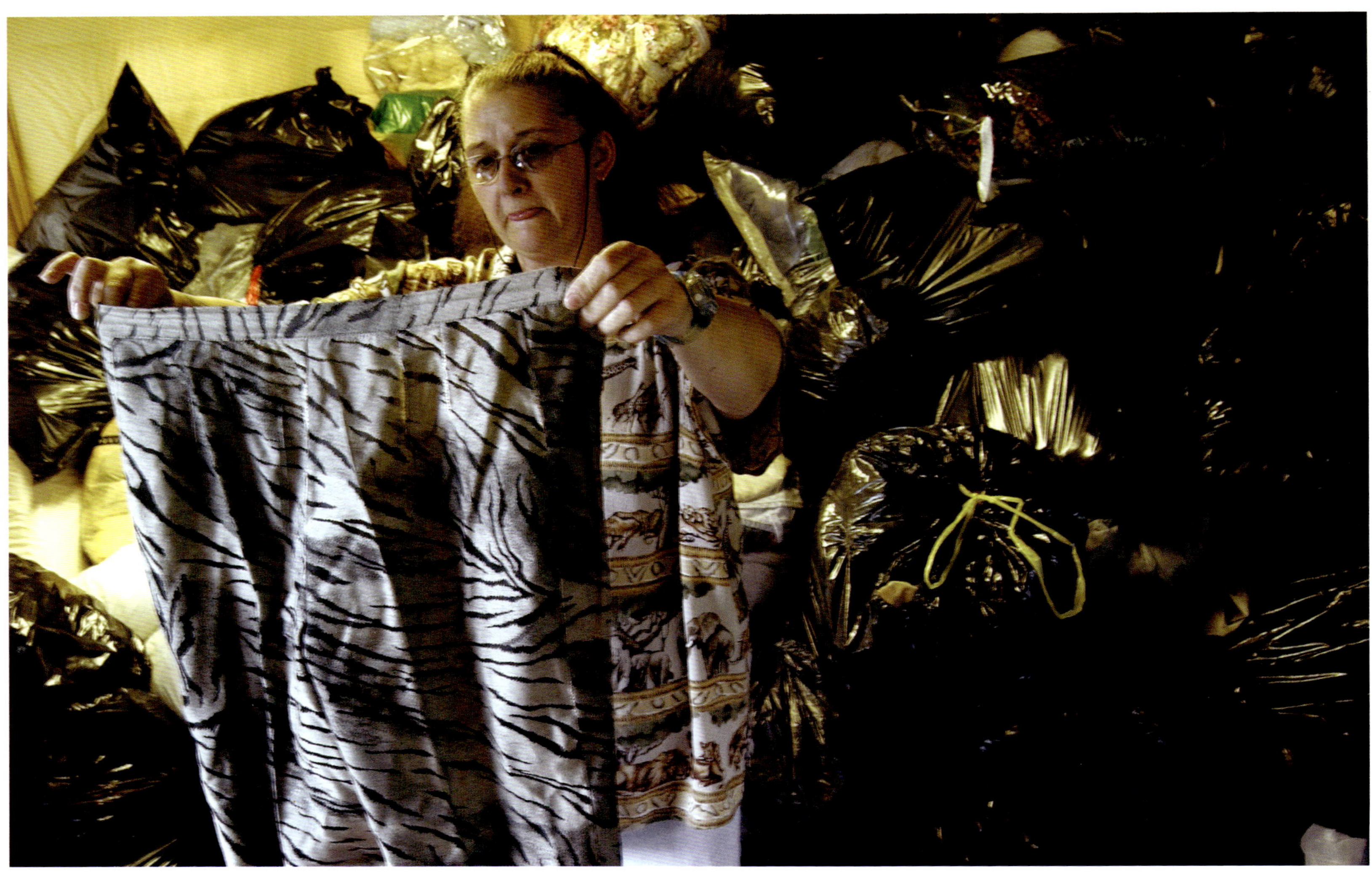

116

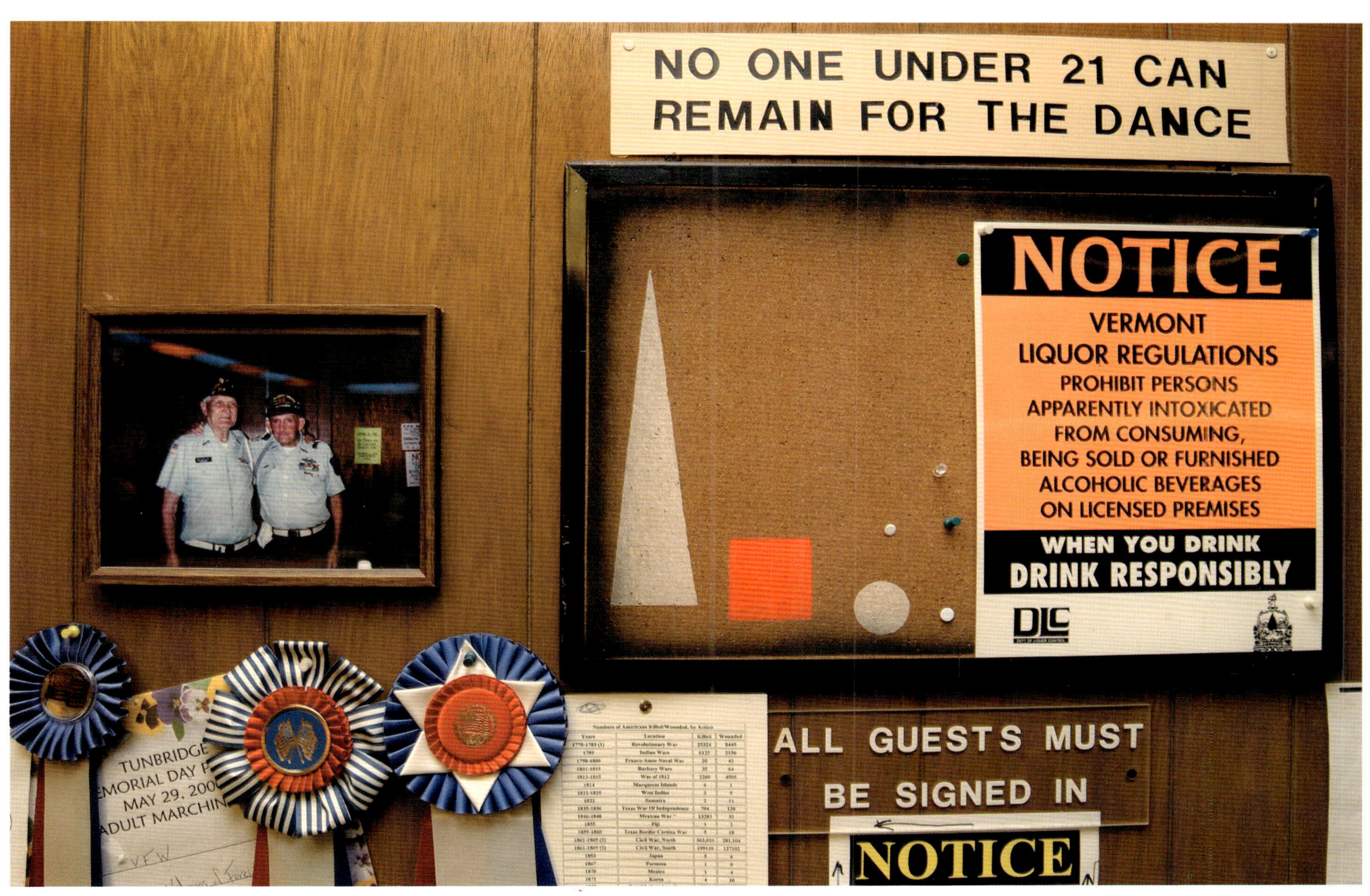

NO ONE UNDER 21 CAN REMAIN FOR THE DANCE
NOTICE
VERMONT LIQUOR REGULATIONS PROHIBIT PERSONS APPARENTLY INTOXICATED FROM CONSUMING, BEING SOLD OR FURNISHED ALCOHOLIC BEVERAGES ON LICENSED PREMISES
WHEN YOU DRINK DRINK RESPONSIBLY
DLC
ALL GUESTS MUST BE SIGNED IN
NOTICE
TUNBRIDGE
MEMORIAL DAY P
MAY 29, 200
ADULT MARCHIN

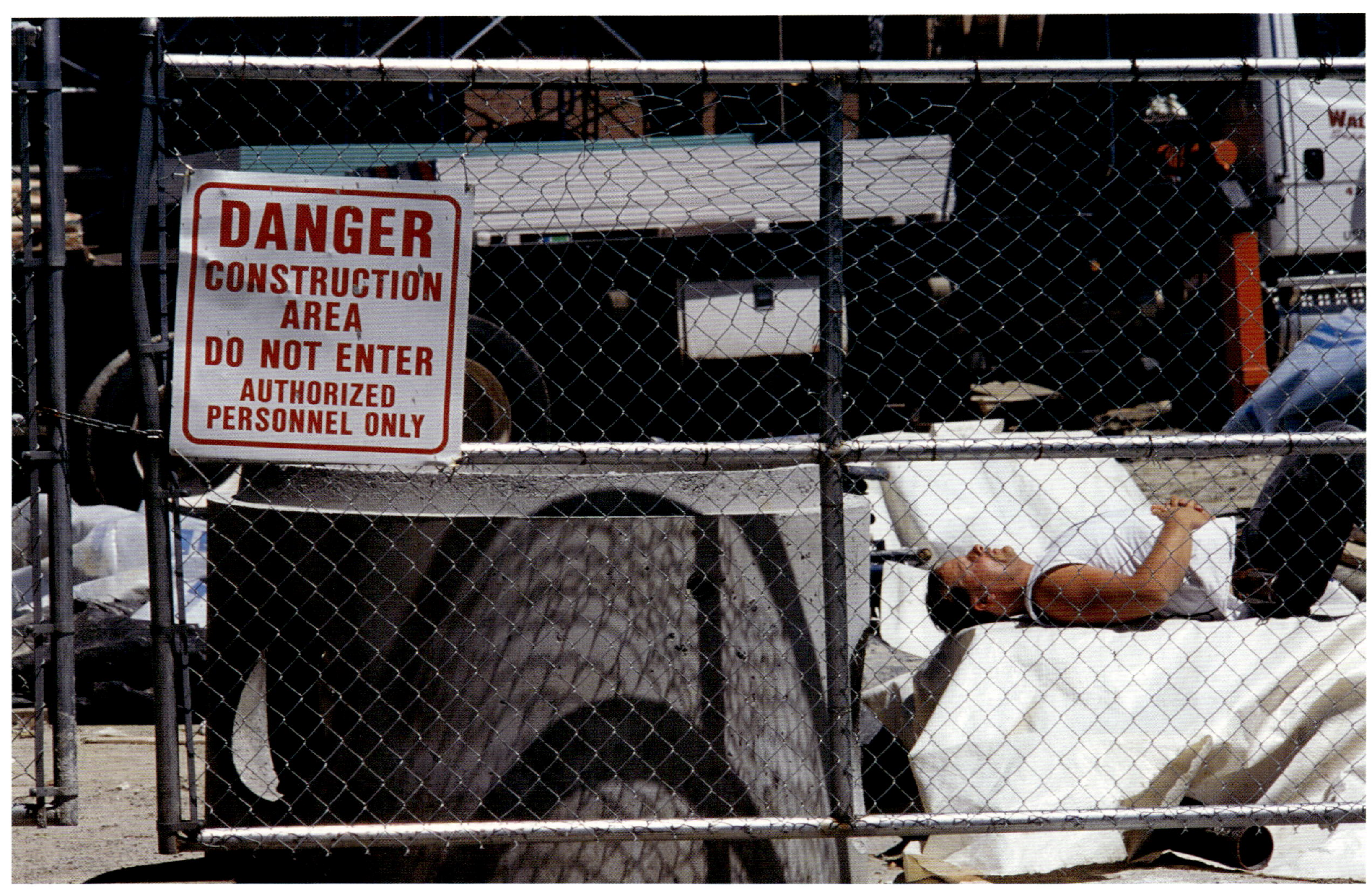

DANGER
CONSTRUCTION
AREA
DO NOT ENTER
AUTHORIZED
PERSONNEL ONLY

118